An Afternoon with C. S. Lewis

McMaster Divinity College Press
McMaster General Studies Series, Volume 20

An Afternoon with C. S. Lewis

Modern Perspectives on Lewis's Life, Work, and Legacy

edited by
STANLEY E. PORTER

☙PICKWICK *Publications* • Eugene, Oregon

AN AFTERNOON WITH C. S. LEWIS
Modern Perspectives on Lewis's Life, Work, and Legacy

McMaster General Studies Series, Volume 20
McMaster Divinity College Press

Copyright © 2025 Wipf and Stock Publishers. All rights reserved. Except for brief quotations in critical publications or reviews, no part of this book may be reproduced in any manner without prior written permission from the publisher. Write: Permissions, Wipf and Stock Publishers, 199 W. 8th Ave., Suite 3, Eugene, OR 97401.

Pickwick Publications
An Imprint of Wipf and Stock Publishers
199 W. 8th Ave., Suite 3
Eugene, OR 97401

McMaster Divinity College Press
1280 Main Street West
Hamilton, ON, Canada L8S 4K1

www.wipfandstock.com

PAPERBACK ISBN: 979-8-3852-5882-6
HARDCOVER ISBN: 979-8-3852-5883-3
EBOOK ISBN: 979-8-3852-5884-0

McMaster General Studies Series
ISSN 2564-4408 (Print)
ISSN 2564-4416 (Ebook)

Cataloguing-in-Publication data:

Names: Porter, Stanley E., editor.

Title: An afternoon with C. S. Lewis : modern perspectives on Lewis's life, work, and legacy / edited by Stanley E. Porter

Description: Eugene, OR: Pickwick Publications, 2025 | McMaster General Studies Series 20 | Includes bibliographical references and index.

Identifiers: ISBN 979-8-3852-5882-6 (paperback). | ISBN 979-8-3852-5883-3 (hardcover) | ISBN 979-8-3852-5884-0 (ebook).

Subjects: LCSH: Lewis, C. S. (Clive Staples), 1898–1963—Religion. | Authors, English—20th century—Biography. | Anglicans—England—Biography.

Classification: BX5199.L53 P67 2025 (print). | BX5199 (ebook).

VERSION NUMBER 11/11/25

Contents

Preface | vii
List of Contributors | xi
List of Tables | xiii
List of Abbreviations | xv

The Life, Work, and Legacy of C. S. Lewis and his Continuing Influence
—*Stanley E. Porter* | 1

Part One: Apologetics and Philosophy

A Virtue Approach to Mass Animal Suffering: or, the Problems and Promise of C. S. Lewis's Theory of Animal Pain
—*Adam Barkman and Tristan Barkman* | 21

Myths, Morals—and—Joy: C. S. Lewis, the *Consensus Gentium*, and Postmodern Thought
—*Mark G. McKim* | 52

Pick your Poison: Revisiting C. S. Lewis's *The Abolition of Man* in a Postmodern Age
—*Jason Vander Horst* | 65

Part Two: Fictional Worlds

Consider the Narnian Birds: Birdsong as Sacrament in C. S. Lewis's *The Chronicles of Narnia*
—*Paul Robinson* | 91

Playing with a Lion: (Christian) Leadership According to *The Chronicles of Narnia*
—*Seán M. W. McGuire* | 108

Regarding *Screwtape*
—*David I. Yoon* | 127

Part Three: Literature and Criticism

What Kind of Scholar Was C. S. Lewis?
—*Stanley E. Porter* | 149

C. S. Lewis and the Art of Criticism
—*Aaron Jung* | 175

Doings, Readings, Thinkings: C. S. Lewis on the Discipline and Reward of Personal Correspondence
—*Dawn R. Berkelaar* | 198

Index of Authors | 217

Preface

THE TITLE OF THIS volume describes the occasion that was responsible for its origins. C. S. Lewis continues to fascinate scholars and non-scholars alike, because he uniquely combined qualities that are rarely found in others. He was a scholar of abiding significance who was widely read, was highly knowledgeable, and did not hesitate to take positions that put him at odds with his contemporaries. He was also a writer of great skill, so that he was able to write not just works of great erudition but works of great popularity, whether these were radio addresses, apologetics, or lay theology. Lewis excelled in all of them, being able to make broadcasts that encouraged a nation during some of its bleakest times, while also engaging with contemporary issues that were of concern not just to Oxford dons but to the entire populace. And then there is his fiction. Lewis is probably best remembered today for his *The Chronicles of Narnia* stories, but he also wrote science fiction and imaginative allegories and even poetry that merit attention. In all these, Lewis comes across as writing effortlessly, with hardly a wrong word chosen or a phrase too long or tortured. But Lewis probably continues to be as popular and widely read as he is because of his Christian faith that pervaded his life and as a result permeates the wide variety of writings that he left as a legacy. Lewis's Christian faith was not easily gained and is not facilely understood. His was a complex faith borne out of deep thinking about fundamental questions regarding God's existence and who Jesus Christ was. His faith was also tested by significant human and spiritual challenges to which he responded, often outwardly and publicly in his writings.

These are just some of the reasons that Lewis continues to fascinate readers, especially Christian readers, who continue to buy, read, and discuss his writings. McMaster Divinity College offered a course in Lewis in the fall 2024 term, taught by adjunct professor Dr. Mark McKim, a local pastor who also has a PhD in theology and a deep and abiding interest in Lewis.

Preface

The occasion was too good to pass up and so we organized what some have called a pop-up conference, an ad hoc afternoon to which we invited both our students and faculty but also anyone in the area to participate. The conference was entitled Faith, Fantasy, and Philosophy: An Afternoon of C. S. Lewis, and was held on December 4, 2024. We arranged for several plenary speakers and then sent out a call for papers, not knowing what the response would be. We were very pleased with the proposed papers and so arranged for several parallel paper sessions. We would have been happy with the conference to have twenty-five attendees, since the conference was only offered in person (a risk in this day and age of livestream on demand). We were pleasantly surprised that we had over 75 total attendees and participants for the day. We all enjoyed the plenary presentations but were forced to choose among the parallel sessions.

Because we made no charge for the conference, we are thankful to the H. H. Bingham Colloquium fund for providing funding to support the inevitable costs of the conference. The Bingham funds were donated by the family of a highly respected CBOQ (Canadian Baptists of Ontario and Quebec) pastor in honor of his ministry in Ontario and as a means of helping to create a meaningful legacy by sponsoring events such as this one. Even if a conference is organized to run as efficiently as possible, there are inevitable costs for advertising, administration, and even refreshments. The Bingham Colloquium enabled us to meet these costs and provide a wonderful afternoon of C. S. Lewis papers and discussion.

As editor of the volume, I wish to thank all who have made the conference and now the volume the successes that they are. I wish to thank the speakers who prepared their papers for the day, and then those who submitted their papers for possible publication in this volume. All the papers included here have met our review standards for inclusion. We realize that there is great diversity in the topics of the papers included in this volume. Our afternoon of Lewis intentionally did not have a designated theme but welcomed papers on any topic directly related to Lewis and his writings. We have attempted to reflect that diversity in this volume, even if we have also tried to group the papers according to some common interests. So, if you are a reviewer of this volume, you need not remind us that the volume lacks a specific theme—we already know that and have consciously taken that approach so that we may include a range of papers that attest to the range of interests of Lewis himself. I think that most readers will find something of interest in this volume.

Preface

I also wish to thank those who attended the conference. The attendees came from far and wide, including not just southern Ontario but other areas of Ontario (Ontario is a very large province, for those who are unaware) and a few places in the United States. Thank you for spending your afternoon with us. We hope that this volume will provide an enduring memorial of that day to which you can regularly return or to prompt further exploration of Lewis and his writings.

Finally, I wish to thank all those at McMaster Divinity College who helped make the day a huge success. These include Melissa Cesar, our Director of Marketing and Communications, and her assistant, Daphne Dyck, for organizing publicity and administering the conference; Sara Fusilier, our Director of Recruitment and Admissions, and her assistant, Janielle Lim, for providing information about McMaster Divinity College for those interested; John Steadman, our Director of External Relations and Operations, for taking care of the physical requirements of the conference, such as setting up rooms; and Melanie McGlynn, my Executive Assistant, for keeping track of everything. I also wish to thank Dr. James Dvorak, our Vice President Academic, for hosting the conference itself.

We trust that this volume will help to encourage further study of Lewis by exploring some well-known and some not so well-known areas of his thought and writing

Stanley E. Porter
McMaster Divinity College
Hamilton, ON, Canada

List of Contributors

Adam Barkman, Redeemer University, Ancaster, ON, Canada

Tristan Barkman, Redeemer University, Ancaster, ON, Canada

Dawn Berkelaar, Redeemer University, Ancaster, ON, Canada

Aaron Jung, McMaster Divinity College, Hamilton, ON, Canada

Seán M. W. McGuire, Wentworth Baptist Church, Hamilton, ON, Canada

Mark G. McKim, First Baptist Church, St. Marys, ON, and McMaster Divinity College, Hamilton, ON, Canada

Stanley E. Porter, McMaster Divinity College, Hamilton, ON, Canada

Paul Robinson, McMaster Divinity College, Hamilton, ON, Canada

Jason Vander Horst, McMaster University, Hamilton, ON, Canada

David I. Yoon, McMaster Divinity College, Hamilton, ON, Canada

List of Tables

C. S. Lewis's Letters to Arthur Greeves mapped over time
(1914 to 1963) | 212

C. S. Lewis and Arthur Greeves—Letters and visits mapped over time
(1914 to 1963) | 214

List of Abbreviations

AI   Artificial Intelligence
PTSD   Post-Traumatic Stress Disorder

The Life, Work, and Legacy of C. S. Lewis and his Continuing Influence

Stanley E. Porter

C. S. Lewis continues to excite the interests of many people, Christians and non-Christians alike. This was witnessed in the afternoon conference that resulted in the diverse collection of essays in this volume. The success of the conference and now, we trust, the resulting compilation of essays, begs that we ask the question regarding why it is that Lewis continues to generate such deep and significant interest. In this introduction, I will first deal with Lewis himself—his life, work, and legacy—before turning to the essays in this volume as a continuation of the discussion of Lewis as a writer and thinker.

THE LIFE, WORK, AND LEGACY OF LEWIS

There are many good reasons for continued interest in Lewis and his writings. Several of these immediately come to mind and are often mentioned in the various biographies of Lewis. I will deal with three of them: his life, work, and legacy.

His Life

I have no intention of recounting the facts of Lewis's life, most of which have become widely known, at least among those who are followers of Lewis.[1] Nevertheless, Lewis's life was unusual, certainly by today's standards and even by the standards of his own time, creating a unique confluence

---

1. I have found Duriez, *Lewis* and McGrath, *Lewis* helpful for their accounts of Lewis's life.

of factors. While these factors could not have predicted who he would become, they certainly contributed to the person we know as C. S. Lewis. Lewis was born in 1898 in Belfast and grew up in a nominally Christian home but by his teenage years had become an atheist. He was inconsistently educated in various schools and especially by an influential private tutor. It would have been difficult to predict from the wide variety of Lewis's educational experiences that he would become the literary figure of significance that he became. Lewis was early on interested in folk tales and mythology, especially the fictional worlds of his Irish heritage. We might be surprised to know that Lewis struggled to be admitted to Oxford (he was apparently not very good in mathematics), where he studied, interrupted by service and being wounded in the First World War. Lewis completed degree exams with first class honours (the highest degree category) in classics, philosophy, and, as a last resort to enhance his chances of employment as an academic, English, which at the time at Oxford concentrated upon the earlier periods of English literature. Lewis wanted to be a philosopher, but he could not secure a permanent position in philosophy. Instead, Lewis found employment as a tutor in English in 1925 at Magdalen College at Oxford University, where he remained until 1954, when he was appointed as Professor of Medieval and Renaissance Literature, a personal professorial chair, at Cambridge University, a position he held until his retirement shortly before his death on November 22, 1963. Early on as an English don, Lewis gradually converted to Christianity, because of his own logical thinking as much as anything else. He admits to being a reluctant convert at the time. However, his conversion became the impetus for most of the activities of the rest of his life. Later in life, Lewis had the unusual experience of falling in love with and marrying Joy Davidman, who then died of cancer. Lewis himself died three years later, also of cancer.

On the one hand, Lewis's early life is full of change, and one might even say unexpected turns, as he moved between various schools and even private tuition. He was fully steeped in the life of a northern Irishman, which provided for major adjustments when he went to England to study. As for many of his time, World War I was a major event in his life, marked by his fighting in the trenches of Western Europe and being wounded and required to return home. By contrast, his time of study at Oxford, followed by his teaching at Oxford and Cambridge, appears to be, at least outwardly, relatively stable and serene, perhaps even the kind of life that any British academic would aspire to. Nevertheless, it was during this time that Lewis began his highly productive academic career, converted to Christianity, became a famous radio presenter of Christian apologetics, especially during the Second World War (some say he was perhaps one of the most widely recognized voices in Britain, second to Winston Churchill), and wrote his beautifully constructed fiction, along with some poetry that has received mixed responses among critics,[2] among other works. He became a husband under exceptionally difficult circumstances that reflect the kind of Christian values that he highly emphasized, including such things as honour, fidelity, and love.

His Work

Despite there being a growing number of biographies of Lewis, with some new and interesting facts still being discovered and published in more recent versions, most attention to Lewis remains upon his writings, particularly his Christian apologetics, lay theology, and fiction, especially his Narnia tales.

I do not attempt to review Lewis's literary corpus, as that would simply be impossible in a single work, to say nothing of an introductory essay. Nevertheless, I wish to categorize his writings in three groups and say a few words about each one. These three categories form the three divisions of this book: Apologetics and Philosophy (Part One), Fictional Worlds (Part Two), and Literature and Criticism (Part Three)—although some of these categories overlap.

Lewis originally wanted to be a philosopher, took a degree in philosophy, and wished to be an Oxford tutor in philosophy, a position he held for a very short period of a year before getting a more permanent position in English language and literature. Lewis never gave up the idea that he was a philosopher, or at least could have been a philosopher, to the point that he continued to engage in a variety of philosophical activities, such as chairing the Oxford Socratic Club for over ten years, a venue for debate over Christian and philosophical issues. Lewis, therefore, was philosophically minded from the outset, and so his Christian conversion provided an opportunity

---

2. Even though many have not highly regarded Lewis's poetry, I note that one of his poems was selected for the most recent version of *The Oxford Book of Twentieth Century English Verse* edited by the renowned twentieth-century poet Philip Larkin. See Lewis, "On a Vulgar Error," in Larkin, *Oxford Book*, 314, reprinted from Lewis, *Poems*, 60. Lewis as a poet loved traditional poetic forms, so it is not surprising that he felt left behind and was seen as out of harmony in a modernist poetic age that was instigated by Eliot's "The Love Song of J. Alfred Prufrock" (1915), in Eliot, *Complete Poems and Plays*, 3–7.

for him to express his philosophical ideas in an appropriate form of apologetics. These tendencies were aided by the exigencies of the Second World War that demanded a Christian response. Lewis continued to write apologetic works his entire life. In fact, one might well argue that most of what Lewis wrote, even if it was cast as fiction, was a form of apologetics.

Those who read Lewis all have their favourite works of apologetics by him. One of my earliest introductions to Lewis was reading his *The Screwtape Letters*, first published in 1942 during the Second World War.[3] I vividly remember reading it one summer and being struck by Lewis's poignant creativity. This example of fictional apologetics has retained its timeless character, since its concern is with how it is that the devils constantly try to entrap the unwary Christian, often by appeal to his own proclivities. As creative as the tale is, the heart of *The Screwtape Letters* is a strong commentary on the contemporary Christian life, in which Lewis, although addressing his own time, reveals uncanny ability to describe our own day and age. Others no doubt will turn to Lewis's *Mere Christianity*, first published in 1952, based upon war-time broadcasts.[4] I read this as an undergraduate contemplating majoring in philosophy. Even though I did not pursue the major in philosophy, I found Lewis's commonsense arguments and appeals to general human nature compelling and reinforcing beliefs that I already had, to the point that I realized that, with Lewis, I found a solid basis for holding to mere Christianity. The enduring significance of Lewis's *Mere Christianity* makes it no surprise that this work is cited by several of our authors in this volume. Another work of Lewis that is discussed by several of our authors is one that is far less well-known, *The Abolition of Man*, published in 1947.[5] In this work, Lewis presents some memorable images, when he characterizes those without moral strength as "men without chests" and instead advocates for following the "Tao," by which he means objective truth or even natural law. Other works could no doubt be mentioned as well, but these are several books of Lewis's apologetics that have continued to have widespread relevance.

I include Lewis's work in theology here as well. Lewis wrote numerous works that have continued to resonate within a church that has often wondered about its theology. We live today within an often-fragmented Christianity, where it is sometimes difficult to find common ground and

---

3. Lewis, *Screwtape Letters*.
4. Lewis, *Mere Christianity*.
5. Lewis, *Abolition of Man*.

even where there are incredible divisions over relatively simple and trivial things. In this regard, on the one hand, Lewis himself would probably not have been welcome in many of our contemporary churches, especially in North America, if for no other reason than his own use of alcohol and tobacco, as well as other elements of his lifestyle. On the other hand, Lewis himself—I speculate here, but I do so based upon what I think is compelling behavioural patterns in his own life—would probably have found even the limited use of social media, to say nothing of its proliferation and even fixation, among Christians as something that was at the least diverting, if not harmful, to Christian faith. I strongly doubt that Lewis would be a blogger or do many podcasts. Remember that Lewis himself did not read a daily newspaper so that he would not have his mind cluttered with the kinds of things that found their way into the contemporary media of his day. Lewis was a person devoted to well-chosen words, and despite his use of radio saw the printed word as paramount. Nevertheless, Lewis's lay theology still speaks to the hearts of many, often because of its deceptive simplicity, in which complex theological ideas are boiled down to relatively straightforward expressions. His *The Great Divorce*, published in 1946, is a case in point.[6] Over the years, and especially when I taught English, I have used this book several times and found that it provokes serious thinking among my students, even in an age that no longer even really understands what a bus ride is. One of the abiding questions in the Christian church—at least until relatively recently, when there seems to have emerged a flaccid universalism—is the question of hell. Lewis addresses this question by means of this apologetic work cast in the form of an allegory about a bus ride, in which the travelers are rewarded with the results of their own choice. Lewis satisfies neither hard nor soft deterministic sides in the debate, but nevertheless creates a compelling, and even emotionally moving, account of how human beings have everything to lose and yet still choose to be divorced from divine love. Lewis's *The Four Loves*, published in 1960, relatively late in Lewis's life, has always been a popular book because of its attempt to differentiate the various ways in which the concept of love—which can be conveyed in the Bible by means of a variety of Greek words—is to be understood.[7] At times, Lewis perhaps presses the distinctions among the meanings of the words too much to make his point, but the result is a much deeper understanding of a fundamental Christian concept that runs the

6. Lewis, *Great Divorce*.
7. Lewis, *Four Loves*.

risk of being diluted by the over-use and cheapening of a common English word.

The next area of Lewis's work to mention, and the next section in our volume, concerns the fictional worlds that Lewis created. These worlds are usually associated with his science fiction trilogy and his Narnia stories. The science fiction trilogy, which makes its own contribution to the sci-fi genre, revolves around a Dr. Ransom, an obvious Christ-figure within these stories of other worldly travel. However, much more widely known and read are *The Chronicles of Narnia*. These seven novels, published over a period from 1950–1956, form a cohesive set of volumes that, at least at first glance, appear to be children's stories.[8] They involve adventuresome children whose explorations of hidden spaces become entrees to an allegorical world of sin and salvation. In these stories, they encounter various figures, in many ways a sort of children's updated version of John Bunyan's *Pilgrim's Progress* (which inspired Lewis in his own work, *The Pilgrim's Regress*, his first novel),[9] but arguably perhaps even more highly allegorical with the anthropomorphized figure of the dangerous lion Aslan. Lewis's Narnia stories are certainly excellent examples of great children's literature, in that they can be read by children as children's stories, but they also have much wider and deeper appeal at all age levels up to and including ostensibly more mature adults. Lewis also wrote other fictional accounts, some of them, as already mentioned above, the means of conveyance of some of his theological and related writings but others of them more simply for the sheer enjoyment. Lewis had a genuine gift for creating fictional worlds, full of atmosphere and inhabited by memorable characters with whom the reader identifies and against whom readers react. Readers and writers continue to be highly interested in Lewis's fiction, to the point that much of the scholarly work written about Lewis has focused upon the Narnia tales. Some of these works provide guides and compendia and analyses of these eloquent examples of children's literature, to the point where I think that there are probably some readers who are unaware of much of the other writing of Lewis.

---

8. Lewis, *Chronicles of Narnia*, including *The Magician's Nephew* (1955—said by Lewis to be the first in the series for reading, even though written much later); *The Lion, the Witch, and the Wardrobe* (1950); *The Horse and his Boy* (1954); *Prince Caspian* (1951); *The Voyage of the Dawn Treader* (1952); *The Silver Chair* (1953); and *The Last Battle* (1956).

9. Lewis, *Pilgrim's Regress*.

The third and final category of Lewis's work is his literary criticism. As mentioned above, the way that Lewis made his living for virtually all his professional life was as a tutor and then professor in English at the universities of Oxford and then Cambridge. His specialization was medieval literature, an area with which he had a great affinity developed from his childhood and his interest in stories that had medieval connections and mythological and other imaginative dimensions to them. This interest no doubt had a direct bearing upon his membership in the group called "The Inklings," an informal group of writers with common interests—such as J. R. R. Tolkien, Owen Barfield, and Charles Williams, among others—who indulged one another by reading and discussing their imaginative writings.[10] Lewis's first major scholarly work, completed relatively soon after his conversion to Christianity, reflects his long-held interest in medieval literature and in particular the medieval Romance and its various conventions, such as courtly love. *The Allegory of Love* continues to be one of the best, if not the best, known of Lewis's scholarly publications.[11] However, during his scholarly career, Lewis was arguably even better known for his theory that—to put it boldly and in its most striking form—the Renaissance never happened. Lewis believed—and on many occasions strongly argued the point—that the dominant worldview, which had come into being with the rise of the Middle Ages, continued long past the Renaissance and even up to the nineteenth century. As a result, the Renaissance, which most scholars characterize as a significant turning point in the re-awakening of learning in the West, was viewed by Lewis as a continuation of this hierarchical and interconnected view of all elements of the world that developed in the Middle Ages and gave medieval and subsequent people a clear sense of their identity and place within the world. Such a view of the world is found in many of Lewis's writings, perhaps most clearly in his late book *The Discarded Image*, where he depicts and describes this image of the universe.[12]

Whereas his *The Allegory of Love* contains a wealth of knowledge of relatively obscure medieval sources, I believe that Lewis's arguably best work of literary criticism is his literary history of the sixteenth century excluding the drama.[13] The scope of this volume, large enough on its own, means that

---

10. Some of Lewis's reactions to these writers are found in the essays in Lewis, *Of This and Other Worlds*.
11. Lewis, *Allegory of Love*.
12. Lewis, *Discarded Image*.
13. Lewis, *English Literature*.

Lewis did not write about the dramatists, such as Shakespeare, who made the sixteenth century as important as it is for English literature. He instead offered a thorough treatment of the other writers, of both prose and poetry, of this period. What emerges is Lewis's very independent judgments on the various English-language authors of this period, including especially the English and Scots. Although not all his judgments have survived the test of time, his arguments continue to merit response. Today, Lewis's English literary scholarship—which encompassed, through book and especially essay form, a good portion of English literature up to the twentieth century—is probably the least well-known portion of his oeuvre, except for those who are specialists in English literature. He is still highly regarded for his literary history and criticism, such as his major article on Chaucer and the Troilus story or his various treatments of Spenser and Milton. It is only recently that English critical scholarship has begun to give Lewis his due as not just a literary historian but as a genuine literary critic of significance.

His Legacy

One would think that the legacy of Lewis would be much more easily determined, now that he has been dead for over sixty years. In some ways, I believe that this is true, although in others I believe that Lewis is just now establishing his reputation and confirming his legacy as his life and literary output continue to be studied in growing detail. In this section, I offer some ad hoc and admittedly personal comments upon what I see as Lewis's legacy in the three areas of his work mentioned above.

So far as Lewis's apologetics and philosophy are concerned, I think that his legacy has been mixed. There are certainly those who know of and recognize Lewis's Christian apologetics, especially during the Second World War, and how important this was for the British nation—that is, having a voice of deep Christian reflection and explanation in the midst of a time of severe testing and trial. Although these talks were published in three separate volumes soon after the talks were given, they were eventually consolidated and supplemented in *Mere Christianity*,[14] which has endured as one of Lewis's most important apologetic and theological writings. Within this historical context, Lewis is certainly to be commended, and he remains highly regarded. However, there are others who are much more guarded in their acknowledgment of Lewis's publications in these areas, since some

---

14. Lewis, *Mere Christianity*, 5, based upon *Broadcast Talks* (1942), *Christian Behaviour* (1943), and *Beyond Personality* (1944).

believe that his ideas have not stood the test of time as well as have his writings in other areas. Most would probably say that, despite his original aspirations, Lewis, even though a quick and sharp thinker, was not a deep and original philosopher. So many of the ideas that he promotes in his works, while they have broad appeal, especially to a lay theological audience, are not as enduring as contributions to other areas in which he wrote. One of the examples of this is his *Mere Christianity*. *Mere Christianity* shows that Lewis, despite whatever else he may have believed, was a commonsense realist who appealed to a general human nature. The kinds of appeals that he often makes in *Mere Christianity* are those of a twentieth-century Western European, especially an Englishman, who assumes that the world is as it appears to be to such an Englishman. As a result, various ethical assumptions rely upon an agreed-upon view of humanity and how it should act, the kind of actions that one would expect of an Englishman, perhaps especially of an Englishman who had spent much of his adult life in such places as Oxford and Cambridge. Similar critiques might be brought of some of his other apologetic and theological writings. However, there are others who would respond that, with advances that we have made in the cognitive sciences, especially in the last half century, we have come to realize that, whereas environment is important in shaping human behaviour, all human beings have a common hard-wiring that makes them think in the same ways using the same cognitive apparatus. If this is true cognitively, it is arguably true spiritually and in other ways as well, thus supporting the notion of a general nature that is common to humanity and the basis of generalization about humans at their most fundamental.

As mentioned above, Lewis's literary historical and critical writings are probably the least well known and where his legacy is the least substantial—again, apart from those within literary circles who study him for professional reasons. However, even here he has never been identified with the major movements in literary criticism of the early to mid-twentieth century but has remained an outsider to many of the major influential ideas within literary criticism. Lewis was best known and continues to be primarily known, where he is known as a literary scholar, as a literary historian, and where his book *English Literature in the Sixteenth Century Excluding Drama* continues to be heralded as a major work of its time and even of subsequent times. Literary historians have only occasionally been known as those who are poised on the cutting edge of literary theory or novel and avant-garde approaches to textual interpretation. In that regard, for the most part, Lewis would probably not have wanted to be identified with such a position, since he preferred simply to endorse good reading. There are instances, admittedly, where he goes against the contemporary interpretive grain and makes comments that place him sometimes at odds with and sometimes in a surprisingly supportive position in relation to English literary theory of his time. Nevertheless, it has been argued, and probably convincingly, that Lewis himself is to be seen as part of the humanist tradition of literary criticism.[15] His works in literary theory are relatively few, and his comments in this regard tend to be more incidental than expansive and well-developed. However, his stance as a literary historian and critic is within the broad humanistic tradition of those who believe in the importance of the attentive reading of the major works of English (and for Lewis often related) literature. This canon of literature formed the backbone of Western civilization (and only relatively recently has come under attack), and so humanistic readers believe that knowledge of this literary tradition has been instrumental in the development of the West. Lewis would not only fit within this picture as avidly embracing such a humanistic approach, but he would promote such a position and its canon of authors. Nevertheless, in a day and age that has moved from modernism to post-modernism, from structuralism to post-structuralism, such views are decidedly in the minority and as a result Lewis's legacy in this area is probably at its least enduring.

Regarding Lewis's fictional writings, this is where Lewis continues to generate the most attention and has created the most enduring legacy. In many ways this is not incidental to who Lewis was. As noted above, Lewis had a great interest in fictional worlds since his childhood. This interest was encouraged and promoted in various ways, both in his own literary writing, where he embraced the Romantic literary tradition, and in his association with other writers who themselves were interested in and developed their own fictional worlds. These are the worlds of Narnia, Perelandra, Middle Earth, and other such fictional worlds where children and hobbits and others occupied them, and their adventures were conveyed in such a way as to continue to arouse the excitement and interest of new reading audiences. However, I would go further and suggest that works that are not strictly within such fictional worlds but that are themselves fiction used for other purposes, such as Lewis's *The Screwtape Letters* or his *The Great Divorce*, to name only a couple, owe much of their enduring significance to the fact

---

15. See Calin, *Twentieth-Century Humanistic Critics*.

that not only are they works of lay theology by Lewis but they are theology written in a fictional key and drawing upon Lewis's great abilities as a great storyteller to give them their enduring importance. Lewis had an ability not just to use the right words and hardly ever the wrong word but to create fictional scenarios that resonated with life situations—and they continue to do so. When we read *The Screwtape Letters*, even though we know that the entire account is a fiction, there is something compelling about the figures of Screwtape and his subordinate Wormwood that draw us into the tale and propel us to continue reading. The same is true of many of Lewis's other works. We too are *Surprised by Joy* and warm to the story of his hard-won conversion to Christianity, and we too grieve with him over the loss of a loved one, Lewis's wife, in his *A Grief Observed*.[16]

Lewis's legacy, therefore, is probably created as much by his power of words as it is by any other dimension of his writing. There is no doubt that Lewis was incredibly knowledgeable, with a deep cultural background and a sharp mind that was able to penetrate issues with keen insight. There is also no doubt that Lewis had a shockingly deep literary knowledge that came about as the result of continued and wide reading especially in English literature from its earliest periods to the present, but also in related literatures, to the point where there were few literary subjects on which Lewis could not speak and write with confidence. And for a person who did not have formal theological education, Lewis also demonstrates a surprisingly mature ability to identify and focus upon the kinds of issues that his readers would find most helpful in the Christian life, whether it is issues of joy or grief or love or pain or simply the grounds of belief and the way they ought to live. These are all important in identifying what makes Lewis the compelling author that he continues to be. However, I believe that it is his winsome style, his ability to turn a phrase, his knack for finding the right word and expressing his thoughts vividly in compelling and smooth prose (and even sometimes in poetry), his adroit depiction of character, and perhaps most of all his ability to weave an interesting tale—in other words, his ability with the English language—that will remain Lewis's greatest legacy and that continually brings readers back to his variety of writings to read and study them further.

---

16. Lewis, *Surprised by Joy*; and Lewis, *Grief Observed*.

LEWIS'S CONTINUING INFLUENCE AND THE ESSAYS IN THIS VOLUME

The essays in this volume reflect the three categories mentioned above under his works: apologetics and philosophy, fictional worlds, and literature and criticism. The presentation of these essays in this volume now becomes part of the continuing influence of Lewis.

Apologetics and Philosophy

There are three chapters in this first section on apologetics and philosophy. In the first, Adam Barkman and Tristan Barkman take up one of the major issues in Christian theology, the problem of evil and suffering. This chapter is both an examination of the thought of C. S. Lewis on the problem of pain and an attempt to address some of the weaknesses in Lewis's argument in an attempt to establish a stronger Christian apologetic. The authors approach this question through one of the areas that Lewis addressed, and that is the question of animal suffering. Whereas most attempts to deal with theodicy—the problem of evil—focus upon the human situation, this essay addresses the question of how we should view animal suffering. This is a particularly poignant topic in light of much recent discussion regarding the relationship of humans to animals over such issues as sentience. The authors respond in detail to four suggestions that Lewis makes regarding animal suffering. Although the authors find shortcomings with the three major arguments that Lewis makes and attempt to remedy them, they find a fourth proposal, intimated by Lewis regarding the role of suffering in developing moral virtue in humans, as the most satisfactory apologetic defense. This essay provides an important starting point for this volume, as it engages fully with both Lewis and his opponents on a topic of abiding significance.

The next chapter, by Mark McKim, addresses the question of post-modernism. This may at first seem surprising, since Lewis died before post-modernism came to be widely recognized. His writings, however, anticipated and responded to the two major characteristics of post-modernism: questioning or even denying the ability of human reason to discern truth, and rejecting the possibility of meta-narrative. A major theme in Lewis's writings, including *The Abolition of Man*, is the conviction that there is a *consensus gentium*. This consensus points to there being a transcendent reality, an authority *external* to humanity, which defines what is good, right, and beautiful, and which makes both discerning truth and meta-narrative possible. The existence of this consensus not only points to the existence of a transcendent reality but also calls into question the two major tenets of post-modern thinking. Lewis's arguments for this consensus are the commonalties of both the myths of every culture and the moral teachings of the world's major religions and philosophies. Although Lewis also views the experience of what he called "joy," a deep, unsatisfied longing, as evidence of the reality of the consensus, he did not develop this line of thought as thoroughly as the other two. In this chapter, McKim enlarges on Lewis's thinking about joy. He argues that *joy* is a very common and widespread experience and that expanding our understanding of it may be a means of persuading others to reconsider their secular and post-modern worldview.

In the final chapter in this section, Jason Vander Horst also discusses Lewis's *The Abolition of Man*. In that book, Lewis warns that the rise of moral relativism brings the risk of people becoming "men without chests"—individuals who have lost the capacity for true moral conviction. Vander Horst sees this problem as more relevant today than ever, especially in education, where students are often encouraged to adopt pragmatic moral frameworks. He labels this the "Pick your Poison" problem: the tendency for individuals to treat moral frameworks like weapons in an arsenal, choosing the one that best suits their immediate interest, often reflecting self-serving biases rather than timeless moral values. In response, Vander Horst turns to Lewis and contemporary psychology to illustrate the tangible harms of moral relativism.

Fictional Worlds

The second part focuses upon Lewis's fictional worlds, especially *The Chronicles of Narnia*, but also *The Screwtape Letters*. There is still much to be learned from reading these various fictional works in new ways and from new vantage points, as several of the essays in this section illustrate.

In the first chapter of this section, Paul Robinson takes a cue from a comment in *The Screwtape Letters* regarding sacramental elements in the world and examines birdsong in *The Chronicles of Narnia*. Robinson goes through the various tales and examines numerous important episodes where birdsong is depicted in sacramental ways that point to another, divine reality. He does not think that every reference to birdsong fits within this category, but once he opens it up for examination, it is surprising how many instances there are to examine. Whereas we may be surprised to read a paper devoted to birdsong, Robinson points out that Lewis himself was a great lover of music and this comes through in various ways in his works. Lewis saw music as providing a means for humans to encounter God, and so it is in the various episodes in the *Chronicles* that Robinson cites, especially, so Robinson contends, if one reads the individual tales in the order in which they were published, rather than in the order that Lewis later recommended. There is a revealing of the sacramental nature of birdsong because of how the tales unfold, with later encounters offering fuller understanding of previous episodes. Birdsong provides an invitation for the human to unite with God's creation in divine communion.

In the next chapter, Seán McGuire also examines *The Chronicles of Narnia*, but he does so for a completely different purpose. He draws upon them as a means of providing guidance for contemporary pastors as they are confronted by the challenges of ministry that require leadership within the church. McGuire does so by invoking what he characterizes as pragmatism that is based in the notion of playfulness, especially as espoused by the contemporary philosopher and hermeneut Hans-Georg Gadamer. McGuire is careful, however, to make a distinction between pragmatism and practicality. He finds fault with the latter, which he sees as being all too prevalent in the contemporary church as leaders go for easy solutions to the problems of leadership. Despite the identification of the problem, however, one might not expect the concept of play to offer a suitable means of addressing the problems. McGuire disagrees, because he sees playfulness as a means of creating virtue. In the same way that play is fundamental to Gadamer's thought about what it means to be fully human, so McGuire uses play to describe a movement out of which emerges a creative and expansive push toward truth.

In the final essay in this section, David Yoon focuses upon *The Screwtape Letters*. At the conference, Yoon outlined his own creative writing project of letters from an angel to his associate, fashioned after the opposite found in *The Screwtape Letters*. These *Letters to Bradus* are currently being written. For this conference volume, rather than presenting a few of the letters of this unfinished project, Yoon instead offers an analysis of Lewis's *Screwtape Letters* and the several features, both good and bad, that make them memorable, instructive, and worthy of imitation. He identifies several of these features, which include subtlety and complacency, pride and self-deception, distraction, and suffering and trials. He defines and depicts them in the collection of letters as forming a means of defining the central themes that he intends to treat in his own fictionalized account of angelic letters.

Literature and Criticism

The third and final section of this volume includes three essays that treat various dimensions of literature and criticism. I mentioned earlier that Lewis's literary criticism, as important as it was in his own professional career, has been relatively less important in studying the life and writings of Lewis, especially by Christians who are not engaged in literary history or criticism. Nevertheless, several of our participants in the conference focused upon Lewis as a literary scholar in either his accomplishments or the making.

In the first essay, Stanley Porter raises the question of what kind of scholar Lewis was. By this, he recognizes that Lewis has been characterized in a variety of ways that attempt to capture how his background contributed to his varied writings. Instead, Porter wishes to examine Lewis as a literary critic and historian by tracing his major ideas through his major book-length treatments of literary subjects. Those who are not familiar with Lewis the literary scholar may be surprised to read the technically sophisticated and highly developed literary works that Lewis produced during his scholarly career—while at the same time he was writing very popular apologetic writings and, even more so, his fictional worlds as found in *The Chronicles of Narnia*. Porter focuses upon Lewis's major works of literary scholarship, beginning with his *The Allegory of Love*, published in 1936 very early in his academic career, and ending with the final work published during his lifetime, *An Experiment in Criticism* (1961), but also including several posthumous works. Several major ideas emerge from this critical survey, including Lewis's view of the medieval world that he believed continued in existence in the West until the nineteenth century, Lewis's major literary-critical ideas and how they related to the predominant patterns in literary criticism of the time, and his enduring contribution especially to literary history as found in his monumental survey of English literature of the sixteenth century (excluding drama).

Aaron Jung focuses upon one of Lewis's works of literary criticism, his *An Experiment in Criticism*, as noted above the last book in literary studies that Lewis published on his own during his lifetime. Jung observes that Lewis was not afraid to read and talk about literature in ways that put him outside the mainstream of his contemporaries in other English departments of the time. In his *Experiment in Criticism*, Lewis reacts against the Romanticism of the nineteenth century while also embracing a mimetic view of literature that dates to ancient times. Jung examines in detail the relationship between art and text as a means of understanding how Lewis placed such value in the mimetic view of literature. Although some might see Lewis as highly objective (while others as highly subjective), Jung sees Lewis as negotiating a mediating position between the two, one that resonates with several of the approaches to literature current during the middle part of the last century. Lewis sees criticism as itself a kind of art form, and so it warrants serious exploration of the ways in which we read and interpret texts.

The final essay of this volume is not focused upon any particular scholarly work by Lewis but upon Lewis's personal correspondence and both what it reveals about Lewis and how it plays a role in his own development as a reader, writer, and thinker. Since Lewis's death, the publication of his letters in three volumes has opened up many possibilities for probing more deeply into Lewis's life. In this essay, Dawn Berkelaar focuses upon the correspondence between Lewis and his friend Arthur Greeves that occurred over the course of nearly fifty years. In many respects, Lewis and Greeves were very dissimilar, to the point that one might legitimately wonder how they could even have become acquaintances, much less life-long friends. Nevertheless, friends they became. As Berkelaar points out, Lewis reveals himself in his letters to Greeves in ways that are profoundly moving and reveal the kind of person he was, especially as a faithful friend who continued to write to his childhood companion, even as their lives in many ways moved further apart. But the letters also reveal many of the qualities that are found elsewhere in Lewis and that constitute the heart of who he was: his seriousness, his faithfulness, his lack of self-focus, his self-awareness, and his honesty. The person who appears as the authorial voice in Lewis's other writings is the same person who engages in faithful correspondence with his life-long friend, even as they lived different lives at distances apart. Lewis reveals through the correspondence that a person is much more than his or her public representation but is to be seen in how he or she lives their daily life in relation to others, especially those for whom there is no apparent advantage in knowing. Lewis was such a person throughout his life.

This brings us to the end of the volume. If I may be excused for speaking on behalf of the contributors to this volume, we recognize that this is not a book that makes any pretense of speaking a final word about C. S.

Lewis. Too much has already been said about him, and he is far too great a figure, as indicated by his life and work, to be able to attempt such a final statement. This book, instead, attempts to identify various interesting features of Lewis's life and work and to comment upon them as a means of exploring tried and true areas regarding Lewis, open up new avenues for further exploration even when we think that we may have exhausted the possibilities of doing so, and bring into new relationships various elements of Lewis's life and work that will prompt further exploration. Lewis had a complex origin and past; however, he also had—despite indicators to the contrary—a complex life that led him to exploration through various media and modalities some of the major ideas of his or any age regarding human existence, the nature of God, and how we understand the world around us, especially in its verbal representations. We trust that this volume will be deemed a worthy contributor to this ongoing exploration of the life and work of C. S. Lewis.

BIBLIOGRAPHY

Calin, William. *The Twentieth-Century Humanist Critics: From Spitzer to Frye*. Toronto: University of Toronto Press, 2007.

Duriez, Colin. *C. S. Lewis: A Biography of Friendship*. Oxford: Lion, 2013.

Eliot, T. S. *The Complete Poems and Plays 1909–1950*. New York: Harcourt, Brace & World, 1971.

Larkin, Philip, ed. *The Oxford Book of Twentieth Century English Verse*. Oxford: Oxford University Press, 1973.

Lewis, C. S. *The Abolition of Man: Or Reflections on Education with Special Reference to the Teaching of English in the Upper Forms of Schools*. New York: Macmillan, 1947.

———. *The Allegory of Love: A Study in Medieval Tradition*. Oxford: Oxford University Press, 1936.

———. *The Chronicles of Narnia*. Reprint, New York: HarperEntertainment, 2001.

———. *The Discarded Image: An Introduction to Medieval and Renaissance Literature*. Cambridge: Cambridge University Press, 1964.

———. *English Literature in the Sixteenth Century Excluding Drama*. Oxford History of English Literature. Oxford: Clarendon, 1954.

———. *The Four Loves*. London: HarperCollins, 1960.

———. *The Great Divorce*. New York: Macmillan, 1946.

———. *A Grief Observed*. New York: HarperCollins, 1961.

———. *Mere Christianity*. Glasgow: Collins, 1952.

———. *Of This and Other Words*. Edited by Walter Hooper. London: Collins, 1982.

———. *The Pilgrim's Regress*. London: Dent, 1933.

———. *Poems*. Edited by Walter Hooper. San Diego: Harcourt Brace Jovanovich, 1964.

———. *The Screwtape Letters*. New York: Macmillan, 1950.

———. *Surprised by Joy: The Shape of My Early Life*. Glasgow: Collins, 1955.

McGrath, Alister. *C. S. Lewis—A Life: Eccentric Genius, Reluctant Prophet.* Carol Stream, IL: Tyndale House, 2013.

Part One

Apologetics and Philosophy

A Virtue Approach to Mass Animal Suffering

or, the Problems and Promise
of C. S. Lewis's Theory of Animal Pain

Adam Barkman and Tristan Barkman

INTRODUCTION

On the surface, there are a number of reasons to doubt the existence of an all-powerful, all-knowing, and perfectly good God. The Bible, among other sources of authority, compares God to a father who cares about his children, and yet at the same time, God seemingly remains very silent and hidden from the experiences of many, even the most devout. Similarly, the sheer amount of evil and horror that the world produces is very hard to square with a good, wise, and powerful father. In recent years, James Sterba, a renowned philosophy professor at Notre Dame University, declared himself an atheist on the grounds that the sheer amount of evil in the world cannot possibly be compatible with theism.[1] Indeed, claims like this often cite new studies coming in from the sciences and social sciences that show nature to be vaster, more ancient, and more uncaring and brutal than we had hitherto believed.

Although rarely topping the list of major objections to the existence of God, the problem of animal suffering, a sub-category of the broad problem of evil, is an issue that has increasingly come to the attention of philosophers and theologians. While some, in Kierkegaardian fashion, celebrate the absurdity of belief in God, and others, like Gijsbert van den Brink, are

---

1. Sterba and Swinburne, *Could a Good God Permit So Much Suffering?*

PART ONE: APOLOGETICS AND PHILOSOPHY

inclined to "skeptical theism" in the face of these sorts of objections,[2] there are others who yet attempt to give rational defences of the God of Christianity in the face of the newest evidence.

C. S. Lewis, who himself occasionally flirted with "skeptical theism" in regard to this problem, nevertheless, is generally seen as one who thinks a rational explanation for mass animal suffering is possible. While Lewis is not the only or even the most thorough defender of the various rational defences that exist, he does raise, in our view, the three most plausible approaches that Christian theists might take in respect to animal suffering and, as such, his views on animal suffering are worth exploring with seriousness. Nevertheless, as we shall argue, while none of Lewis's explicit suggestions in respect to mass animal suffering are entirely satisfactory, he does provide, in works unrelated to animal suffering per se, the seeds of a fourth explanation that we think both original and defensible, namely, that mass animal suffering can extend the possibility of the greatest goods, which is to say, moral virtues in rational creatures.

LEWIS'S FIRST SUGGESTION: ANIMAL SUFFERING IS NOT AS OBVIOUS AS WE MIGHT THINK

Although we remain flexible in regard to whether God uses or does not use macroevolution to create, we agree with Lewis that our planet is very old and that animals have existed on it for hundreds of millions of years before humans ever appeared.[3] What many would add, however, is that animals that lived hundreds of millions of years before humans came on the scene were designed by God to suffer and that hundreds of millions of years of this suffering is a "serious problem."[4] God being the architect of animal suffering and his apparent indifference with respect to the sheer amount of animal suffering, however, are two points that Lewis is not willing to concede easily.

Regarding the first point—the apparent divine blueprint for animal suffering—there is an additional point that Lewis thinks pushes the problem back even further, and this is what we would like to discuss in this section. Both in his early work relating to the problem of animal suffering, such as *The Problem of Pain* in 1940, and in his later writings, such as in a

2. van den Brink, *Reformed Theology*, 134.

3. "[W]e have good reason to believe that animals existed long before men. Carnivorousness, with all that it entails, is older than humanity" (Lewis, *Problem of Pain*, 542).

4. Cf. Illingworth, "Problem of Pain," 113.

letter written in 1962—just one year before his death—Lewis consistently highlights our general ignorance of what an animal *is*. He writes, "How strange that God brings us into such intimate relations with creatures of whose real purpose and destiny we remain forever ignorant.... What is a flea for, or a wild dog?"[5] Here Lewis is talking about the final cause or purpose in God creating animals, and Lewis, in an Aristotelian fashion, suggests that ignorance of this significantly hinders subsequent discussions surrounding animal ethics.

We are partly sympathetic to Lewis's broad Aristotelian comment here. To illustrate our appreciation of Lewis's point about final cause, consider ancient cave art. It is a well-known phenomenon for those who study cave art to find both guides to these sites and even the anthropologists studying them exaggerating the level of certainty that exists with respect to the purpose of particular cave paintings. Is the man in the headdress a shaman? Is his standing behind the antelope his attempt to appropriate the animal's power? Does his before-and-after positioning show his increase in status and power? Perhaps. If this sort of explanation of the art's purpose and meaning is accepted, then we certainly can say many things about the culture that produced it; but if this explanation is mistaken—if we get the intentionality of the artist wrong—then this will necessarily affect our subsequent explanation for the worse. To Lewis's point, then, given that God has not explicitly told us his purpose in creating animals (and especially ones "off the grid" like prehistoric beasts), we should be cautious in our ethical judgments concerning them. Cautious—we agree with Lewis—yet perhaps not as cautious as Lewis himself is.

In addition to forwarding some doubts about the final cause of animals, Lewis also thinks that a significant problem relating to alleged animal suffering comes from a faulty view of the formal cause or specific nature of animals: "We know neither what [animals] are nor why they are."[6] Thinking along Aristotelian lines, Lewis seemingly classifies biological life into sentient (feeling) and non-sentient (non-feeling), and then further distinguishes sentient life into those capable of reasoning about their sentience and those incapable of so reasoning.

Plants, on this model and according to Lewis, are non-sentient, and so, thinking purely in terms of plants being harmed and dying, there is

---

5. "26th October 1962" (Lewis, *Collected Letters—Volume III*, 1377).

6. Lewis, "Pains of Animals," 192–93. This was written in 1950, ten years after *The Problem of Pain*, and ten years before the letter quoted earlier.

no moral problem per se. Although not a zoologist much less one up-to-date on the latest research on animality, Lewis further adds that likely the vast majority of animals (insects, for instance) are, in fact, closer to non-sentience than sentience, and their alleged suffering is not something that Lewis—unlike Charles Darwin and his caterpillar—is morally bothered by.[7]

Animals that seem incapable of reflecting on their sentience include a vast host of creatures more complex than insects but less complex than humans (whom we can classify as "rational animals" if we like or simply something higher than animals). Humans are clearly creatures that are capable of reflecting on their pain sensations, and the purpose of this reflection appears to be for the benefit of the human in terms of aiding the survival and fitness of the human in the biological sense (for example, knowing that a nail in your foot hurts helps you to avoid stepping on one in the future) and, far more importantly, to aid human moral development—that is, pain, for imperfect creatures, is a necessary means to the production of moral virtue (more on this later). Where Lewis is controversial—although we also think somewhat misunderstood—is in his questioning of whether animals do in fact *suffer*; that is, whether sentient creatures—animals capable of feeling pain (we may include or exclude insects if we like)—can be said not simply to feel pain, but to suffer it.

Lewis's suggestion here is that perhaps higher animals, while certainly having the biological mechanisms to register pain sensations in their brains, do not have the capacity to make sense beyond the moment of said pain. A goat being eaten alive by a Komodo dragon feels "P" at t_1, "A" at t_2, "I" at t_3, and "N" at t_4 before it finally dies.[8] On Lewis's initial suggestion—in his first and unqualified remarks in *The Problem of Pain*—the goat might not be in a position to spell out "PAIN" since this spelling out requires a psyche that can unify the various pain-sensations over time. For Lewis, the spelling out of "PAIN" is what we call "suffering," and this might—he says in a tentative fashion—only occur in the higher types of beings.

Christopher Southgate[9] and Michael Murray,[10] arguably the most authoritative voices with respect to the problem of animal suffering, both classify Lewis in this respect as a neo-Cartesian, presumably since

---

7. Lewis, "Pains of Animals," 194.
8. Lewis, *Problem of Pain*, 545.
9. Southgate, *Monotheism*, 8.
10. Murray, *Nature Red*, 43. See also Devries, "Andrew Linzey."

Descartes argues that biological bodies (the human body and animals, for example) are more like machines than souls: "The body of a man is a kind of machine equipped with ... bones, nerves ... in such a way that even if there were no mind in it, it would still perform all the same movements as it now does ... even without will."[11] Descartes is often misunderstood here as if he were saying that animals *are* machines and the pain within them is not morally significant. But what he in fact claims is that the human bodies, like higher animals, have sense perceptions and something like an Aristotelian sensitive imagination,[12] and so are able to receive pain sensations and hold them inwardly in the form of "images," and that these images presumably aid the body or animal in its adaptability. The human body in its own right, and the higher animals in general, thus "avoid what induces a feeling of pain and seek out what induces feelings of pleasure," and it does not appear to be Descartes's purpose—no more than it was Aristotle's—to regard the mangling of a dog and the mangling of a machine as equally morally significant.[13] Certainly, this is not Lewis's point as we shall see. Rather, Lewis is interested in arguing that given a real distinction between a rational creature like a human, and a merely sentient creature or higher biological organism like an animal, we should be cautious to avoid a real category mistake that would distort the problem of animal suffering.[14] Not being a rational will (Descartes) or a "[Self]-Consciousness or ... [Rational] Soul" (Lewis), a higher animal is not the same as a human, and so the suffering humans feel when their bodies are mangled is likely different and greater than that which the higher animals undergo.[15] We must not make the problem of animal suffering greater than it is if, again, we have reason to think animals are different from humans or at least if we do not have reason to think them sufficiently similar to humans. Some ignorance of animal nature should make us cautious not to overstate the problem.

Lewis's cautionary tone with respect to the purpose and nature of animals is one that we appreciate, and we certainly agree that the distinction between humans and animals—rational-willed, self-conscious, choosing creatures and those that are not—is central and non-negotiable regarding

11. Descartes, "Meditations," 58 (see esp. §6.84).
12. See Aristotle, *De anima*, 680 (3.3/428a1–21680; Barnes, Bollingen).
13. Descartes, "Meditations," 58 (see esp. §6.84).
14. "I myself am inclined to think that far fewer animals than is supposed have what we should recognize as consciousness" (Lewis, "Vivisection," 694).
15. Lewis, *Problem of Pain*, 541.

the problem of pain in general and the problem of animal suffering specifically. We also think that the literature that dismisses Lewis as a neo-Cartesian (whatever this means exactly) inadequately represents him since there are, even in *The Problem of Pain*, times when Lewis is open to non-rational-but-higher-animals, such as bears and wolves,[16] being capable of spelling "PAIN" or suffering in a morally significant sense.[17] Indeed, in his 1948 essay denouncing vivisection, Lewis writes of his own experience with animals, "They certainly behave as if they [are suffering]."[18]

Our disagreement with Lewis, then, is not as significant as that by those that would have him claiming that animals do not suffer at all. Rather, our critique is more limited and centres around two smaller but real objections.

First, even if we are right in attributing a kind of Aristotelian psychology to Lewis, seeing higher animals as capable of imagining[19] their pain, and so, for the purposes of adaptability, possibly "suffering" in a limited sense, the individual pain units felt by low-to-mid-range animals who might lack an imagination are still, in our opinion, experiencing something bad and it is not obvious that this is morally insignificant.[20] The self-conscious nature of man, which makes him like God and unlike the animals, certainly extends man's ability to suffer well beyond a pain-feeling-and-painful-image-possessing bear or wolf. But what of a small-to-mid-range creature like a sparrow? Suppose for the sake of argument that a sparrow can neither rationally reflect on its pain as a man nor can it "imagine" as a bear or wolf might—suppose that a sparrow merely experiences Lewis's sequence of "P," "A," "I," and "N," or what some call "first-order" pain detection.[21] Is this lack of durability or continuity of the felt-pain morally insignificant? The pain felt seems to be, in some sense, against the flourishing of the sparrow's nature, and, in itself, is a kind of badness. It might be a necessary badness

---

16. "By the way read Lorenz's *King Solomon's Ring: New Light on Animal Ways* on animal—especially bird—behaviour. There are instincts I had never dreamed of: big with a promise of real morality. The wolf is a v. different creature from what we imagine" ("28th May 1952" [Lewis, *Collected Letters—Volume III*, 195]).

17. See Murray, *Nature Red*, 44.

18. Lewis, "Vivisection," 694.

19. For Aristotle, the sentient or sensitive imagination simply provides the creature with "an image of x," and this faculty should not be confused with that which can creatively construct original images or mental pictures.

20. See Murray, *Nature Red*, 48–49.

21. See Murray, *Nature Red*, 56.

(as we will later argue), but it is still a kind of badness. Assuming, as we do, that God is morally good, then he likely could not cause a sparrow (which he is always mindful of [Luke 10:29]) to feel even pain without any trade-off or greater purpose in mind.[22]

Connected to this is our second objection, namely, that there is something about the way that Lewis talks about animal suffering in some parts of *The Problem of Pain* that is—with the greatest respect to him—lacking in common sense, out-of-step with his own later insistence on how these senses can and should elicit "stock responses" in us,[23] and, in all this, potentially inattentive to God's goodness due to this. Descartes himself provides some of the initial pushback here since it is Descartes who makes one of the pillars of his philosophy that God is good and this entails that he is essentially not a deceiver. God not being a deceiver applies to those who would defend the strong thesis that animals do not suffer *and* those who, with our more generous interpretation of Lewis, think the pain sensations of low-to-mid-range animals is morally insignificant. We ourselves think that God can, and does, have good reasons for hiding himself at times, and we would not agree with the tradition that thinks all deception is blanketed injustice. Rather we accept the Cartesian insight behind Richard Swinburne's "Principle of Honesty," which states, "God has an obligation not to make a world in which agents are systematically deceived on important matters without their having the possibility of discovering their deception."[24]

Applied to our critique of Lewis, we think that since God is the morally perfect being who gives us common sense[25] and expects of us certain stock responses with regard to the world he has made, then what appears clear to properly functioning senses in an environment they are designed to function in[26] should, as a tentative or default position, be believed to be

---

22. We agree with Schneider that "the appearance of animal suffering is extremely strong," but voice his unspoken assumption here that this appearance is something that we generally ought to trust (see Schneider, *Animal Suffering*, 59).

23. Three years after writing *The Problem of Pain*, Lewis approvingly cites Coleridge when the poet suggests that the experience of a waterfall ought to produce in us a kind of stock, objective, common, proper, or God-designed response, in this case, sublimity (see *Abolition of Man*, 399).

24. Swinburne, *Providence*, 139.

25. We use "common sense" here to mean something like the faculty that provides us with "properly basic beliefs" or beliefs that are reasonable to hold in a default manner or before philosophical argumentation. These beliefs often work as the foundation of our other beliefs.

26. Here we borrow a number of insights from Plantinga and the common-sense

true and something God wants us to believe to be true. We do not deny that what appears to us by default could, ultimately, turn out to be different upon closer examination. But we distinguish between overly easy denials of the reports of common sense and those that approach such denials with fear and trembling. For example, a Niels Bohr thinking the universe is radically hostile to all belief in regularity due to quantum mechanics, or a George Berkeley thinking that an unperceived tree that falls in a forest did not actually fall would both be examples of those radically opposed to common sense in their various ways, and would, in this radicalness, indirectly implicate God in unjust deception, while an Albert Einstein, on the other hand, who thinks quantum mechanics can be reconciled with a common sense belief in a hidden regularity, or a Thomas Reid, who thinks a real tree has actually fallen, would be better attuned to the reports of God-given common sense and so are more in keeping with belief in a good God.[27]

As has been argued elsewhere, although Lewis himself often defends commonsensical beliefs, he never entirely left behind the influence of his former Idealism, especially Berkeleian Subjective Idealism, and it is possible that this caused him to be, at least in places, more skeptical of animal pain than he ought to have been.[28] But whatever the reason is for his apparent skepticism in respect to pain in low-to-mid-range animals at least, we think that common sense inclines us to believe that the pain-signaling or pain-guarding behaviour of animals is reasonable evidence that they are in fact experiencing pain, that this pain likely hinders their flourishing, and that this is morally significant as a result. Thus, we stand with Lewis in asserting that animal pain and suffering is perhaps not as clear or as much as some might think (we are in no danger of becoming a Sterba here), but against Lewis in thinking that more animals experience pain and suffering than he supposes, and that God wants us to believe that this pain and suffering is both real and bad.

Reformed epistemologists (Neo-Calvinist students of Thomas Reid if one likes). See Plantinga, *Warranted Christian Belief*.

27. The debate between Bohr (the denier of all regularity) and Einstein (the defender of a hidden regularity behind quantum irregularity) is the basis of Einstein's famous saying, "God doesn't play dice." Cf. Lehner, "Einstein's Realism," 307.

28. Many years after his conversion to a kind of Neo-Platonic Christianity, Lewis could still be heard saying things like, "I still think Berkeley is unanswerable" ("15th February 1946" [Lewis, *Collected Letters—Volume II*, 70]). And remnants of Lewis's idealism can also be found in his much later works, such as *Prayer*. For more on this, see Barkman, *C. S. Lewis*.

LEWIS'S SECOND SUGGESTION: GOD DOES NOT WILL MOST ANIMAL SUFFERING

When Lewis became a teenager, he lost his nominal faith in God and became a kind of Epicurean or a metaphysical materialist (who thought moral rightness resides in maximizing pleasure and minimizing pain for the individual).[29] Part of his reason for this atheistic conversion was due to what he called his "Argument from Undesign,"[30] namely, that the physical world or nature is so full of imperfections and evils that there could not possibly be a good, wise, and powerful Creator behind it. Even when Lewis returned to Christianity, he insisted that all arguments from nature that try to prove the existence of a good God fail since nature is plainly imperfect and corrupt.[31] Here, then, we can see the seeds of Lewis's second approach to animal suffering, namely, that if many animals *do* in fact suffer, the cause of this suffering needs to be compatible with a good God.

In 1932, around the time of his conversion to Christianity, Lewis wrote of his visit to Whipsnade Zoo that the combination of birds, summer flowers, and the zoo's bear (which he called "Bultitude") was a portrait that "came nearer to one's idea of the world before the fall than anything [he] ever hoped to see."[32] This warm, harmonious, and cheerful environment later fit with Lewis's 1943 description of the un-fallen Perelandra or Venusian Eden.[33] Both of these instances suggest that there is a part of Lewis strongly attracted to the vision of a once-harmonious union of humanity and nature that was subsequently lost. This vision had support from the older Chrisitan tradition that read Gen 1–8 as strict history wherein, due to Adam's unjust rebellion against God, God justly cursed man by causing all those things below Adam to rebel against him, and part of this rebellion included animals now trying to kill one another and humans (hence producing, among other things, animal suffering). While Lewis clearly believes Adam and God's curse upon him to be historical,[34] he denies that Adam's sin and God's curse produced animal suffering. Lewis's reason for rejecting

---

29. Lewis's Epicurean phase has been described as "Lucretian materialism" since it was the Epicurean poet-philosopher Lucretius who had influenced Lewis. See Barkman, *C. S. Lewis*, 23.
30. Lewis, *Surprised by Joy*, 1281.
31. See Lewis, *Problem of Pain*, 473.
32. "14th June 1932" (Lewis, *Collected Letters—Volume II*, 84).
33. Lewis, *Perelandra*, 182.
34. Lewis, *Problem of Pain*, 505–15.

the once-majority view is because he believed the earth to be old, and carnivorous or suffering-causing animals to have lived on it long before God created humanity. Thus, despite his attraction to the story of humanity and nature having once lived in a state of harmonious non-violence, Lewis ultimately rejects the strong version of this as history. Perhaps unfallen humanity's influence on the wild, carnivorous beasts might have had some taming effect on them,[35] but even if so, the earth as a whole has never been a suffering-free Eden.

As a reluctant skeptic of a young earth and a world-wide-Eden, Lewis, who believes God to be atemporal such that everything is present to him in an Eternal Now, might have been attracted to the more recent theory that claims God's curse on Adam is retroactive,[36] God seeing the "future" sin of Adam "before" he "created" anything and "then" baking this into the "original" creation wherein animal pain and suffering is, in one sense, unintended by God and yet in another sense, entirely so. While Lewis probably would have liked the metaphysical gymnastics exhibited here,[37] we ourselves tend to agree with Alvin Plantinga, Nicholas Wolterstorff, and other recent Christian philosophers in seeing this approach to God, time, and causation—with the deepest respect to this tradition—as incoherent.[38] Be this as it may, even if Lewis were aware of the retroactive theory of Adam's sin and animal suffering, we suspect he would have rejected it on moral grounds. That is, while Lewis agrees that sin deserves to be punished and humanity's authority over the beasts can lead to humans harming the beasts, Lewis probably would not have liked the idea of God himself—even if driven by justice—directly designing carnivorousness and animal suffering as a punishment. This sort of hands-on construction of carnivorousness and animal suffering is, for Lewis, better suited to demons than to God—a claim to which we now turn.

Lewis's demonic corruption approach to animal suffering starts with two premises that we ourselves agree with. First, belief in angels and demons (fallen angels) is not an essential Christian doctrine, yet belief in these creatures has widespread support from the Bible—including Jesus

---

35. "Wholly commanding himself, [paradisical humanity] commanded all lower lives with which he came into contact. Even now we meet rare individuals who have a mysterious power of taming beasts" (Lewis, *Problem of Pain*, 510).

36. See, e.g., Dembski, *End of Christianity*.

37. Among other places, see "Appendix B" in Lewis, *Miracles*, 1232–37.

38. See Plantinga, "On Ockham's Way Out," 262. See also Wolterstorff, "Unqualified Divine Temporality."

himself—the Christian tradition at large, and even pagan literature with its gods and titans. While we could demythologize the Bible to some extent, and, as Lewis himself admits, even acknowledge that Jesus in his humanity might be mistaken about certain things,[39] including, perhaps, demons and demonic causation, our hermeneutics—and certainly Lewis's—resists quick attempts to purge Scripture of the supernatural. The commonsense principle known as Ockham's Razor tells us not to postulate entities needlessly, but it is not obvious to Lewis or us that this applies to angels and demons wholesale. Possibly—probably, in our opinion (though we do not defend this opinion in this chapter)—these sorts of creatures exist. Second, Lewis accepts most of what the tradition has said about the nature of angels and demons, namely, that these creatures are more ancient than humans, extremely powerful, and potentially harmful to God's creation. While we agree with Lewis in attributing these characteristics to demons, we would register our surprise that Lewis, who was seemingly quite skeptical about the nature and purpose of animals (with which he interacted regularly), seems to be less skeptical about the nature and purpose of angels (with whom he seems never to have interacted and whose very existence could be doubted on Lewis's hermeneutics). Lewis's somewhat imbalanced emphasis on the mythological over and against the scientific likely propelled him to his fairly radical suggestion about demons corrupting animal nature.[40]

In *The Problem of Pain*, Lewis cites Scripture in support of the demonic corruption of the natural world, in particular, pointing to Jesus' attribution of some diseases to demonic causation. Developing this notion, we can see Lewis putting forward a kind of a fortiori argument, namely, that if humanity, being only slightly intelligent and powerful, is able to cause great harm to the natural world, how much more could demons, being more intelligent and powerful, cause greater harm? Indeed, Lewis encourages us to consider what the upper limits of this potential harm and corruption might look like. Lewis himself imaginatively develops some of these thoughts in his cosmic trilogy, wherein, for example, Satan is responsible

---

39. "I certainly think that Christ, in the flesh, was not omniscient. . . . [T]hus if Our Lord had committed Himself to any scientific or historical statement which we knew to be untrue, this would not disturb my faith in His deity" (Lewis, *Problem of Pain*, 543).

40. While we agree with Peter Harrison that "An ad hoc hypothesis which invokes mythological beings lacks a certain credibility," we do not think Harrison properly appreciates how essential, and not accidental or ad hoc, mythology is to Lewis's theology (Harrison, "Theodicy," 80).

for killing a number of prehistoric creatures on Malacandra (Mars),[41] the Satanic-possessed Un-man seemingly introduces animal death (and suffering?) to Perelandra (Venus),[42] and demons appear to have been largely responsible for wiping out ancient lunar vegetation.[43] The cosmic reach of Satanic corruption is more than a passing thought in Lewis's work; thus, "If there is such a power, as I myself believe, it may well have corrupted the animal creation before man appeared."[44]

The particulars of how Lewis imagines this starts with his aforementioned Aristotelian psychology, which classifies terrestrial lifeforms into vegetative, sentient, and rational lifeforms, respectively. Vegetative lifeforms seek to survive and reproduce, and not being able to experience pain or suffering, unproblematically—in a moral sense—kill other vegetative lifeforms in order to fulfill their basic directives. Sentient lifeforms—animals, and especially higher animals—possess the vegetative drives, but they are also able to feel. Rational terrestrial lifeforms (humans) possess the vegetative and sentient drives. But they also have rational wills, which allow them to act against the deterministic drives within them, thus freeing humans to be genuine moral agents. Lewis suggests that perhaps as Satan was able to lead man to act against his higher nature (that is, to act irrationally by disobeying God's commandment not to eat the fruit), so, too, perhaps was Satan able to lead the sentient animals to act against their higher natures, "encouraging" them toward their vegetative drives alone, wherein killing and suffering is proper to the vegetables but improper to the beasts.[45]

At an arm's length, there is a kind of broad plausibility here, just as there is with Saruman twisting the Uruk-hai into a new kind of corrupted existence. Yet similar to how Tolkien ultimately struggles to explain clearly and consistently the details surrounding the corrupt nature of his Uruk-hai (without resorting to Manicheanism[46]), so, too, does Lewis fail to develop his thoughts on demonic corruption of animals in light of scientific research. Had Lewis looked into the science more than he did, he might have grown uncomfortable with his own suggestion in terms of how it,

41. Lewis, *Out of the Silent Planet*, 88.
42. Lewis, *Perelandra*, 243, 265.
43. Lewis, *That Hideous Strength*, 531.
44. Lewis, *Problem of Pain*, 543.
45. Lewis, *Problem of Pain*, 543.
46. Tom Shippey argues that Tolkien's poetic vision in *The Lord of the Rings* oscillates between a "Boethian" view of evil and a "Manichean" one (*J. R. R. Tolkien*, 157).

weakly speaking, seems to smuggle a young earth creationist vision into an old earth framework, and, strongly speaking, violates one of Lewis's oft-repeated beliefs, namely, that only God can create: "I don't think evil, in the strict sense, can *create*. It can [just] spoil something that Another has created."[47]

In terms of the weak objection, consider that given the ancient earth thesis, Lewis accepts both that animals have lived on our planet for hundreds of millions of years before humans came on the scene, and that these animals appeared over long, punctuated periods of creation (either through direct creation or via guided evolution). Here we would need to imagine that nearly every time God created a new sentient creature—for example, a eurypterid during the Ordovician period, a Tyrannosaurus during the Cretaceous period, and a megalodon during the Miocene epoch—that Satan was there to distort their herbivorous natures into carnivorous ones. This would not be a matter of the White Witch waving her wand at one moment and covering Narnia in snow as it were, but Satan consistently seizing on, and being allowed to distort, God's new creatures nearly every time they appeared over hundreds of millions of years. This, of course, is possible to believe, yet one gets the sense from Lewis—as we noted earlier—that he has in the back of his mind an imaginative young earth creationist model wherein Adam's sin causes instantaneous and worldwide distortion. We rest nothing on this weak objection, yet we think it another possible instance in this debate where the famed "romantic rationalist" occasionally emphasized the romantic over the rational to the detriment of his theory.[48]

In terms of the strong—or more serious—objection, there is the direct charge that Lewis's theory implies Satanic creation, not mere corruption or distortion. When Lewis asserts that only God can create, he seems to think, first and foremost, that only God can bring forth something out of nothing. While we need not compel Lewis to agree with Thomas Aquinas's claim that on the "seventh day" God rested "from creation of any new genera and species"[49] in the sense that God stopped creating new essential natures at a fixed time in the past, we do think Lewis's insistence that only God creates implies that only God can create new essential or formal natures (genus and species, if one likes). Thus, Lewis would likely deny that even the greatest

---

47. "1st November 1954" (Lewis, *Collected Letters—Volume III*, 520).
48. See Reilly, *Romantic Religion*.
49. Aquinas, *Summa Theologica*, 1:576 (1.118.3).

advances in genetics and synthetic biology in the future will see humanity himself creating a new species.[50]

The evidence that shows Lewis inconsistent in at once maintaining that only God creates essential natures and yet demons can bring forth carnivorousness in beasts is found in the nature of the humble ferret, whose current carnivorousness really seems to be caused by God himself. The ferret, a small mustelid, has a range of anatomical and physiological adaptations that has led it to being classified as an obligate carnivore. Ferrets produce virtually no amylase[51] or lactase,[52] which are enzymes responsible for breaking down complex carbohydrates and lactose, respectively. They lack a cecum and the necessary microbial flora to ferment plant matter,[53] and they have an exceptionally short digestive tract that is well-suited to the rapid absorption of meat protein and fat.[54] Ferrets require preformed taurine,[55] vitamin A,[56] and vitamin B12[57]—nutrients that are found almost exclusively in animal tissues. And their dentition, which includes prominent canines and carnassial blades, along with powerful jaw musculature, helps the creature in seizing and shearing flesh.[58]

A ferret is not merely an herbivorous animal taught, like Gray's monitor lizard,[59] to eat meat; rather, all biological evidence suggests the ferret to be a predator designed to hunt and consume other animals. Ferrets cannot

---

50. Nowadays some biologists question the truth of Aristotle's ontological distinction between "species and genus" (and, to some extent, Linnaeus's binomial nomenclature thereupon), seeing the boundaries between species as fluid. We make no attempt to weigh in on this debate, but rather note, more broadly, that at least as things stand right now, geneticists do not seem to be able to create new lifeforms so much as modify, within certain fixed boundaries, old ones. But if things change, a more nuanced Christian philosophical response will be required if one wants to agree with Lewis—so understood—here. See J. Davies, *Synthetic Biology*, 10–27.

51. Fox, *Biology*, 113–14.

52. Johnson-Delaney, "Ferret Nutrition," 449.

53. Johnson-Delaney, "Ferret Nutrition," 449–50.

54. Johnson-Delaney, "Ferret Nutrition," 449.

55. Emudianughe et al., "Utilization."

56. Lederman, "Ferrets."

57. Fox, *Biology*, 164.

58. Johnson-Delaney, "Ferret Nutrition," 450.

59. In the wild, Gray's monitor lizard appears to be exclusively a fruit-eating reptile with "no rodents ever found in [its] intestines"; however, in captivity it was "successfully" taught to eat meat, especially rodents (Auffenberg, *Gray's Monitor Lizard*, 208).

thrive on a vegetarian or vegan diet (as lions can for a time[60]) since plant-based foods contain only trace amounts of the essential vitamins they require. Furthermore, ferrets lack the ability to efficiently digest plant matter or dairy, making it virtually impossible for them to meet their nutritional needs on a non-carnivorous diet. If a ferret were to achieve the necessary adaptations to survive on a vegetarian or vegan diet, it would no longer belong to the same species, as its entire morphology would need to be altered. This transformation would not be a case of rehabilitating the Mares of Diomedes into oat-eaters; rather, it would involve a fundamental restructuring of the ferret's genotype.

Thus, if Lewis were to stick with his Satanic corruption model, he would need to attribute creative—and not merely distortive—powers to Satan. While we cannot be sure whether Lewis would hold more strongly to his belief that God is the essential Creator or Satan is the corruptor of animal natures, we, at any rate, would support the former over the latter, even if we agree with Lewis that demons do exist and can, in a more modest sense, distort creation through tempting, possessing, disease-inflicting, destroying, and generally causing suffering.

LEWIS'S THIRD SUGGESTION: NOT ALL ANIMAL SUFFERING ENDS IN SUFFERING

"Everything," Lewis summarizes approvingly in his edition of Boethius's *De Consolatione Philosophiae*, "desires to realize its own proper nature."[61] This, again, is Aristotle's theory of final causation, wherein the philosopher insists that we cannot understand a thing truly until we understand that at which it aims or, in theistic language, God's intention for it. As we know, Lewis expressed some doubt about God's intention for animals, and we, though a little sympathetic, think Lewis overstated things. Part of our reason for thinking so is that we do not think Lewis spends enough time—though certainly more time than most philosophers— considering how animals fit into the purpose of creation as whole. To clarify our position on this,

---

60. The story of "Little Tyke," the vegetarian lioness, offers some hope to those who would take Isaiah's heavenly vision of the lion lying down with the lamb literally, for here we do have a case of a lion who was able to survive without meat for some time; however, the lioness does not appear to have flourished in this diet as it required a steady supply of eggs for supplementation. See Westbeau, *Little Tyke*.

61. Lewis, Marginalia (*King Alfred's Old English Version of Boethius*).

we propose a comparison between Lewis and Aquinas on the final cause of creation.

Citing Matt 23:37, Lewis maintains that the purpose or final cause of creation exists for God's pleasure: "Thou has created all things, and for thy pleasure they are and were created."[62] Agreeing with this, Aquinas understands God's pleasure here as consisting in him seeing his own "goodness" or "perfection" reflected.[63] As reasonable as this might seem to many of us, objections have been raised against Aquinas on this point, noting that God's goodness or perfection on his model is not necessarily the same as his moral goodness.[64] If one reads Aquinas in asserting God to be simple, then God's goodness or perfection expresses a Oneness that admits no absolute distinction (and hence prioritization) between his various attributes such as his moral goodness, beauty, and understanding. And if this is correct (and we make no insistence that it is), then the problem would be that Aquinas's God does not necessarily prioritize moral goodness over and above, say, aesthetic goodness in cases where the two might conflict. We are not Thomists and do not weigh in on how to read him on points of controversy; however, supposing this were the case, then one could argue for a kind of aesthetic goodness in the soil existing for the sake of grass, the grass for the sake of the donkey, and the donkey for the sake of the lion, and wrongly imagine—in our opinion—that this aesthetic goodness somehow justifies the pain and/or suffering of the donkey.

While not as sophisticated as Aquinas, Lewis is superior to the Angelic Doctor in clearly prioritizing God's moral goodness or holiness above his other (presumably real and distinct) attributes. Thus, "We were made . . . that God may love us."[65] Or again, "God became Man for no other purpose [than to draw us to Him]. It is even doubtful, you know, whether the whole universe was created for any other purpose."[66] Indeed, while Lewis often insists that moral duty is not supreme, the perfected moral law—the "deeper magic" of agape love, martyrdom and self-sacrifice, which presupposes and completes the law—is God's supreme concern, and it is only through this

---

62. Lewis, *Problem of Pain*, 493.

63. Aquinas, *Summa Theologica*, 1:246 (1.47.1).

64. "Aquinas' definition of 'all-good' refers to metaphysical goodness and not necessarily moral goodness" (Keltz, "God's Purpose," 487). See also B. Davies, *Reality of God*.

65. Lewis, *Problem of Pain*, 493.

66. Lewis, *Mere Christianity*, 448.

that the greatest effects of creation can be brought forth and the highest happiness can be achieved.[67]

With Lewis, then, we assert both that the purpose of creation as a whole lies in expressing God's perfection and that this perfection is hierarchically ordered, prioritizing moral goodness or excellence above all other types of goodnesses or excellences when they come into conflict. Yet while God's chief priority in creation must never be lost sight of, we must not suppose that other goods that contribute to God's perfection are unimportant. Indeed, many of God's other attributes and values find expression in creation; hence, Lewis states:

> Everything God has made has some likeness to Himself. Space is like Him in its hugeness. . . . When we come to the animals, we find other kinds of resemblances in addition to biological life. The intense activity and fertility of the insects, for example, is a first dim resemblance to the unceasing activity and creativeness of God. In the higher mammals we get the beginnings of instinctive affection. . . . When we come to man, the highest of the animals, we get the completest resemblance to God which we know of.[68]

With thinkers as diverse as Aquinas and Descartes, Lewis believes in a "hierarchical order of creation,"[69] where every rung of creation reflects God in some way, but also where the higher one moves up this ladder, the more God is reflected in the creation with all this culminating in creatures that are most able to reflect back God's highest qualities. Thus, to take Aquinas's example, soil reflects God more than nothingness since existence is better than non-existence; grass reflects God more than soil in that grass both exists and has life; donkeys reflect God more than grass since donkeys have existence, life and sentience; and humans reflect God more than donkeys since humans have existence, life, sentience, and rational will. "We are 'worth more than many sparrows,' and in saying this we are not merely

---

67. "'It means,' said Aslan, 'that though the Witch knew the Deep Magic, there is a magic deeper still which she did not know. Her knowledge goes back only to the dawn of time. But if she could have looked a little further back, into the stillness and the darkness before Time dawned, she would have read there a different incantation. She would have known that when a willing victim who had committed no treachery was killed in a traitor's stead, the Table would crack and Death itself would start working backwards'" (Lewis, *Lion, the Witch, and the Wardrobe*, 148).

68. Lewis, *Mere Christianity*, 422.

69. "5th April 1961" (Lewis, *Collected Letters—Volume III*, 1252).

expressing a natural preference for our own species simply because it is our own but conforming to a hierarchical order created by God."[70]

All things being equal, the creation is better—that is, more like God as a whole—for having soil then for having none, and the plurality or diversity of soil types, furthermore, increases the beauty of creation and so better reflects God than a creation with only one soil type. This is true also for vegetation, animals, and even rational creatures: the creation is better for having both Kentucky bluegrass and crabgrass than for having just the one; the creation is better for having donkeys and mules than only one of the two;[71] and the creation is better for having humans and angels than for just having angels. Nevertheless, the "better-ness" of creation here is "all things being equal," and must not be confused for moral "better-ness." It would not be a better creation if the donkey suffered at the claws of the lion *and* no moral good could ever plausibly come from this, for to say this, again, would be to elevate the aesthetic above the moral. We stand with Lewis on this point.

If God were chiefly concerned with simply creating and loving in a lesser sense, he could have created a world where only soil and vegetation exist in vast diversity with him, Demeter-like, cultivating this cosmic garden with loving concern. But a better world than this would be one that included herbivores capable of sentience and the lower loves (such as storge and eros[72]). While the Christian philosophical tradition has been skeptical about God's ability to feel, Scripture is not; moreover, feeling and loving have a greater intuitive value than mere life. This herbivorous world would host ample play and revelry among its inhabitants and would fit with Lewis's idea that "When you study any animal you know—what at once strikes you is their cheerful fatuity. . . . [T]he world is sillier and better fun than [scientists] make out."[73] Yet in this vegetarian-world, the beasts, being

---

70. Lewis, "Vivisection," 226.

71. We agree with Christopher Southgate when he writes, "We might also ask why we so lament the extinction of species in the present day. Is this simply for their instrumental value to humans—and something for our children and grandchildren to experience (or exploit)? Or do we recognise any extinction as an irreversible loss of a whole way of being alive in God's creation, and a loss of a particular song of creaturely praise to God? On balance I am inclined to think that the extent of non-anthropogenic extinction over evolutionary time, the loss of so many ways of being alive, is a disvalue, an aspect of the problem an evolutionary theodicy must tackle" (*Monotheism*, 12).

72. We follow Lewis's classification of the loves here. See Lewis, *Four Loves*.

73. "4th April 1949" (Lewis, *Collected Letters—Volume II*, 930). Consider also the wisdom of Denniston's words: "'The grown-ups are all going about with long faces, but

able to feel, would likely need to feel pain since pain helps them navigate their environment. "There are such things as necessary evils," writes Lewis, [But pain] always requires justification."[74] We could try to argue that the pain would be less than what we see now (for example, every time a cat were to step on a sharp rock a literal light would go off in its brain to tell it to avoid stepping there in the future),[75] but here Lewis's skepticism about animal nature is warranted and we are not in a great position to judge what minimal-but-necessary pain might look like. Yet even so, since existence is better than non-existence, even if an animal in this universe were to experience tremendous pain leading to its death, God would likely ensure that the animal, phoenix-like, rose again.[76]

Nevertheless, a better world than these two alternatives is not only one where God lovingly cultivates the land and ensures weak forms of love is expressed among its lower inhabitants, but also one in which there are creatures who are able to love in the highest, moral sense. This world would include not only pain but also suffering since these higher creatures or rational wills would have not only higher levels of understanding and memory but also the power of choice, and choice entails the power to produce pain and suffering in itself and others. And while entirely decontextualized pain and suffering are bad and we ought to believe them to be bad, a lot of pain, and quite possibly, suffering, is likely necessary to achieve the ends of a God who prioritizes moral goodness above all else. This God would not want to see rational wills occasionally choose what is morally good but would want them to become good or virtuous in character—indeed, godlike in the greatest sense of the word. Yet since no created rational will can be good as God is, without choice and practice, these created rational wills

---

look at the children—and the dogs. *They* know what snow's made for'" (Lewis, *That Hideous Strength*, 464).

74. Lewis, "Vivisection," 225.

75. Cf. White and Sweet, *Pain*, 68.

76. On the badness of decontextualized or unnecessary death, consider this passage from *Perelandra*: "Ransom had as yet seen nothing dead or spoiled in Perelandra, and it was like a blow in the face. . . . He told himself that a creature of that kind probably had very little sensation. But it did not much mend matters. It was not merely pity for pain that had suddenly changed the rhythm of his heartbeats. The thing was an intolerable obscenity which afflicted him with shame. It would have been better, or so he thought at the moment, for the whole universe never to have existed than for this one thing to have happened. Then he decided, in spite of his theoretical belief that it was an organism too low for much pain, that it had better be killed" (Lewis, *Perelandra*, 241).

must practice choosing to do the right thing, and this entails, for so many of the virtues, obstacles and difficulties, and, in fact, pain and suffering.[77]

Would the world described above entail absolute vegetarianism and animal immortality? To answer this, we need to consider two Lewisian principles with which we agree. The first principle states that the highest things—rational wills or agents or souls—ought to elevate the lower things, that the strong should take care of the weak, and that agape love descends to save or improve.[78] In this spirit, Lewis suggests that perhaps as Christ came down to bring humanity up to God, so too might humanity stoop down to the level of beasts and bring some of them up to be with Christ. Lewis restricts[79] this elevation of the beasts to only the beasts loved by humans—family pets as it were—and he would not go along with Swinburne, who sometimes speaks of some animals going to a temporary heaven as moral compensation for a disproportionate amount of suffering in this life.[80] Lewis is unwilling to allow moral rights to be claimed by anything that is not a moral agent or rational will, and so even if animals suffer and this is a moral problem, it is not so much a problem of the animals being wronged as potentially God and humans being cruel. Lewis's objection to vivisection accords with Immanuel Kant's objection to cruelty to animals, arguing that this cruelty makes us flawed moral agents, and not that the animals themselves are wronged.[81] Thus, in terms of the pets that might be able to go to heaven, Lewis speaks of this possibility in terms of the unmerited grace and love of the superior that might see the inferior elevated and brought into a state where the present suffering is the necessary context for a greater joy. Based on this principle, then, we can postulate some animal immortality, and since this is an immortality that comes through the moral

---

77. Cf. "Perhaps there is an anguish, an alienation, a crucifixion involved in the creative act. Yet He who alone can judge judges the far-off consummation to be worth it" (Lewis, *Prayer*, 586).

78. Lewis, *Problem of Pain*, 545. Also, in Christ, "We catch sight of a new key principle—the power of the Higher, just in so far as it is truly Higher, to come down, the power of the greater to include the lesser" (Lewis, *Miracles*, 1184).

79. In fairness, Lewis does add a further suggestion about how animal immortality might be a kind of collective immortality, but this in no way helps with the problem of the individual animals that suffer and die. See Lewis, *Problem of Pain*, 547.

80. "But, if the earthy life of some animal is not on balance good, God would have an obligation to give that animal another compensatory life of some finite duration either on this earth or on another planet; and that in his omnipotence he could do" (Swinburne, *Could a Good God Permit So Much Suffering?* 131).

81. Lewis, "Vivisection," 226.

cultivation of rational wills, we think Lewis is largely right in this unique assertion.

The second principle moves in the opposite direction, stating that the lesser things of creation, being truly lesser (that is, less reflective of God), properly serve the higher things, and this harmony among unequals is part of the general beauty of the creation. Thus, Lewis ("All is righteousness and there is no equality"[82]), Aquinas ("God made the universe to be best as a whole.... He did not make each single creature best, but one better than another"[83]), and Descartes ("Whenever we are inquiring whether the works of God are perfect, we ought to look at the whole universe, not just at one created thing on its own. For what would perhaps rightly appear very imperfect if it existed on its own is quite perfect when its function as a part of the universe is considered"[84]). This principle, in itself, neither justifies the lion preying on the donkey nor the vast amount of animal suffering and death in history; however, this principle does assume that while rational beings should, in Kant's phrase, "never be treated merely as a means to an end," non-rational beings can be.[85] It asserts that rational, moral agents, sharing in God's rational, moral nature, have not merely a degreed superiority to sentient creatures (as Naturalist philosophers like Peter Singer imagine) but a near infinite superiority to them. Thus, on this principle, if carnivorousness and animal death can somehow be shown to cultivate the moral character of rational beings, then this suffering could possibly be justified. And this leads to Lewis's final, implicit, suggestion.

LEWIS'S FOURTH (IMPLICIT) SUGGESTION: THE DEVELOPMENT OF MORAL VIRTUE IN RATIONAL CREATURES JUSTIFIES ANIMAL SUFFERING

So far, we have argued that Lewis is mistaken when he seemingly discounts the bulk of animal pain and suffering, but correct in reminding us that animal nature—with its pain and suffering—is not as clear as we might think. We have also argued that Lewis is mistaken in suggesting that demons can radically alter animal natures but correct to remind us not to neglect

---

82. Lewis, *Perelandra*, 340. Cf. "Part of the excellence of a good man is that he is not an angel, and of a good dog that it is not a man" ("5th April 1961" [Lewis, *Collected Letters—Volume III*, 1252]).

83. Aquinas, *Summa Theologica*, 1.47.2.

84. Descartes, "Meditations," 39 (see esp. §§4.55–56).

85. Kant, "Groundwork," 80 (§4.429).

demonic causation as a real factor in the problem of pain, and, especially, animal suffering. Finally, we think Lewis correct in asserting that the chief purpose of creation is for God to promote the highest good, namely, moral goodness—from which the highest happiness flows—and, from this, we also agree with Lewis's unique proposal that some animals that suffer in this life might enjoy a non-suffering or less suffering life in the next. Lewis's suggestions found in his major works on animal suffering end here, but we think that throughout his other works, he actually provides a fourth explanation for animal suffering, which we want to develop, namely, that God may have designed a vast amount of animal suffering to help rational creatures develop morally. Although they are scattered, tentative, and far from worked out in his writings, Lewis alludes to three moral virtues that can be cultivated in rational creatures vis-à-vis animal suffering: compassion, humility, and courage.

The love that a pet owner has for his or her pet is, when it is most perfectly expressed, a weak form of agape love in that through the sacrifice of the owner's time and money, the animal is elevated to the very best version that the animal in question can be. Lewis takes much of this from Aristotle's *Politics*, wherein he notes, "The same holds good of animals in relation to men; for tame animals have a better nature than wild animals and all tame animals are better off when they are ruled by man; for then they are preserved."[86] This elevation of the beasts, wherein their best versions are drawn out by rational humanity, is a central theme in *That Hideous Strength*, where, we are told, in Ransom's "presence Mr. Bultitude [the bear] trembled on the very borders of personality."[87] The key take away, however, is not that human encounters with animals provide the opportunity for animals to be happier (we can remain agnostic on this point if we like[88]), but rather that encounters with animals provide rational creatures the opportunity to love them. Through books or binoculars or in our own backyards, when we, even at a distance, encounter animals that are in pain, these encounters provide significant opportunities for us to develop compassionate responses and, eventually, compassionate characters.

Compassion is the excellence in respect to feeling-with-others and wanting, if possible and proper, to alleviate their suffering. The

---

86. Lewis, Marginalia (Aristotle, *De Re Publica*, 54b).

87. Lewis, *That Hideous Strength*, 671–72. Lewis named this bear after the one in Whipsnade Zoo.

88. For a critique of this Aristotelian point, consider Jamieson, "Against Zoos."

compassionate person is neither a "bleeding heart" who would risk his life (a thing more valuable than the life of an animal) to save the family dog[89] nor a person cold or insensitive to the sufferings of others, such as the vivisectionists at N.I.C.E. (National Institute of Co-ordinated Experiments). Do we need animals to suffer in order for rational creatures to develop compassion? It is logically possible for rational creatures to develop compassion simply through encounters with other rational creatures; however, as we have argued, a better world is one that includes sentient creatures in addition to vegetation and rational creatures, and given this better world, it is right that the pain of animals serves not simply themselves, but also their superiors through their superiors having the opportunity to develop compassion in response to their pain and suffering. More and different opportunities for a person to develop compassion are desirable if compassion, as a moral good, is one of God's highest concerns.[90] Thus, for example, a little girl with six siblings has many opportunities to experience suffering in her family, yet it remains true that if she also happens to have a pet hamster and this hamster suffers from proliferative ileitis, this different and additional opportunity for her to show compassion makes this world preferable to the world without the hamster-suffering. Yet here we caution against a misuse of 1 Cor 9:9–10 ("Is it for oxen that God is concerned? Or does he not speak entirely for our sake?"), for if we rightly praise the compassion of the little girl, it is only because we first praise compassion itself, which belongs to the very nature of God qua the moral good. To think about this correctly, we assert, pace Lewis, that even as God designed the hamster to feel pain and is very possibly the direct cause of the pain and suffering, yet, with Lewis, God both feels compassion for the hamster and believes that this pain and suffering is a worthwhile means to provide the little girl with greater and more diverse chances for her to become compassionate: "I will never laugh at anyone for grieving over a loved beast. I think God wants us to love Him *more*, not to love creatures (even animals) *less*."[91]

To some, our argument may appear both "anthropomonistic"[92] and unacceptably silent in regard to the suffering of animals separated from us

---

89. Some interpret Jonathan Kent in the 2013 film *Man of Steel* doing this, but we do not.

90. Recent studies in psychology show the prosocial benefits that come from pet-owners empathizing with the suffering of their pets. See Faner et al., "Pet Attachment."

91. "18th August 1956" (Lewis, *Collected Letters—Volume III*, 782).

92. Visscher, "Listening to Creation Groaning," 21.

in space and time. To these, we note that our theory is not concerned with human moral development per se but moral development as such, which is to say, taking a cue from Lewis, that if there are other rational creatures besides humans in creation, then the trials and pains of creation could also be for their betterment. Thus, for example, it is possible that the pain and suffering of prehistoric creatures might have helped angelic beings to become more, or less, compassionate. But even if we bracket this, it is possible to see the suffering and death of prehistoric beasts as relevant to humans.[93] Swinburne argues that our eventual coming-to-know of prehistoric animal suffering through the fossil record can aid us toward compassion:

> It is good that if pain exists, compassion exists, whether or not it can lead to action.... Some pain and some compassion is at least as good as a world with no pain.... It is good that the range of our compassion should be wide—extending far in time and space. Good for those who suffered long ago that they are not forgotten; good for us to react with love to distant creatures about whom we know little.[94]

Even for animals that are separated from us, not by time but by space—animals that suffer and die in the wild and forever remain unknown to all rational creatures—their suffering and deaths are likely necessary, for, given the Principle of Honesty, wherein God, being morally good, cannot exercise widespread deception, the suffering and deaths of wild animals might be a necessary consequence of human beings being able to trust the reports of common sense and make their way through the world, developing in virtue as we go. Certainly, God could do select miracles for special purposes to spare a given animal suffering and death—for example, God might spare Draper's fawn at the request of the righteous man[95]—but to posit too many miracles such that common sense could no longer be trusted would be counter to God's greater purpose, which is to draw us to him, not spare animals suffering and death. Once again, we must remind ourselves that Aslan "is not a tame lion, but good."[96]

Humility, which has to do with the correct lowering of the self in respect to one's betters, is another virtue that can be better realized through animal suffering and death. How? Lewis's philosophy is greatly indebted

---

93. Lewis, *Problem of Pain*, 547.
94. Swinburne, *Providence*, 161.
95. See Draper, "Pain and Pleasure."
96. Lewis, *Lion, the Witch, and the Wardrobe*, 75, 166.

to Rudolf Otto's *The Idea of the Holy*,[97] especially Otto's discussion of the *numinous* or the profound "creature-feeling" that overcomes the individual when he "is submerged and overwhelmed by [his] own nothingness."[98] This "creature-feeling" arises when the individual encounters the sublime or unbounded, such as the depth of antiquity, the vastness of space, or the darkness of the woods and the mysteries therein. These sublime instances are for Otto, but more clearly for Lewis, instances of God—not yet known to be morally good, but certainly felt to be vast, infinite, and terrible—awesomely reflecting through his creation, and, in the process, making us feel our relative smallness. As we have already argued, all things in creation reflect God to some extent, and many of these reflections can act as signposts to direct our attention to He-Who-Stands-on-the-Other-Side-of-the-Mirror; thus, Lewis writes, "I do not see how we could have come to know the greatness of God without that hint furnished by the greatness of the material universe."[99] For the Oxford don, this feeling of awe, fear, or terror is not a pleasant feeling, but it does furnish us with the opportunity to properly understand ourselves in respect to the divine, and, in this sense, can give us an opportunity to become humble. Hence, for example, in *The Great Divorce*, thundering unicorns are summoned by the saints to scare the ghosts out of themselves and toward God.[100]

Along these lines, we believe that the pain and deaths of prehistoric creatures have the potential to produce in humans the sense of the sublime or *numinous*. Anecdotally speaking, we ourselves have felt this—this sense of the vastness of time and the awe-fulness of God—when digging for Paleozoic fossils in Hungry Hollows, Ontario and, later, collecting prehistoric shark teeth in Calvert Cliffs, Maryland. And we suspect we are not unique in this—that quite possibly some who visit natural history museums today and see reconstructed skeletons of dinosaurs experience this pre-religious

---

97. For more on this debt, see Barkman, "Rudolph Otto."

98. Otto, *Idea of the Holy*, 10.

99. Lewis, "Dogma," 121. Even proud Kant was awed by the cosmos: "Two things fill the mind with ever new and increasing admiration and reverence the more often and more steadily one reflects on them: the starry heavens above me and the moral law within me" (Kant, "Critique," 269 [§5.162]).

100. "'This put me in mind to ask my Teacher what he thought of the affair with the Unicorns. 'It will maybe have succeeded,' he said. 'Ye will have divined that he meant to frighten her; not that fear itself could make her less a Ghost, but if it took her mind a moment off herself, there might, in that moment, be a chance. I have seen them saved so'" (Lewis, *Great Divorce*, 4).

feeling. Certainly, many ancient peoples, including the Greeks and Chinese, were horrified, fascinated, and—note the word, humbled—when they found the bones of "monsters" from the distant past.[101] Given that cultivating moral goodness in creatures that are capable of cultivating moral goodness is chief among God's concerns, it is possible that God may have designed and instigated millions of years of animal suffering and death to bring about, millions of years later, the sense of the sublime and *numinous* in rational creatures, which in turn would increase and diversify our chances of cultivating a humble character. This would allow us to say in the spirit of Job, "My ears had heard of you but now my eyes have seen you. Therefore, I despise myself and repent in dust and ashes" (Job 42:6).

Yet once again, we anticipate some incredulity. Some might argue that even if fossils can produce sublime or *numinous* feelings in us, and even if these feelings can lend themselves to the cultivation of humility, why could God not simply have faked the bones? Why cause real suffering and death in billions of animals over millions of years? The Principle of Honesty rules this out since if God were to have faked the millions of bones found in the earth, it would not have produced in us sublimity, but profound distrust. Such a mass deceiver would not be God and, in saying all this, we would have lost sight of the primary purpose of creation as a whole. Thus, the fossils, needing to be real, entail real animal pain and death, and, moreover, we need lots of it since it is the particular mixture of vastness, antiquity, mystery, and awe-fulness that provides the glow of the fossils, and which properly elicits sublime or *numinous* feelings in us. Consequently, as anguishing as all the pain and death of the prehistoric world is, God's priority is for rational creatures to become the sort of creatures—moral creatures, here, humble creatures—who, being like God, can live like God, that is, forever, for certainly the five major extinction events our planet has undergone have taught us the truth of Augray's words, "'A world is not made to last forever . . . that is not Maledil's way.'"[102]

Courage—roughly, the disposition to take action when it is wise to do so—is another virtue that likely has a greater chance of being cultivated in a world with animal suffering than in one without. In the appendix to *The Problem of Pain*, Lewis's friend and physician Robert Harvard notes the

---

101. "Big vertebrate fossils, even isolated bones and teeth, were objects of intense curiosity and speculation in Greco-Roman times" (Mayor, *First Fossil Hunters*, 5).

102. Lewis, *Out of the Silent Planet*, 89.

obvious truth, "Pain provides an opportunity for heroism."[103] Even though in *The Problem of Pain* Lewis does not discuss how human encounters with animals could facilitate heroism or even courage, he does so in *Out of the Silent Planet*. In this novel, Lewis suggests both that God created the fierce *hnakra* and that this sea monster was created partly or primarily to try to kill the rational *hross* of Malacandra. Thus, the *hross* Hyoi says:

> Maledil has let in the *hnakra*.... I long to kill this *hnakra* as he also longs to kill me.... And if he kills me, my people will mourn me and my brothers will desire still more to kill him. But they will not wish that there were no *hnéraki*; nor do I. How can I make you understand, when you do not understand the poets? The *hnakra* is our enemy, but he is also our beloved.... I do not think the forest would be so bright, nor the water so warm, nor love so sweet, if there were no danger in the lakes.... I drank life because death was in the pool.[104]

Lewis's idea here accords with the way many of the world's cultures have justified some forms of hunting, namely, to prove the valor of the human. Maasi boys, for example, would not be declared men—that is, males with a character strong enough to lead their families—until they could kill a lion. This reason for hunting is far from a rich dentist using, in Lewis's phrase, "a coward's weapon"[105] to trophy-hunt Zimbabwean big cats.

Yet this is also distinct from a man hunting a deer because he needs food to eat. Our theory, elevating rational creatures far above animals and allowing for animals to be used for human flourishing, does allow for humans to kill animals for food and shelter; however, mere biological survival is a lesser reason for hunting, and in many cases humans could flourish in their biological lives on a vegetarian diet. Indeed, when this is so, it might sometimes be better to opt for vegetarianism since compassion for animals could be a greater consideration than maximizing our protein intake.

Thinking along these lines—thinking in terms of conflicting interests—we might have further situations where compassion for the animal and courage to face it come into conflict; in a case like this, we would need to be wise (another virtue that can be cultivated vis-à-vis animal suffering) in deciding which of the two virtues to focus on at the moment. For example, we might approve of the matador fighting the bull (courage) but

---

103. Lewis, *Problem of Pain*, 555.
104. Lewis, *Out of the Silent Planet*, 65–66.
105. Lewis, *Out of the Silent Planet*, 112.

disapprove of the matador seriously injuring or killing it (compassion). Nevertheless, as with all virtue development, it would really depend on what the individual in question most needs to cultivate.[106]

As we have seen throughout this section, there are many virtues that can be cultivated through our interaction with animals, and there are many more besides these. When a skunk digs up our backyard, we can develop temperance by refraining from poisoning it. When a dog barks at us while we are jogging, we can become good-tempered, and not irascible, as we breath and jog on. When an antisocial child gets a pet cat, she can become more friendly with other humans as a result. When we observe the ridiculousness of many animal behaviours, we can acquire material to become tactfully witty. When we study the bodies and behaviour of animals, we can become wise in the ways of medicine and even martial arts. And when we contemplate the goodness of God and our love for our departed pets, we can practice being hopeful—cultivating the rational desire for a world where virtue ends in the highest happiness, which, found in God and being like him, we might reasonably suppose includes all those lower joys that were not the necessary means—the necessary pains and scars—to that supreme joy.

CONCLUSION

In this chapter, we have explored the problems and promises of C. S. Lewis's theory of animal suffering. Despite his insufficiency in respect to the science of animality and his excessive emphasis on angelology, we think Lewis's theory of animal suffering is on the right track. Indeed, beyond his explicit writings on animal pain, we found in many of Lewis's other works helpful clues toward a more complete explanation of animal suffering, namely, that animal suffering can help to promote moral excellence in rational creatures. Our modified and developed Lewisian theory, then, claims that God is the designer of the structures of pain, suffering, and death and, indeed, that he is a major contributor to these, yet it also asserts that unlike

---

106. "But I mean moral virtue, for it is concerned with passions and actions, and it is in these that excess, deficiency, and the middle term reside. For example, it is possible to be afraid, to be confident, to desire, to be angry, to feel pity, and, in general, to feel pleasure and pain to a greater or lesser degree than one ought, and both cases this is not good. But to feel them when one ought and at the things one ought, in relation to those people whom one ought, for the sake of what and as one ought—all these constitute the middle as well as what is best, which is in fact what belongs to virtue" (Aristotle, *Nicomachean Ethics*, 34 [2.6/1106b17–24; Bartlett and Collins).

much of the pain and suffering that rational creatures cause animals, God, prioritizing the cultivation of virtue in rational creatures, can only cause animal suffering and death with this greater purpose in mind. We end this chapter, then, with a final thought experiment to drive home our virtue approach to mass animal suffering. Suppose you had to choose between saving the life of your child or saving an entire planet of sentient creatures. What would you choose? Or suppose further you could provide your child with a one-in-a-million chance to repent and live forever or you could save the lives of all the sentient creatures in the entire cosmos. What would you choose? We know what we would choose.

BIBLIOGRAPHY

Aquinas, Thomas. *The Summa Theologica*. Translated by the Fathers of the English Dominican Province. 10 vols. Allen, TX: Christian Classics, 1981.

Aristotle. *De Anima*. In *The Complete Works of Aristotle: Volume One—The Revised Oxford Translation*. Edited by Jonathan Barnes, 641–92. Bollingen Series 71.2. Princeton: Princeton University Press, 1984.

———. *Nicomachean Ethics*. Translated by Robert Bartlett and Susan Collins. Chicago: University of Chicago Press, 2012.

Auffenberg, Walter. *Gray's Monitor Lizard*. Gainesville: University of Florida Press, 1988.

Barkman, Adam. *C. S. Lewis and Philosophy as a Way of Life*. Allentown, PA: Zossima, 2009.

———. "Rudolph Otto, The Idea of the Holy." In *C. S. Lewis's List: The Ten Books That Influenced Him Most*, edited by David Werther and Susan Werther, 113–34. New York: Bloomsbury, 2015.

Brink, Gijsbert van den. *Reformed Theology and Evolutionary Theory*. Grand Rapids: Eerdmans, 2020.

Davies, Brian. *The Reality of God and the Problem of Evil*. New York: Continuum, 2006.

Davies, Jamie. *Synthetic Biology: A Very Short Introduction*. Oxford: Oxford University Press, 2018.

Dembski, William. *The End of Christianity: Finding a Good God in an Evil World*. Nashville: Broadman and Holman, 2009.

Descartes, René. "Meditations on First Philosophy." In *The Philosophical Writings of Descartes: Volume II*. Translated by John Cottingham et al., 1–62. Cambridge: Cambridge University Press, 1984.

Devries, Ben. "Andrew Linzey and C. S. Lewis's Theology of Animals." *Journal of Animal Ethics* 3.1 (2013) 25–40.

Draper, Paul. "Pain and Pleasure: An Evidential Problem for Theists." *Noûs* 23 (1989) 331–50.

Emudianughe, T. S., et al. "The Utilization of Exogenous Taurine for the Conjugation of Xenobiotic Acids in the Ferret." *Xenobiotica* 13.3 (2008) 133–38.

Faner, Jhon Marc V., et al. "Pet Attachment and Prosocial Attitude toward Humans: The Mediating Role of Empathy to Animals." *Frontiers in Psychology* 15 (2024). No pages. DOI: https://doi.org/10.3389/fpsyg.2024.1391606.

Part One: Apologetics and Philosophy

Fox, James. *Biology and Diseases of the Ferret*. Baltimore: Williams & Wilkins, 1998.

Harrison, Peter. "Theodicy and Animal Pain." *Philosophy* 64.247 (January 1989) 79–92.

Illingworth, J. R. "The *Problem of Pain*: Its Bearing on Faith in God." In *Lux Mundi*, edited by Charles Gore, 113–26. London: John Murray, 1890.

Jamieson, Dale. "Against Zoos." In *In Defence of Animals*, edited by Peter Singer, 108–17. New York: Blackwell, 1985.

Johnson-Delaney, Cathy. "Ferret Nutrition." *Veterinary Clinics of North America: Exotic Animal Practice* 17 (2014) 449–70.

Kant, Immanuel. "The Critique of Practical Reason." In *Practical Philosophy*, edited by Mary J. Gregor, 133–272. Cambridge: Cambridge University Press, 1999.

———. "Groundwork of the Metaphysics of Morals." In *Practical Philosophy*, edited by Mary J. Gregor, 37–108. Cambridge: Cambridge University Press, 1999.

Keltz, Kyle. "God's Purpose for the Universe and the Problem of Animal Suffering." *Sophia* 58 (2019) 475–92.

Lederman, Janine. "Ferrets (Mustela Putoius Furo) Inefficiently Convert β-Carotene to Vitamin A." *Journal of Nutrition* 128 (1998) 271–79.

Lehner, Christopher. "Einstein's Realism and his Critique of Quantum Mechanics." In *The Cambridge Companion to Einstein*, edited by Michael Janssen and Christopher Lehner, 306–53. Cambridge: Cambridge University Press, 2014.

Lewis, C. S. *The Abolition of Man*. In *Selected Books*, 395–442. London: HarperCollins, 2002.

———. *The Collected Letters of C. S. Lewis: Books, Broadcasts, and the War, 1931–1949— Volume II*. Edited by Walter Hooper. HarperSanFrancisco, 2004.

———. *The Collected Letters of C. S. Lewis: Narnia, Cambridge, and Joy 1950–1963— Volume III*. Edited by Walter Hooper. HarperSanFrancisco, 2007.

———. "Dogma and the Universe." In *C. S. Lewis: Essay Collection and Other Short Pieces*, edited by Lesley Walmsley, 118–26. London: HarperCollins, 2000.

———. *The Four Loves*. In *Selected Books*, 1–88. London: HarperCollins, 1999.

———. *The Great Divorce*. In *Selected Books*, 1023–94. London: HarperCollins, 1999.

———. *The Lion, the Witch, and the Wardrobe*. London: Fontana Lions, 1980.

———. Marginalia in Aristotle, *De Re Publica*, edited by Immanuel Bekker. Oxford: Oxford University Press, 1837. The Rare Book Collection, The University of North Carolina at Chapel Hill.

———. Marginalia in *King Alfred's Old English Version of Boethius De Consolatione Philosophiae*, edited by Walter John Sedgewick, 4. Oxford: Clarendon, 1899. The Rare Book Collection, The University of North Carolina at Chapel Hill.

———. *Mere Christianity*. In *Selected Books*, 311–466. London: HarperCollins, 1999.

———. *Miracles*. In *Selected Books*, 1095–238. London: HarperCollins, 1999.

———. *Out of the Silent Planet*. In *The Cosmic Trilogy: Out of the Silent Planet; Perelandra; That Hideous Strength*, 1–144. London: Pan Books, 1990.

———. "The Pains of Animals: A Problem in Theology; the Reply by C. S. Lewis." In *C. S. Lewis: Essay Collection and Other Short Pieces*, edited by Lesley Walmsley, 187–96. London: HarperCollins, 2000.

———. *Perelandra*. In *The Cosmic Trilogy: Out of the Silent Planet; Perelandra; That Hideous Strength*, 145–348. London: Pan Books, 1990.

———. *Prayer: Letters to Malcolm*. In *Selected Books*, 223–304. London: HarperCollins, 2002.

———. *The Problem of Pain*. In *Selected Books*, 467–556. London: HarperCollins, 1999.

———. *Selected Books: The Four Loves, Mere Christianity, The Problem of Pain, Prayer: Letters to Malcolm, Reflections on the Psalms, The Pilgrim's Regress, The Screwtape Letters with Screwtape Proposes a Toast, Till We Have Faces, The Great Divorce, Surprised by Joy, Miracles.* London: HarperCollins, 1999.

———. *Surprised by Joy.* In *Selected Books*, 1239–1382. London: HarperCollins, 1999.

———. *That Hideous Strength.* In *The Cosmic Trilogy: Out of the Silent Planet; Perelandra; That Hideous Strength*, 349–753. London: Pan Books, 1990.

———. "Vivisection." In *C. S. Lewis: Essay Collection and Other Short Pieces*, edited by Lesley Walmsley, 693–97. London: HarperCollins, 2000

Mayor, Andrienne. *The First Fossil Hunters: Dinosaurs, Mammoths, and Myth in Greek and Roman Times.* Princeton: Princeton University Press, 2023.

Murray, Michael. *Nature Red in Tooth and Claw: Theism and the Problem of Animal Suffering.* Oxford: Oxford University Press, 2008.

Otto, Rudolf. *The Idea of the Holy: An Inquiry into the Non-Rational Factor in the Idea of the Divine and its Relation to the Rational.* Translated by John W. Harvey. Oxford: Oxford University Press, 1958.

Plantinga, Alvin. "On Ockham's Way Out." In *The Analytic Theist: An Alvin Plantinga Reader*, edited by James F. Sennett, 258–92. Grand Rapids: Eerdmans, 1998.

———. *Warranted Christian Belief.* Oxford: Oxford University Press, 2000.

Reilly, R. J. *Romantic Religion: A Study of Owen Barfield, C. S. Lewis, Charles Williams and J. R. R. Tolkien.* Great Barrington, MA: Lindisfarne, 2006.

Schneider, John. *Animal Suffering and the Darwinian Problem of Evil.* Cambridge: Cambridge University Press, 2020.

Shippey, Tom. *J. R. R. Tolkien: Author of the Century.* London: HarperCollins, 2000.

Southgate, Christopher. *Monotheism and the Suffering of Animals in Nature.* Cambridge: Cambridge University Press, 2023.

Sterba, James, and Richad Swinburne. *Could a Good God Permit So Much Suffering? A Debate.* Oxford: Oxford University Press, 2024.

Swinburne, Richard. *Providence and the Problem of Evil.* Oxford: Oxford University Press, 2011.

Visscher, Lukas. "Listening to Creation Groaning: A Survey of Main Themes in Creation Theology." In *Listening to Creation Groaning*, edited by Lukas Visscher, 11–31. Geneva: Centre International Réformé John Knox, 2004.

Westbeau, Georges. *Little Tyke: The Amazing True Story of the World-Famous Vegetarian African Lioness.* Mountain View, CA: Pacific Press, 1956.

White, James C., and William H. Sweet. *Pain and the Neurosurgeon: A Forty-Year Experience.* 2nd ed. Springfield, IL: Charles C Thomas, 1969.

Wolterstorff, Nicholas. "Unqualified Divine Temporality." In *God and Time: Four Views*, edited by Gregory Ganssle, 187–213. Downers Grove, IL: InterVarsity, 2001.

Myths, Morals—and—Joy

C. S. Lewis, the *Consensus Gentium*, and Postmodern Thought

MARK G. MCKIM

INTRODUCTION

C. S. LEWIS IS almost certainly the most widely read lay theologian today. Indeed, it is probably not going too far to suggest that he is the *only* Christian theologian—lay or otherwise—being widely read today by the general public. Over sixty years after his death Lewis's books still sell millions of copies annually in multiple languages. Although Lewis died well before it became a clearly recognizable school of thought, much of what he wrote was surprisingly prescient and anticipated much of what we now call "postmodernism."

POSTMODERNISM

Postmodern thought has multiple complex variations, but two major characteristics stand out. *First*, postmodern thought calls into question the ability of human reason to discern truth. Enlightenment thinkers had held an extremely high estimation of the ability of human thought and reason. Indeed, in its most extreme expressions Enlightenment thought asserted that the *only* way of knowing—of ascertaining truth—was by means of the empirical method. If something could not be touched, heard, seen, tasted, or smelled by human senses, it either was not true or, at least, it was not important. That Western Christians and Western Christian theology largely accepted this worldview was disastrous; it meant, among other things, accepting that revelation was *not* a valid means of knowing and greatly deemphasizing, if not entirely eliminating, all supernatural elements in Christianity, even though such elements were a critical part of the biblical narrative and worldview. One of the most extreme examples of this was the work of Rudolf Bultmann, who, notoriously, insisted that to make the gospel acceptable and relevant to modern people, the New Testament had to be "demythologized." According to Bultmann, the authors of the New Testament had used the only terms and concepts they had available to them. Unfortunately, however, these terms and concepts were inextricably bound to the miraculous and supernatural, notions which were anathema to modern or Enlightenment thought. Consequently, such elements needed to be reinterpreted in such a fashion as to remove the supernatural, so the universal truth underlying the stories could then be seen and accepted by modern people. That such a proceeding not only involved a priori assumptions about the nature of reality but also gutted Christianity of much of its meaning and raison d'être, which stems from the historicity of the gospel accounts, were not things Bultmann regarded as valid concerns.

Insofar as postmodern thought takes a humbler view of the ability of human reasoning, it can be seen as a positive development. Postmodern thought is much more modest in its assessment of human ability to discern truth, and it allows that there may be ways of knowing outside the empirical method.

However, postmodern thought, like many over-reactions, resembles Luther's proverbial drunk man who mounts his donkey on the right and falls off on the left, only immediately to mount on the left and then fall off on the right. Having called into question the Enlightenment's overly generous estimate of human reason, postmodern thought falls off the other side of the donkey. Thus, the *second* major characteristic of postmodern thought is the insistence it is virtually impossible to discern *any* universal truth by means of reason and empiricism. Postmodernism rejects the possibility of there being any single, foundational, overarching story, or meta-narrative, which makes sense of all human life. Hence the French philosopher and literary theorist Jean-François Lyotard wrote, "Simplifying to the extreme, I define postmodern as incredulity towards meta-narratives."[1] Indeed, for many postmodernists, any attempt to create a meta-narrative is seen as nothing more than me, or my group, trying to impose my or its view

---

1. Lyotard, *Postmodern Condition*, xxiv.

on others—a "power play" to dominate or oppress others and impose my, or our, story on others. The notion that no meta-narrative is possible is utterly at odds with the biblical insistence that there *is* an overarching story, a *divine* narrative that explains the universe and gives meaning to human life, a narrative that centres on God, whose inmost nature is love and who became one of us in Jesus Christ.

CONSENSUS GENTIUM

This is where Lewis's startling prescience at times becomes important. A major theme in Lewis's writings is the conviction that there is a *consensus gentium* (a "consensus of humanity"). This consensus, Lewis believed, pointed to the conclusion that there is a transcendent reality, an authority *external* to humanity, which defines what is good, right, and beautiful, and which makes both discerning truth (to some degree) and meta-narratives possible.[2] The existence of such an authority means it is *not* necessarily just personal preference or subjective opinion to say something is good, right, or beautiful, nor is asserting such, automatically, my attempting to impose my group's views on you and everyone else; I may instead be expressing objective truth in line with what the transcendent authority defines as good, right, or beautiful.[3] *If* such a consensus really exists, pointing to the existence of a transcendent reality, it calls into question the two major tenets of postmodern thinking. So, the critical issues are: Does such a consensus exist? What evidence is there for it?

Lewis asserted that not only did a *consensus gentium* exist, but that it was evidenced in the myths of every culture, in the moral teachings of all the world's major religions and philosophies, and in the experience of what Lewis called "joy." The existence of such a consensus was a "clue to the meaning of the universe" and pointed toward some authority beyond us.

It is entirely worth exploring, then, what evidence Lewis presented to demonstrate that such a consensus exists. He gave three arguments to support his case. The first two—myths and morals—which I will review briefly, are fairly well known. The third, however, the experience of joy, is both less well known, and I will contend, not as fully developed as it could be.

---

2. I am here especially employing the phrasing and thought of American sociologist James Davison Hunter (*Culture Wars*, 47) and Canadian sociologist Reginald W. Bibby (*Fragmented Gods*, 111, 136, 138, 140).

3. Lewis, *Abolition of Man*, esp. 7–16.

Myths

To avoid confusion, we need to be clear that Lewis rarely, if ever, uses the word "myth" in the popular sense of a false, untrue, foolish, superstitious, or ridiculous story. Rather he uses the word in a technical, literary sense, meaning, "a story told to make a point." A "myth" does not have to be historical to be true. No one, for example, on hearing Aesop's fables about a race between a tortoise and a hare, or the little boy who cried "wolf," is likely to insist these stories are untrue unless we can pinpoint the precise date and place where the race occurred or prove there was an actual boy, in a specific Greek village, on a particular day, month, and year whose flock was eaten by a wolf. That one should be wary of strangers is not dependent on being able to verify the names of a little girl wearing a red hood and her grandmother, the location of the house where the grandmother was eaten by a wolf, or on producing a police record giving the exact date of the tragedy! These "myths" are true without being *historical* events. Historicity is not integral to the truth of the story.

Lewis believes that there is a great divide between those he deems the "ancients" and the "moderns," between those who believe there is a transcendent reality and try to order their lives by it and those who do not. That divide Lewis identifies as occurring sometime after the Enlightenment, when its tenets had become widely accepted, part of the *Zeitgeist*.[4] In his inaugural address as Professor of Medieval and Renaissance Literature at Cambridge University in 1954, titled "*De Descriptione Temporum*," Lewis speaks about this great divide. It shows up, he says, in politics, modern painting, poetry, and the role of machines.[5] However, the most important aspect of this division is the underlying spiritual or religious one. Specifically, Western society, argues Lewis, has moved from being pagan to being in some vague sense Christian, and is now becoming post-Christian or secular.[6] Until very recently in human history, Lewis argues, faith *of some sort*, belief in *myth* of some sort—such as Christianity in the Western world—was the norm. Consequently, the Nordic pagan who worshipped Odin, Loki, or Thor and the ancient Greek who worshipped Zeus, Poseidon, Athena, or Apollo, had far more in common with the Christian than either had in common with the *modern* person who worships nothing at

---

4. Lewis, "*De Descriptione Temporum*," 17–22.
5. Lewis, "*De Descriptione Temporum*," 17–22.
6. Lewis, "*De Descriptione Temporum*," 19–20.

all.[7] Both the Christian and the pagan believed there was a reality, an external reality beyond that which he or she could see and touch, a reality which impacted human life and defined what was good and right and beautiful. The postmodern secular person regards this notion as "primitive" and thinks the idea of any authority external to him- or herself, particularly if that authority demands adherence to any kind of moral code, to be oppressive and almost certainly the result of some group trying to *impose* its view on others.

Lewis argues the side of the ancients, or "Old Western Man" as he calls it, over that of what *we* would call postmodern man [sic]. Lewis allies himself with all the northern myths, with the tales of the ancient Greeks and Romans, with medieval and Renaissance Europe, and with the world's great faiths, over against secular humanity, what he calls "modern" or "subjective" and we would likely call "postmodern" man. Lewis's pointed question is this: Was it realistic to believe that virtually *all* of humanity, Western and otherwise, both pagan and Christian, had been inexplicably and totally wrong until the last one hundred and fifty years or so? Specifically, was it sensible to believe that the overwhelming majority of humanity—and its mythology—had been wrong in asserting there was some kind of transcendent reality which defined rightness and wrongness, moral good and moral evil in absolute terms, and beauty? Such a notion, Lewis argues, is both unlikely and arrogant. It is a prime example of what he calls "'chronological snobbery, the uncritical acceptance of the intellectual climate common to our own age and the assumption that whatever has gone out of date is [solely] on that account discredited."[8]

Instead, Lewis asserts, it makes far more sense to conclude the many "stories scattered all through the heathen religions about a god who dies and comes to life again and, by his death, has somehow given new life to men [sic],"[9] though unhistorical, are a sort of distant early warning that God sent to humanity. They were the "good dreams" that God had sent leading and pointing toward the real thing.[10] That real thing was that once, and only once, a "myth"—the incarnation of Jesus Christ—had been more

---

7. Lewis, "*De Descriptione Temporum*," 14.
8. Lewis, *Surprised by Joy*, 167.
9. Lewis, *Mere Christianity*, 54.
10. Lewis, *Mere Christianity*, 54.

than just another story, but a *historical* event.¹¹ The incarnation "myth" was "a true myth: a myth . . . that . . . *really happened.*"¹²

Morals

It was not, however, just humanity's myths that, for Lewis, demonstrate the reality of the *consensus gentium*. The consensus also can be seen in the millennia long, near universal conviction, held by both pagans and Christians, that there is a moral code—certain moral laws or rules—known by all, or almost all people everywhere, which laws ought to be obeyed and which were believed to have *come* from an external authority.

This moral code contrasts sharply with the view of the typical modern, subjective, secular person (as Lewis puts it) or the typical postmodern, secular person (as we shall put it) who asserts there never were and never can be unchanging, universal moral absolutes. For the postmodern person, morals emerge from human experience, not from any outside authority. Because human experience is constantly changing, it is impossible for there to be permanent or absolute moral laws. Lewis, with considerable foresight, raises objections to and rejects this view.

There is, he argues, clear and convincing evidence for the existence of what he calls "the Tao," more usually called "natural law." Lewis in fact took very seriously the biblical witness to natural law, expressed particularly strongly by the apostle Paul in his letter to the Romans (see Rom 1:18–32; 2:14–15), that there is within human beings an innate sense that some things are always right and some things are always wrong, a sense placed in humans by God. Thus, in *The Lion, the Witch, and the Wardrobe*, we encounter Edmund, who betrays his brother and sisters to the White Witch. Repeatedly, Edmund is shown trying to convince himself that she really is a nice person and that everyone who says she is quite nasty and evil—which she is—is just being unfair about her. Deep down, however, Edmund *knows* very well that she really is evil, and he cannot convince himself otherwise, no matter how hard he tries. This, of course, is an entirely relatable description of a very common human experience. Few there are who have not at some point tried, unsuccessfully, to convince themselves that something they knew to be wrong was, in fact, right.

---

11. See, e.g., Lewis, *Surprised by Joy*, 188–89; "Myth Became Fact."
12. Lewis, "Letter," 977.

Part One: Apologetics and Philosophy

In *The Abolition of Man*, Lewis includes an appendix citing multiple examples of widespread agreement on a variety of moral issues in ancient Egyptian and Jewish writings, from Babylonian instructions, Greek and Roman thinkers, old Norse and Anglo-Saxon texts, to Confucius, Hinduism's sacred Bhagavad Gita, and Australian aboriginal lore.[13] Given this reality, to argue, as postmodernism does, that moral judgments in fact mean nothing more than the opinion of my group means making the incredible assertion that almost all humanity, including our most revered thinkers, philosophers, and writers of great literature, somehow, for millennia, have not only been wrong but were babbling utter nonsense.[14]

Lewis's best-known treatment of the evidence for the existence and reality of a universal moral law is the line of reasoning he presents in *Mere Christianity*. There Lewis points out, "First, human beings all over the earth have this curious idea that they ought to behave in a certain way, and cannot really get rid of it. Secondly, they do not in fact behave in that way. They know the Law of Nature [or the natural law, or the moral law, or the Tao but] they break it."[15] "These two facts," Lewis writes, "are the foundation of all clear thinking about ourselves and the universe we live in."[16] Thus, Lewis notes that people quarrel. They have moral arguments. They do not merely fight physically as animals do. Instead, human beings try to *justify* their behaviour by appealing to a moral law or standard. Everyone in the world, insists Lewis, does this, except the subjectivist or, as we today might say, the postmodernist.[17] Moreover, Lewis observes, "Whenever you find a man [sic] who says he does not believe in a real Right and Wrong, you will find the same man going back on this a moment later. He may break his promise to you, but if you try breaking [yours] to him he will be complaining 'It's not fair' before you can say Jack Robinson."[18] The offended party, to whom you have broken your promise, is appealing to some standard which he expects you both to know and meet, a standard which is *external* to and *above* either of you. Yet, according to postmodern thinking, there is no such externally given standard or morality. Morality is not external to humanity; instead, it develops from ever changing human experience. But

---

13. Lewis, *Abolition of Man*, 49–59.
14. Lewis, *Abolition of Man*, 14.
15. Lewis, *Mere Christianity*, 21.
16. Lewis, *Mere Christianity*, 21.
17. Lewis, *Mere Christianity*, 17–21.
18. Lewis, *Mere Christianity*, 19.

what then are we to make of the fact that for countless centuries, humans, whilst quarrelling, have almost always appealed to an external standard? Has practically everyone who has ever lived, until very recently, been utterly, entirely, wrong whenever they did so?[19] That Lewis thought implausible and scarcely credible. He therefore relentlessly keeps pushing this question: From whence did that standard to which we almost all appeal come? It cannot have come from ourselves since we appeal to it and think of it as something over and beyond ourselves. If this standard is merely a "social convention," that is, "something human beings have made up for themselves,"[20] we could, during any quarrel, simply say we do not accept the convention. But we do not do that. Instead, the way we speak, argue, and behave betrays that we really do think the standard is much more than simply "social convention." Moreover, if in fact there is a standard to which almost all of us appeal and to which the vast majority of humans in the past have appealed, is it not obvious there must be some kind of authoritative standard giver—someone or something—outside of ourselves? To quote Peter Kreeft, a prominent Lewis scholar:

> No one in our time has ever faced and answered the question: "If there is no God [or as we might put it no universal ethical code given by a transcendent authority] why shouldn't I do as I please if I can get away with it? Because it's not acceptable, nice, humane, human, democratic, fair, just, community building, helpful, survival-enhancing, practical and approved? But suppose I don't want to be [any of these things]? I have never heard any reply [to this"] . . . And of course, there never will be a reply. For if there is no. . .outside, independent authority to give us a natural law, then there is no reason *why* I shouldn't do [exactly] as I please.[21]

Joy

In his autobiography, Lewis describes three experiences, as a boy, of intense desire or longing.[22] He describes these experiences as "an unsatisfied desire which is itself more desirable than any other satisfaction."[23] Joy is an inconsolable, haunting yearning for something unknown, something

19. Lewis, *Mere Christianity*, 17–21.
20. Lewis, *Mere Christianity*, 24.
21. Kreeft, "'Darkness at Noon.'"
22. Lewis, *Surprised by Joy*, 18–20.
23. Lewis, *Surprised by Joy*, 20.

beyond current experience, something which cannot be fully described or explained, a sensation both bitter and sweet, perhaps with some affinity to nostalgia. This powerful sense of longing Lewis calls "joy,"[24] writing that the search for it was "the central story of my life."[25]

A number of characters in Lewis's fictional works experience this intense longing. John, the protagonist in *The Pilgrim's Regress*, has visions of an island which create an indescribable yearning that, at first, he confuses with sexual desire. The children in *The Lion, the Witch, and the Wardrobe*, or at least all of them except the traitor Edmund, long for Aslan, even before they meet him. At the mere mention of his name the children experience a "strange feeling—like the first signs of spring, like good news [which came] over them."[26] The two talking horses in *The Horse and his Boy*, Bree and Hwin, make "Narnia and the North" their rallying cry; both have a deep longing to get back home to Narnia, their homeland. Prince Caspian, the rightful but usurped heir to the throne of Narnia, is schooled by his tutor, Dr. Cornelius, in the history and lore of Narnia—in the time before the talking animals and mythical beings faced oppression and possible extinction—and the Prince longs for a return to such, to what Aslan had intended all along for Narnia. In *The Voyage of the Dawn Treader*, Reepicheep, the fearless, loyal, and noble mouse—who is most sensitive of his own dignity—yearns to find the end of the world and Aslan's country. In *The Last Battle*, Emeth discovers, to his very great surprise, that in his service to the false god Tash, he has, all along, been seeking and desiring Aslan. The experience of longing also appears in Lewis's science fiction trilogy. It has been argued, for example, that in both *Out of the Silent Planet* and *Perelandra: Voyage to Venus*, "the result of this longing is a relentless quest,"[27] undertaken in both books by Dr. Elwin Ransom, a philologist at Cambridge University. *That Hideous Strength* might well be described as an extended commentary on longing gone wrong. Mark Studdock's acute desire to be part of the inner circle of Bracton College leads him to the verge of being totally co-opted by the hellish leadership of the N.I.C.E. (National Institute of Co-ordinated Experiments).

Lewis both describes his own experience of "longing" and imaginatively pictures the experience as normal and more or less universal in his

24. Lewis, *Surprised by Joy*, 20.
25. Lewis, *Surprised by Joy*, 20.
26. Lewis, *Lion, the Witch, and the Wardrobe*, 74.
27. Dennis, "Sehnsucht."

fiction. Moreover, he also argues, in *Mere Christianity*, "If I find in myself a desire which no experience in this world can satisfy, the most probable explanation is that I was made for another world."[28] Given all this, it is odd that Lewis gave relatively little attention to the experience of longing as evidence for the existence of the *consensus gentium*. Why he did not do so is a serious puzzlement; if the experience of longing and desire—joy—is indeed near universal, as Lewis pictures it to be, then surely this too is evidence for a *consensus gentium* and in turn is suggestive *of* a transcendent reality, an authority *external* to humanity, for which we long. Indeed, such a universal sense of longing is the same kind of evidence for consensus as is a universal moral code or commonalities in mythology. And if such a consensus exists and points to an external authority, the assertions of postmodernism are called into serious question. We simply do not know why Lewis did not employ, as prominently as he did with myth and morality, the experience of longing—or joy—as evidence for the *consensus gentium*. Nevertheless, doing so is a reasonable extension of his thinking in part *because* there is very considerable attestation that the experience of longing is not only very common but also widespread across many different time periods, cultures, and worldviews. Here are but a few examples:

In ancient Greek mythology, humans once had four arms and legs and two faces, fused together. Either as a punishment for pride or out of fear of human power, Zeus split humans in half, condemning us to searching and longing because we were no longer complete. The idea of longing is also found in Greek Neoplatonic philosophers who believed that we had been trapped in physical, material bodies but yearned and longed to return to our original higher, non-physical reality. In that state, humans would attain beauty and knowledge impossible in our enfleshed, lower mode of existence. The wisdom literature of the Hebrew Scriptures often describes something akin to Lewis's "joy." The psalm writer compares his longing for God to a deer longing for flowing streams of water (Ps 41:1 NRSV). Ecclesiastes describes all humanity as having had "a sense of past and future [put] into their minds" (Eccl 3:11 NRSV) by God. The exilic books of the First Testament repeatedly describe a longing for Zion or Jerusalem, which is often pictured in terms far more mystical than simply a rebuilt or restored city. The great medieval rabbi, Maimonides, wrote of a longing to know God's name. New York-born Orthodox Rabbi Yitzchok Adlerstein writes, "Longing and yearning are unrecognized essentials of life. Few pleasures

---

28. Lewis, *Mere Christianity*, 120.

compare to the sweetness of a longing derived from desire that is pure and holy."[29] The Christian tradition is, of course, filled with references to a sense of longing—for something indescribable and never fully found. Jesus, before his crucifixion, tells his anxious disciples that not only is there plenty of room for them in "my Father's house," but that he will both go "to prepare a place" for them and return to take them there (John 14:2–3 NRSV). The author of Hebrews writes of the desire for a better, heavenly country—which his readers had never seen or visited (Heb 11:16). Augustine, in his *Confessions*, famously wrote that human hearts are restless until they find rest in God, while Pascal describes a craving which demonstrates that we were once happy but are now empty. Sufi Muslims describe longing—understood as longing for God, for home—as the basis of their entire practice. The experience of intense longing in Hinduism is also well recognized and is usually understood to be a yearning for the divine. Even among the self-proclaimed non-religious, this sense of longing may be seen. For example, Carl Sagan (1934–1996) was an astronomer and planetary scientist who widely popularized these fields through his books and notably through his award-winning TV series, *Cosmos*. Although Sagan was an agnostic, a sense of longing appears early in his book of the same name:

> The surface of the Earth is the shore of the cosmic ocean. From it we have learned most of what we know. Recently, we have waded a little out to sea, enough to dampen our toes or, at most, wet our ankles. The water seems inviting. The ocean calls. Some part of our being knows this is from where we came. *We long to return.* These aspirations are not, I think, irreverent, although they may trouble whatever gods may be.[30]

Similarly, Stephen Hawking (1942–2018), a theoretical physicist, cosmologist, and firm atheist, spent decades pursuing what sounds in many respects remarkably akin to Lewis's "joy." In Hawking's case, it was a search for the so-called "theory of everything" which would, supposedly, provide a framework for understanding all of physics and all the "laws" of the universe.

The point is that there seems to be a plentitude of evidence that Lewis's sense of joy—an unfulfilled longing for *something*—is extremely widespread across multiple cultures and eras and that this longing—just as much as the commonalities Lewis found in mythology and morality—is

---

29. Adlerstein, "Desire and Longing."
30. Sagan, *Cosmos*, 2 (emphasis mine).

also "a clue to the meaning of the universe." More still, this "joy" or longing clearly seems to be experienced even by the most secular.

CONCLUSION

One of the most important themes in Lewis's writings is that there is a *consensus gentium*, consensus of humanity, expressed in the great myths of every culture and found in the moral teachings of all the world's major religions. This consensus points to there being a transcendent reality which defines what is good, right, and beautiful. Lewis provides his readers with strong evidence that this consensus exists *and* that it runs deeply through all the world's great myths and worldviews, Christian and otherwise, as well as in a commonly recognized moral code. It would therefore be profoundly unwise, not to mention arrogant, Lewis believed, simply to dismiss this consensus out of hand *or* what the consensus pointed toward. Presciently, Lewis's argument from the existence of the consensus, in our era, presents postmodernism with a challenging problem: Has most of humanity, including most of humanity's greatest thinkers, been wrong in believing that there is a transcendent reality which defines what is good, right, and beautiful? Is it only very recently that a tiny portion of humanity has gotten it right that no such reality exists?

Although Lewis does not give as much attention to what he called "joy" as evidence for the existence of the consensus and the transcendent reality toward which it points, as he does with the commonalities he sees in both myth and morals, "joy" or longing, in fact, is *also* a very widespread human experience, crossing multiple cultures and centuries. It too is a "clue to the meaning of the universe," pointing us toward the existence of a transcendent authority. Deepening our understanding of "joy," and how it appears in the lives of our contemporaries in Western society, may very well be an important means of challenging the major tenets of postmodernism and persuading at least some to reconsider their secular and postmodern worldview based on those tenets.

BIBLIOGRAPHY

Adlerstein, Yitzchok. "Desire and Longing: Parshas Vayikra." *torah.com* (March 14, 2019). No pages. Online: https://torah.org/torah-portion/mei-marom-5779-vayikra.

Bibby, Reginald W. *Fragmented Gods: The Poverty and Potential of Religion in Canada.* Toronto: Irwin, 1987.

Part One: Apologetics and Philosophy

Dennis, Sherry K. "Sehnsucht and the Island Motif in C. S. Lewis' *Out of the Silent Planet* and *Perelandra*." MA thesis, Florida Atlantic University, 1978.

Hunter, James Davison. *Culture Wars: The Struggle to Define America*. New York: HarperCollins, 1991.

Kreeft, Peter. "'Darkness at Noon': The Eclipse of 'The Permanent Things.'" *EWTN (Eternal Word Television Network)*. No pages. Online: https://www.ewtn.com/catholicism/library/darkness-at-noon-the-eclipse-of-the-permanent-things-10026.

Lewis, C. S. *The Abolition of Man*. 1947. Reprint, Glasgow: Collins, 1982.

———. "*De Descriptione Temporum*." In *They Asked for a Paper: Papers and Essays*, 9–25. London: Geoffrey Bles, 1962.

———. "Letter to Arthur Greeves, Oct. 18th, 1931." In *The Collected Letters of C. S. Lewis: Family Letters, 1905–1931—Volume I*, edited by Walter Hooper, 426–28. London: Harper Collins, 2000.

———. *The Lion, the Witch, and the Wardrobe*. 1950. Reprint, London: Collins, 1989.

———. *Mere Christianity*. 1952. Reprint, New York: Macmillan, 1977.

———. "Myth Became Fact." In *God in the Dock: Essays on Theology and Ethics*, edited by Walter Hooper, 63–67. Grand Rapids: Eerdmans, 1978.

———. *Surprised by Joy: The Shape of My Early Life*. 1955. Reprint, Glasgow: Collins, 1978.

Lyotard, Jean-François. *The Postmodern Condition: A Report on Knowledge*. Translated by Geoff Bennington and Brian Massumi. Theory and History of Literature 10. Minneapolis: University of Minnesota Press, 1979.

Sagan, Carl. *Cosmos*. New York: Ballantine, 1985.

Pick your Poison

Revisiting C. S. Lewis's *The Abolition of Man* in a Postmodern Age

Jason Vander Horst

INTRODUCTION

The Abolition of Man is one of C. S. Lewis's most darkly prophetic works, envisioning the practical consequences of a world stripped of objective value. His warning is chillingly persuasive: he sees moral collapse, combined with the unchecked progression of science, culminating not in a utopia of freedom but in a dystopian future where a powerful few exercise absolute control over the many.[1] Without objective values, these few will seize the moral vacuum as an opportunity to indoctrinate society with values derived only from their own instinctive desires.[2] Lewis fears that humanity itself will be rendered as a mere product, ruled by the conditioners, who in turn are ruled by their own nature.[3]

Today's educational environment has grown unapologetically subjective. Theoretical perspectives are so numerous that pursuing just one seems almost reductive and perhaps even intellectually irresponsible, as though one were ignoring the rich complexity of human thought. The pursuit of truth appears hopeless in the face of such diversity, and it can seem like no single tool can truly do justice to the world. The average student is led to

---

1. Lewis, *Abolition of Man*, 28–40.
2. Lewis, *Abolition of Man*, 31–34.
3. Lewis, *Abolition of Man*, 31.

believe that all these tools are, in some way, valid and that they can pick and choose whichever they resonate with most; in short, "Pick your poison!" This approach can appear tremendously liberating but perhaps too much so.

In this paper, I contend that the "Pick your Poison" approach to ethics subtly erodes the importance of moral consistency and trains students to rationalize behaviour rather than seek timeless truth. This education produces individuals who are particularly susceptible to manipulation and control by predatory corporations who weaponize vice to acquire profit.

In this essay, I first elaborate Lewis's unifying principle of objective value and the subtle disruption of this perspective that he already observed in the 1940s. Second, I discuss how this disruption is mirrored in modern education, as postmodernism dismantles meta-narratives and leaves decision-making up to students. Third, I explore psychological evidence that reveals this decision-making process to be far less reasonable than educators might hope—and in real life is often used to justify theft, cheating, and hypocrisy. Fourth, I examine how selfish tendencies are worsened as corporations fill the resulting moral vacuum with values of their own. Finally, I offer some level of comfort to those who still operate under a higher moral law.

THE DOCTRINE OF OBJECTIVE VALUE

Bridging the Moral Divide

In *The Abolition of Man*, Lewis masterfully bridges the divide between East and West, unifying traditions across time and culture by uncovering a single yet profoundly important philosophical commonality. This is the doctrine of objective value, the idea that some things truly are right, good, beyond reproach, and others wrong, bad, and contemptible.[4] This standard was not just normative, it was universally respected throughout human history.[5] He unifies this timeless, universal principle under the banner of the "Tao" (道)—a term borrowed from the ancient Chinese tradition meaning nature itself, the way that ought to be followed, and the reality beyond all predicates.[6] The Tao represents the *ought* behind existence itself that ev-

---

4. Lewis, *Abolition of Man*, 9.
5. Lewis, *Abolition of Man*, 7, 9.
6. Lewis, *Abolition of Man*, 8.

eryone, regardless of status, race, or creed, is subject to.[7] It is not something to be refuted; it can only be debated, clarified, or misunderstood but never truly overthrown.

This presents a potential problem; history is full of disagreements about what ought to be, and every culture seems to have a unique conception of truth. Lewis recognizes this: "If we lump together, as I have done, the traditional moralities of East and West, the Christian, the Pagan, and the Jew, shall we not find many contradictions and some absurdities? I admit all this."[8] These contradictions are even present within the same cultural epoch. Confucius, for example, argues that if your father commits a crime, you *ought* to cover it up, placing loyalty to family above duty to the state.[9] Mozi, his first known critic, sees this partisan mentality as the very root of all societal evils, saying that we *ought* to turn him in.[10] Both are objective claims to right and wrong, yet both cannot be true.

Lewis responds to these criticisms, insisting that "Some criticism, some removal of contradictions, even some real development, is required."[11] He compares this process to a poet making affectionate modifications to his mother tongue that preserve and honour the spirit of its origin.[12] Much like language, moral thinking is not stagnant; it is a living tradition that evolves through careful refinement over time rather than wholesale rejection.

While Mozi, Confucius, Plato, Aristotle, Locke, and others may disagree on particular duties or applications, they all affirm that something *ought* to be. Lewis cites Confucius: "It is upon the trunk that a gentleman works."[13] The unique claims of each thinker are like branches growing from the same tree—each one rooted in shared practical axioms such as "*society ought to be preserved.*"[14] What differed were their interpretations of how these axioms should manifest in practice. The real debate is not over whether objective value exists, but over how best to nurture or prune its branches.

---

7. Lewis, *Abolition of Man*, 8.
8. Lewis, *Abolition of Man*, 21–22.
9. Ivanhoe and Van Norden, eds., *Readings*, 39.
10. Ivanhoe and Van Norden, eds., *Readings*, 72.
11. Lewis, *Abolition of Man*, 22.
12. Lewis, *Abolition of Man*, 22.
13. Lewis, *Abolition of Man*, 14.
14. Lewis, *Abolition of Man*, 19.

Through time and refinement, some branches have grown so universally strong that they have become nearly synonymous with fact. Children are rightly loved, old men are rightly honoured, and justice is not merely a useful convention but a moral obligation to "render to things their due esteem."[15] These are not whims, inferences, or evolutionary accidents; they form the very basis of what might be called moral mathematics.

This understanding extended beyond questions of ethics to those of beauty and aesthetic judgment. When someone says that a waterfall is "sublime" or that a landscape is "beautiful," they were not merely reporting a private feeling; they are making a claim about the nature of reality itself.[16] Beauty, like justice or loyalty, is seen as an objective quality—something that called for a right and fitting response.

Challenges to the Tao

This traditional way of thinking did not go completely unchallenged, as historical figures did at times reject that values were embedded in reality. In ancient Greece, Protagoras claimed, "Man is the measure of all things," implying that truth is subjective and individually determined.[17] A similar view is found in the writings of the Chinese philosopher Zhuangzi, who contended that all perspectives are inherently limited, that rigid distinctions are illusions, and that what one considers right may just as well be seen as wrong[18]. In the nineteenth century, Friedrich Nietzsche radicalized this idea, unapologetically mocking the search for truth, arguing that uncertainty or even ignorance might as well be preferable.[19] For him, even the greatest philosophical writing is nothing more than "the personal confession of its author and a kind of involuntary and unconscious memoir."[20]

Although these early challenges to objective value were largely confined to philosophy, Lewis, writing in the 1940s, was greatly alarmed to observe that such subjectivism began to bleed into education itself.[21] He demonstrates this subtle attack on objectivity with passages taken from an English textbook he refers to as "The Green Book." In this book, the authors

---

15. Lewis, *Abolition of Man*, 45, 7.
16. Lewis, *Abolition of Man*, 7.
17. Plato, *Theaet.* 152a (Horan).
18. Zhuangzi, *On Equalizing Things*, 232.
19. Nietzsche, *Beyond Good and Evil*, 1.
20. Nietzsche, *Beyond Good and Evil*, 14.
21. Lewis, *Abolition of Man*, 1, 4.

teach that waterfalls have no objective qualities of their own, and that our attempts to describe them are really only describing our own feelings.[22] A waterfall is not sublime, nor is it pretty; it may be accurately described as majestic, shabby, beautiful, or even ugly so long as the emotions evoking such descriptions are present at the time of viewing.

However, as Lewis points out, "This is a philosophical and not a literary position."[23] For most of human history, it was understood that when someone said, "This waterfall is sublime," or "This waterfall is pretty," they were not merely describing a feeling—they were making a claim about reality.[24] Augustine would call this an act of rightly ordered love: loving things according to their place in the created order. If we withhold awe from what is genuinely awe-inspiring, our hearts are not just mistaken—they are disordered.[25] Plato and Aristotle similarly believed that the purpose of education is to teach students the right way to respond to reality.[26] For these thinkers and many others, to say a waterfall is "sublime" is not simply to say "I like it"—it is to say, "This is worthy of awe."

These English school teachers may have subtly introduced a claim about the subjectivity of inanimate objects, but are its implications truly so dire as to inspire an entire book? Lewis argues that regardless of pedagogical intent, students will—beyond their own awareness—learn to treat all value judgments as both subjective and trivial.[27]

The authors of "The Green Book" go on to critique an advertisement for a cruise, mocking its sentimental language: "Those who buy tickets for this cruise will go 'across the Western Ocean where Drake of Devon sailed,' 'adventuring after the treasures of the Indies,' and bringing home themselves also a 'treasure' of 'golden hours' and 'glowing colours.'"[28] Lewis agrees that this is poor "bathetic" writing but argues that the proper educational response is not to ridicule the emotion it evokes, but to compare it with good literature that rightly stirs the same feelings.[29] Instead, the authors dismiss

---

22. Lewis, *Abolition of Man*, 1.
23. Lewis, *Abolition of Man*, 6.
24. Lewis, *Abolition of Man*, 7.
25. Lewis, *Abolition of Man*, 7.
26. Lewis, *Abolition of Man*, 7–8.
27. Lewis, *Abolition of Man*, 3.
28. Lewis, *Abolition of Man*, 3.
29. Lewis, *Abolition of Man*, 3–4.

the emotional appeal as false simply because it is not literally true, implying that such language is merely a tool to manipulate action.[30]

Lewis argues that this kind of education implicitly teaches students to "debunk" emotional sentiment and approach literary criticism from a superficial "commonplace rationalism."[31] This kind of education leads to the creation of what Lewis provocatively called "men without chests": individuals who have become emotionally detached from the timeless values that were once held to be reflections of an objective order.[32] What was once esteemed is now rendered trivial, contrary to reason, and contemptible.[33] Beauty, honour, courage, and love are no longer ideals to admire, but naive illusions to be unmasked. In this way, subjectivism enters not through debate but through pedagogy—bypassing rational scrutiny and silently reshaping the student's moral framework.[34] What was once openly contested is now absorbed without awareness.

Subjectivist Education and the Problem of Control

Lewis doesn't really try to dispute the claim that value judgments are subjective on a philosophical level; his argument is merely descriptive. He points out that the very authors who debunk traditional emotions, like the authors of "The Green Book," still presume to *educate* the young toward some end.[35] That contradiction is Lewis's target: if values are merely subjective, then their book has no right to ask anything of anyone.

Lewis clearly illustrates this difficulty with an example. During times of war, society relies on the belief that courage and honour are in themselves desirable virtues. Lewis speaks from personal experience: "In battle, it is not syllogisms that keep the reluctant nerves and muscles to their post in the third hour of the bombardment." Heroism would be scarce, perhaps forgotten, if divorced from emotional sentiment. You cannot tell a soldier to throw himself upon a grenade with an appeal to utility; a mathematical equation is laughable when you are facing death. As such, a society that treats objective values like courage, honour, love, and loyalty must also recognize that teaching these becomes a matter of persuasion, not principle.

30. Lewis, *Abolition of Man*, 4.
31. Lewis, *Abolition of Man*, 6.
32. Lewis, *Abolition of Man*, 11.
33. Lewis, *Abolition of Man*, 3–4.
34. Lewis, *Abolition of Man*, 3.
35. Lewis, *Abolition of Man*, 14.

Any attempt to impose them on the impressionable minds of the next generation would not be the propagation of timeless truths, but rather a matter of mere conditioning.[36] The old kind of educator could be likened to old birds teaching young birds how to fly, whereas the new is comparable to poultry keepers manufacturing their subjects into what they please.[37]

CONTEMPORARY MORAL EDUCATION

Postmodernism and the Collapse of Metanarratives

The concerns Lewis had over seventy years ago are decidedly more important today. The rise of postmodernism marks a kind of inverted Enlightenment where certainty is suspect, and meaning is not discovered but endlessly deferred or created. Any attempt to find a unifying theory of truth is drowned out by the myriad voices claiming objectivity. This is especially apparent in the social sciences whose bird's-eye view of humanity reveals the tremendous variance in opinions across societies and even social groups. Perched atop the mountain of history, equipped with the latest scientific discoveries and cultural knowledge, we can now view sentiments rooted in the so-called "Tao" as nothing more than an archaic relic of naivety. It is a monument to an evolutionary history that served its purpose and a sentimental keepsake of our humble beginnings.

However, what also remains is the disturbing words of Lewis, likening educators of the new world to poultry keepers "making them thus or thus for purposes of which the birds know nothing."[38] To a culture that idolizes autonomy and literally builds monuments to freedom, this is a prophecy of doom and an unacceptable threat to the ideal of self-determination. To its credit, postmodern education has found a reasonable solution. The modern educator should, to the best of their ability, take a step back, check their biases at the door, and teach without relying on value-laden judgments. Emotions among students are not to be ordered but validated as subjective experiences.

---

36. Lewis, *Abolition of Man*, 10.
37. Lewis, *Abolition of Man*, 10–11.
38. Lewis, *Abolition of Man*, 11.

Part One: Apologetics and Philosophy

Practical Pedagogy amidst a Moral Vacuum

Even without a commitment to neutrality, there are some perspectives that are in some way deemed neutral, convincing, and practical enough to be included into a curriculum. Ethics, for example, might be argued to be a subjective social construct devoid of objective value, but that's not to say that we should throw out all ethical values. Still, what values are to structure an ethics course when the prevailing social dogma sings only "You do you"? This song, while pleasing, delivers no insight beyond autonomy.

This leaves society in a moral vacuum at a most inopportune time. We now seriously grapple with questions drawn from the most provocative science fiction thought experiments: superhuman genetic modifications, AI-driven consciousness transfers, synthetic wombs for designer babies, memory modification, brain-computer interfaces, and end-of-life decisions outsourced to algorithms. These discussions vindicate Lewis's haunting prophecies as more than just the prophetic ramblings of a man still married to tradition. The educators of today have a serious decision to make. The tools we choose to solve these problems will reverberate through time, shaping all future generations. What moral frameworks are we to provide students to answer such complex predicaments?

To illustrate, I will draw from a bioethics course I took during my undergraduate studies. I enrolled in the course shortly after reading *The Abolition of Man*, which led to the development of what I now call the "Pick your Poison" approach to ethics.

The professor in this course first set out to determine what moral frameworks ought to be avoided in essays and discussions. Religious tradition is fine as long as it stays in its own lane, tolerated as a private belief system but unwelcome in the classroom. Even the ancient Greeks are too old-fashioned; after all, what can antique virtue say about genetic modifications and designer babies? These problems demand efficiency, neutrality, and moral scalability—not transcendentals, not emotion, not metaphysics, and certainly not Gods.

Mixing Utility and Deontology

The safest bet of course lies in utility. Who would take issue with an axiom that espouses happiness and abhors pain? This is both universally agreeable and easily digested by the average student. However, the cold calculus of utility is to be rejected when taken to its logical conclusion, as it permits or even requires acts that violate individual rights and dignity if doing so maximizes overall happiness.[39] Theft, eugenics, government surveillance, torture, organ harvesting, and even slavery are all actions that can be potentially defended on the grounds that they lead to a higher good, yet are simultaneously repugnant and contemptible. As such, the principle of utility must be balanced.

Deontological ethics, particularly from Immanuel Kant, is the obvious choice to fill this void. Autonomy under Kant is paramount; coercion, deceit, and theft cannot be universalized and therefore violate the moral law.[40] Similarly, treating others as ends in themselves rather than simply as means is an excellent way to restrain utilitarian ethics when it seems to go "too far."[41] Unfortunately, however, the categorical imperative also fails in isolation, as an unwavering commitment to principle becomes objectionable when applied to the extreme. A proud Kantian will squirm when asked if they'd lie to save the life of a dear friend when a murderer comes knocking.[42] For Kant, the moral law admits no exceptions, even here, as duty to truth trumps all consequentialist sentiment. Utility then becomes the perfect counterbalance to make up for the unyielding stubbornness of the categorical imperative.

The combination of these two philosophies potentially seems to be perfect, with each making up for the other's absurdities. The theories, being polar opposites, also allow for the expression of all opinions on even the most controversial topics in a more value-neutral, logical, and practical language. As someone who works within the Tao, I believe that the best answer to ethical dilemmas can, in a sort of brutish reductionism, lie somewhere between these two opposing theories. This is not because of their happy union, but rather because they are founded upon opposing metaphysical assumptions. Utility depends only and entirely on outcomes, while deontology cares only about the action itself. Imagine being told that your destination lies somewhere between the North and South Poles—this tells us nothing about where to go.

I won't delay over the attempt these theorists make to compress the complexities of the Tao into a single maxim—such a critique exceeds the

---

39. Rachels and Rachels, *Elements*, 112–15.

40. Kant, "Groundwork," 41–42, 12.

41. Kant, "Groundwork," 36. The application to restraining utility is my own interpretation

42. Rachels and Rachels, *Elements*, 130–32.

scope of this chapter. The biggest problem lies in the uncritical assumption that these two viscerally opposed ethical systems can suddenly be combined by undergraduates on a whim. If John Stuart Mill and Kant were to engage in conversation, they would agree on very little; but within the ethics classroom, their ideas are presented as compatible and interchangeable.

The educator seemingly has all they want and nothing they do not want. All opinions are respected as students are encouraged to pick and choose whichever theory that seems to provide the most logical solution to each given issue. The messiness of emotions can be quieted, leaving room for discussions that are guided by reason rather than sentiment. At this point, I am assuming that the professor is, to some degree, holding onto the belief that such pluralism is valid or practical on the grounds that students are capable of using reason to come to somewhat rational or even preferable combinations of them. However, this assumption can be questioned.

THE ILLUSION OF MORAL REASONING

The Rationalist Approach

The belief that students can use reason to come to logical ethical conclusions stems from the rationalist approach to ethics. It assumes that reason and logical deduction are the primary pathway used to identify moral solutions.[43] Originating in classical philosophy, this view was famously upheld by Plato. He likened the soul to a charioteer with two horses: one noble and obedient, representing the spirited part of the soul, and the other unruly and rebellious, symbolizing desire. Reason, embodied by the charioteer, must skillfully guide both toward truth and harmony.[44] This model was still widely used academically in the 1950s–1980s, when Lawrence Kohlberg argued that moral thinking developed alongside intellect.[45] Whether it is a Greek senator weighing the cost of a bribe or a modern teenager debating whether to outsource their essay to AI, the rationalist vision maintains reason as the primary defense against vice.

This assumption has not been left unscrutinized. Epicurus argued that our moral compass stems not from rationality but from the twin poles of

---

43. Haidt, "Emotional Dog," 1026.
44. Plato, *Phaed.* 246a–249d.
45. Haidt, "Emotional Dog," 1026–27.

pleasure and pain.[46] David Hume pushed this skepticism further, famously declaring, "Reason is, and ought only to be the slave of the passions, and can never pretend to any other office but to serve and obey them."[47] For Hume, morality is not deduced but rather projected through feelings.

Similarly, Lewis rejects rationalism in *The Abolition of Man*, arguing for the mediating role of trained emotion: "The head rules the belly through the chest."[48] His claim here is that our intellect can recognize what ought to be liked or disliked, but only when the chest has been properly refined through education.

Empirical Findings: The Social Intuitionist Model

Jonathan Haidt is a well-known social psychologist who has conducted numerous cross-cultural studies addressing the psychological foundations of ethical reasoning. His work has led him to propose the social intuitionist model, which posits that in most cases, ethical judgments take place rapidly and automatically, like a reflex before any conscious processing even takes place.[49] These judgments arise from deeply embedded sentiments like empathy, love, guilt, shame, remorse, and disgust.[50]

This stands in sharp contrast to the idyllic plains of rationalism; the picture seems almost painfully outside of our control. Haidt inverts Plato's analogy of a horse and rider: rather than a rational rider directing wild horses, he introduces the elephant: powerful, emotional, and stubborn.[51] The rider's job is not to guide the elephant to a destination but to scramble together reasons to explain why the elephant chose to go where it already went.[52]

But where do these sentiments come from? Besides what is innate, Haidt argues that moral beliefs arise from two primary sources: social interaction and culture.[53] The actions and beliefs of one's family, friends, media, and peers describe which emotional reactions are fitting or not fitting in any given scenario. These interactions, or rather internalized observations,

---

46. Epicurus, *Letter*, §7.
47. Hume, *Treatise*, 415.
48. Lewis, *Abolition of Man*, 11.
49. Haidt, "Emotional Dog," 1028–31.
50. Haidt, "Emotional Dog," 1039.
51. Haidt, *Righteous Mind*, 20, 69, 73, 80.
52. Haidt, *Righteous Mind*, 70.
53. Haidt, "Emotional Dog," 1042, 1043.

are mediated by cultural values.[54] A child who grows up in a community that values independence, for instance, will learn that pride is an acceptable response when expressing their autonomy. A child raised in a culture that values interdependence may learn to feel guilt under the same conditions. In both cases, the emotional reaction elicits a post hoc justification that feels like objective reasoning.[55]

These intuitions form the emotional backbone of moral judgment and, in time, become the gut feelings that drive our ethical decisions. In this light, what Lewis calls the "chest"—a seat of trained sentiment—finds its empirical counterpart. To the disappointment of many (including myself), reasoning is not in the driver's seat, it is merely a passenger.

Social Intuitionism and the "Pick your Poison" Approach

Given that ethical judgments are typically born of intuition rather than rationality, what does this mean for students in the bioethics class? Let us consider the Canadian cultural context and assume that these values are normative. Canadian culture is famously, and proudly, inclusive of all ideas and lifestyles. A strong emphasis is placed on the autonomy of the individual to choose how to live life as they see fit, so long as it does not impinge upon the rights of others. Further, both in law and in public sentiment, Canadian society tends to prioritize policies and attitudes that are perceived to reduce suffering, preserve dignity, and protect the vulnerable.

When analyzing ethical issues, these sentiments will play a central role. Take medically assisted death, for example. When students are presented with videos of veterans struggling with PTSD and abandonment by the healthcare system, or disabled individuals fearing they have become burdens to their families, their moral judgment is often made before any analytical reasoning takes place. In such cases, they may naturally be drawn to argue from a utilitarian perspective, where the alleviation of suffering provides a compelling and emotionally satisfying justification.

However, if students are asked to write a paper on whether non-consensual euthanasia is appropriate in extreme cases, where the individual is in deep pain but unable to give assent, the situation provokes deep emotional discomfort. The idea of acting without an individual's informed consent feels repulsive, as autonomy is so deeply cherished. In such cases,

---

54. Haidt, "Emotional Dog," 1042, 1043.
55. Haidt, "Emotional Dog," 1028–31.

it seems fitting to argue from a deontological perspective, asserting that it is categorically wrong to make such a decision without the individual's direct involvement. Similarly, genetic engineering of embryos to prevent disease may invoke an argument from utility, whereas designer babies for intelligence or beauty may invoke deontology. Students become adept at reinforcing their existing views with arguments that *seem* more credible, simply because the theories they employ demand significant cognitive effort to apply.

This may not yet be a problem, however, at least as far as modern education is concerned. These cultural values might well be the most practical intuitive guides humanity has ever seen before. Within the structured prompts of the course, they may well lean towards the "best" answers. Further, ethics courses are not meant to convert students to a particular moral view but to introduce the fundamentals of ethical reasoning. That is the assignment.

For now, I will assume this to be true. However, I am not overly concerned about what happens within the walls of the ethics classroom. Much like Lewis, I am far more concerned with the actual effect of this kind of education on the student's mind.

Moral Fluidity and the Disintegration of the Chest

Lewis would likely see this entire process as a subtle yet significant extension of the problems that inspired his critique of subjectivism in *The Abolition of Man*: an education that cultivates cleverness and skilled rationalization, producing individuals he described as "men without chests."[56] For most, these theories are not integrated; they are swapped according to a kind of emotive pluralism. Their foray into ethics teaches them that virtually any opinion they might hold can be justified. Not merely because all opinions ought to be respected, but because theirs are vindicated by what appears to be the logical combination of two reason-based ethical theories. This "Pick your Poison" approach to ethics will be with them for the rest of their lives, seeping into the deep, perhaps hidden corners of their mind, provoked to the surface only when justification is needed.

I should clarify that I am not concerned with the few students who are truly passionate about philosophy. I know there are some students who take great pride in building and refining a cohesive ethical system that guides

---

56. Lewis, *Abolition of Man*, 12.

them even outside the classroom. They know these and other theories well, and they genuinely wrestle with the tension between them. But they are the exception, and it is the effect on the majority that now concerns me.

Perhaps the professor is not worried. Students are still guided by the values of autonomy and happiness for all, and this should be expected to extend beyond the classroom. But there are no clear guidelines or expectations in the real world, only grey areas and a ticking clock. Worse still, autonomy and happiness often conflict. One person's freedom may depend on another's compliance, and happiness for one may mean harm for another. As reason has been discredited, the modern educator may take the same path as the innovator from *The Abolition of Man*; they will look to instinct.[57] The hope is that even as rational application falters, students will generally lean towards a natural prosocial instinct: a spontaneous impulse towards goodness. This is an encouraging thought, but its truth needs to be questioned.

HUMAN NATURE AND MORAL JUSTIFICATION

Selfish Genes and Cognitive Biases

If the student's reliance on instinct was their position all along, I will first point out that it is a psychological and not a philosophical position. Philosophers have debated this nature back and forth for thousands of years to no satisfying conclusion. The answer must be found empirically.

I allow that my own subscription to the doctrine of original sin may predispose me to interpret human nature as fundamentally flawed, and this reinforces my inclination to doubt instinctive altruism. As such, it seems necessary to draw from the work of an evolutionary biologist whose philosophical outlook stands in sharp contrast to my own and whose focus lies on the cold, hard facts beneath the microscope.

Richard Dawkins argues that the best way to describe our genes—the very coding behind our existence—is to say that they are ruthlessly selfish.[58] This selfishness is what categorizes the entire animal kingdom, giving rise to things like cannibalism, resource competition, and mate rivalry.[59] On a

---

57. Lewis, *Abolition of Man*, 16.
58. Dawkins, *Selfish Gene*, 2.
59. Dawkins, *Selfish Gene*, 5, 6.

genetic level, human beings are said to be no different.[60] He argues against the notion of "universal love," claiming this makes zero evolutionary sense. He claims that a society based solely on the "gene's law of universal ruthless selfishness" would be "very nasty."[61] This description, though chilling, is abstract enough to be dismissed and should be followed with something of more substance.

The observable effects of this selfish nature are seen in the very architecture of our brains. Our judgments, for example, are often quietly shaped by "cognitive biases" operating outside our awareness. One of the most relevant is the self-serving bias, which is the tendency to attribute successes to our deep character traits and failures to external circumstances.[62] When we act well, it is because we are good: "I told the truth because I'm honest," or "I helped because I'm compassionate." But when we act poorly, we blame circumstances: "I was rude because I was stressed," or "I cheated because the test was unfair." Yet we rarely extend the same grace to others.[63] When others lie, we call them deceitful. When they are rude, we call them cruel. Their failures, unlike ours, are attributed to flaws of character, not to the pressures of circumstance.

In the real world, studies consistently reveal that people are masters of self-serving rationalization. We lie, cheat, and steal for personal gain, but not enough to taint our notion that we are good and decent people.[64] We commit our own sins, then soothe our conscience by comparing ourselves to those whose wrongdoings seem greater.[65] Even our good deeds are used as fuel to justify future wrongdoings.[66] When children are caught teasing their peers, they point fingers. Our nature still mirrors the same ancient deflection seen in the Garden of Eden: Adam points to Eve, and Eve points to the serpent.

Thus, if we are to boil down humanity to mere biology, it would be accurate to say that we are geared towards selfishness and spontaneous post-hoc justification; even the very existence of true altruism is still debated.[67]

---

60. Dawkins, *Selfish Gene*, 2.
61. Dawkins, *Selfish Gene*, 2.
62. Zuckerman, "Attribution of Success and Failure," 246.
63. Berry, "Explanations and Implications," 45.
64. Mazar et al., "Dishonesty," 633.
65. Bandura, "Moral Disengagement," 196.
66. Blanken et al., "Meta-Analytic Review," 1.
67. Haidt, "Emotional Dog," 1039.

Our cognitive arsenal is built to preserve self-interest. This is what we have by nature.

Hidden Consequences of the "Pick your Poison" Approach

In a time where objective value is slowly eroded, how are these selfish tendencies to interact with being trained to treat moral theories like tools in a toolbox?

Months after the final exam, much of the content of the ethics course will be largely forgotten; but perhaps too much will remain. The main lesson learned from this ethics course is that pleasure is not merely desirable, it ought to be maximized. Other acts, however, depending on one's feelings at the time, are labeled unethical and contemptible. The key point here is that students are trained to use logic to justify actions, bypassing the emotional core of morality—but as Lewis says, "The intellect is powerless against the animal organism."[68] Although they may not know it, the student's already powerfully selfish arsenal has gained two powerful tools of vindication that operate under the deceitful guise of reason.

This becomes apparent when examining a growing trend—theft from corporations.[69] A student with a penchant for theft, who is trained under the "Pick your Poison" model, may justify stealing from a corporation like Walmart with an appeal to utility. The satisfaction that a brand-new watch would provide, combined with a devious adrenaline rush, is a clear indicator of the action's utility. Meanwhile, the student may say, "They're billion-dollar companies. They won't notice a $50 watch. It won't even show up in the system." But if we apply Kant's logic here, the whole system collapses. If everyone did this, retail would implode, and so the categorical imperative rejects it. And yet, that doesn't matter. In this instance, the student is not invoking deontology. They are invoking vengeance, pleasure, and moral convenience. Guilt and shame are thus bypassed through selective reasoning.

Now let us reverse the situation. If that same student has their wallet stolen—say $5 is pickpocketed by a homeless man—they might respond with outrage. "This is what's wrong with society. Imagine if we were all so selfish!" What happened to maximizing happiness? It may well be argued that the homeless man would benefit more than $5 than he would. What

---

68. Lewis, *Abolition of Man*, 11.
69. National Retail Foundation, *Impact*, 7.

happened to utility? In this instance, the student is not invoking utility but invoking deontology.

Let us look at another case: cheating on online exams. The justification may be, "I don't have time. I'm overwhelmed. It will all be worth it when I get my degree and use it to do some real good in this world." Utilitarianism, again, comes to the rescue. But ask that same student how they would feel if their future child's heart surgeon passed their exams using AI and they will be horrified: "Lying to achieve power is blatantly unacceptable."

Atrophy of the Chest

The absurdity becomes clear when we take a step back. Yet these selective arguments are not irrational in form; the logic is sound provided that the premises are accepted. But this is where the problem lies. Consistency is nowhere to be found. What is missing is the chest, as Lewis would say—a moral centre trained to recognize that our own happiness or convenience does not take precedence over the objective moral order that binds us all. This reversal of values is exactly what Lewis warns against: "We make men without chests and expect of them virtue and enterprise. We laugh at honour and are shocked to find traitors in our midst. We castrate and bid the geldings be fruitful."[70] The students can hardly be blamed when their very nature and education are cultivating such mentalities.

I do not mean to suggest that those who recognize the Tao are immune to the self-serving rationalizations underpinning human nature. But they are restrained by the understanding that actions like cheating and stealing are objectively dishonourable—the sort of things one *ought* to avoid. Even as they transgress, guilt festers. They are painfully reminded of a standard that exists beyond self-interest. This standard calls them to be better and to do better, not because it feels good, but because it *is* good. They are under no illusion that pleasure, convenience, or anticipated outcomes can make the action right.

But the student trained in the "Pick your Poison" model? They will stumble from theory to theory like a drunkard in a tavern—slurring metaphysics, wielding duty when it suits them and pleasure when it does not, stumbling between logic and impulse, all the while believing that they are good, reasonable people. And this is the heart of the problem. When we allow or even encourage students to mix deontology and utilitarianism at

---

70. Lewis, *Abolition of Man*, 12.

will, they will extend this notion to their lives and moral chaos is the natural consequence.

The Educator's Response

The modern educator is likely to also view these tendencies as a problem, which presents a potential path forward. While it would be silly to think that students would abandon their ethical system entirely, it is reasonable to think that, at the very least, the dangers of moral pluralism will be explicitly discussed and even emphasized in the future. The combination of opposing ethical theories is not for the faint of heart; it is dangerous and requires precision even at the highest levels. The use of utilitarianism should be made with caution, and it should be presented as a necessary evil within ethics—not a refinement but rather a denigration of morality that should not find its way into everyday life. Students should be taught to recognize that these reason-based ethical systems are guided by something deeper: the chest.

The problem however is likely to endure, as picking and choosing values at will provides a comforting sense of freedom and control. The education system will likely continue stepping away from teaching values, presenting them as relative and based upon preference. However, as Lewis warns, "By starving the sensibility of our pupils we only make them easier prey to the propagandist when he comes. For famished nature will be avenged and a hard heart is no infallible protection against a soft head."[71] Humanity lives by value judgments, and no amount of rationality will eliminate this inclination. When educators take a back seat to value propagation, others will greedily step in to take their place.

The question is—who are these others?

THE RISE OF THE CONDITIONERS

Lewis's Prophecy of Technological Conditioning

Throughout history, there have been those who use what power they have to mold the values of others according to their own ideals.[72] Yet even at their most domineering, these attempts to sculpt the soul were checked by what Lewis called "beneficent obstinacy": a stubbornness within human

---

71. Lewis, *Abolition of Man*, 6–7.
72. Lewis, *Abolition of Man*, 31.

nature that resisted such reshaping.[73] However hard they tried to manipulate conduct, these educators were always frustrated and ultimately stopped in their tracks.

Lewis argues on two key grounds that the *conditioners* of the modern age are radically different from any social engineers of the past. The first, and perhaps most striking, difference is that their power is massively increased: "The man molders of the new age will be armed with the powers of an omnicompetent state and an irresistible scientific technique."[74] In contrast to the fumbling manipulators of past generations, the conditioners of the future will possess technological and psychological tools so precise, so far-reaching, and even perhaps so tempting, that they would be nearly impossible to resist.

Their methods of control will likely not at first resemble traditional tyranny.[75] There might be no visible oppressor, no iron boot. As Lewis predicts, people subjected to this regime will not necessarily be unhappy, but this is because they are mere "artefacts"[76]; objects created and distilled behind the walls of a laboratory. The meaning found by these artefacts is merely an illusion, engineered by those in power.

The second key distinction Lewis draws is that the conditioners are no longer guided by any objective moral framework. In previous eras, even the most ambitious educator operated within the constraints of moral tradition.[77] Not so with these conditioners. They recognize no higher law, no sacred boundary; the very notion of goodness is definable on their own terms.[78] Lewis warns of the natural consequences of this motivational trajectory: "When all that says *it is good* is debunked, what says *I want* remains."[79]

The Conditioners of the New Age: Power, Seduction, and Control

This dark prophecy of conditioned comfort and simulated purpose is no longer mere speculation. In *The Age of Surveillance Capitalism*, Shoshana Zuboff provides disturbing evidence that Lewis's prediction has already

---

73. Lewis, *Abolition of Man*, 31.
74. Lewis, *Abolition of Man*, 31.
75. Lewis, *Abolition of Man*, 37.
76. Lewis, *Abolition of Man*, 33.
77. Lewis, *Abolition of Man*, 31.
78. Lewis, *Abolition of Man*, 32.
79. Lewis, *Abolition of Man*, 33.

come true, showing how large corporations like Google, Facebook, and Apple have become tremendously powerful through the extraction of user data from everyday online interactions. These surveillance systems are designed to "feed on every aspect of every human's experience."[80] Whether we are watching YouTube, browsing Facebook, or scrolling Instagram, every click, pause, and hesitation is quietly harvested and transformed into exploitable data.

These companies are not motivated by truth, justice, or even democratic values. Government regulation, individual rights, moral reflection, and autonomy are seen as "friction" that gets in the way of their true motive: profit.[81] They use their unprecedented and intimate knowledge to cater to our every whim under the guise of "personalization."[82] Whether we are drawn to sports, video games, sex, politics, or conspiracy theories, the algorithms employed by these companies are meticulously engineered with scientific precision to serve our individual appetites. Outrage becomes profit, lust fosters engagement, sloth begets retention. The kind of individuals these companies hope to produce are those who are, much like the conditioners themselves, ruled by their own desires. Whatever desires lay hidden, they will be hunted down and exploited, as this data is used not merely to serve instinct but to *predict* and *influence* it in ways that align with profit.[83] It is the seductive whisper that tells us what to want before we know what we are wanting.

The potency of this manipulation lies in its subtlety. Indeed, we are given exactly what we want. We are never coerced, and we sign away our rights in knotty user agreements that are slipped into every download. Every interaction feels like an act of personal agency, seemingly intuitive rather than oppressive. As technology advances and human data is harvested, these humanity-moulders gain ever greater power to trivialize virtue and inculcate new values.

Although Lewis's concerns are quickly becoming reality, and our current moral trajectory is suspect, we have not reached the point of no return to which he alludes.[84] He recognizes that the greedy domineering character of science itself has potentially made way for this kind of technological

---

80. Zuboff, *Age of Surveillance Capitalism*, 14.
81. Zuboff, *Age of Surveillance Capitalism*, 164.
82. Zuboff, *Age of Surveillance Capitalism*, 164.
83. Zuboff, *Age of Surveillance Capitalism*, 21.
84. Lewis, *Abolition of Man*, 35.

manipulation, but that maybe it too will be capable of redemption.[85] While he does not provide a clear resolution to the problem, he does suggest that "from science herself the solution might come."[86] It is with this hope in mind that I now turn to a possible solution.

HOPE BEYOND RELATIVISM: THE RETURN TO THE TAO

The Power of Virtue

The result of the "Pick your Poison" approach is real world moral inconsistency. As individuals promiscuously shuffle between different moral frameworks with no stability, there are both personal and social consequences that social science illuminates with the kind of empirical urgency that demands recognition by all parties.

In *Mere Christianity*, Lewis writes of the tangible significance of virtue cultivation: "Moral rules are directions for running the human machine. Every moral rule is there to prevent a breakdown, or a strain, or a friction, in the running of that machine."[87] This claim is profoundly true, and moral psychology points to the benefits of cultivating a strong moral identity. This is something that, while not easy, is found to be strongly associated with living a happy and purposeful life.[88] Those who swap moral frameworks in pursuit of convenience may feel something is missing and may start to look to others.

Even in a morally flexible age, consistency still commands respect. People tend to recoil at the kind of hypocrisy brought on by the "Pick your Poison" approach.[89] Struggling to live up to one's values—even imperfectly—is seen as more trustworthy than shifting standards to suit the moment.[90] It is both easy and common to claim virtue, but in many instances it is cast aside when things get difficult. As a result, only those who are able to make the sacrifices demanded by principled consistency are the ones who will be recognized, trusted, and even admired.[91] The cultivation of the

---

85. Lewis, *Abolition of Man*, 38.
86. Lewis, *Abolition of Man*, 38.
87. Lewis, *Mere Christianity*, 41.
88. Goering et al., "Moral Identity," 1.
89. Monin and Merritt, "Moral Hypocrisy," 6.
90. Monin and Merritt, "Moral Hypocrisy," 11.
91. Bai, "Beyond Dominance and Competence," 208.

chest and submission to the imperatives of the Tao are therefore not merely right; they pave the way to deep social connections and to conversations that help to illuminate the very source of value.

This is an encouraging thought, but it also speaks to the importance of sacrifice. Preaching lofty values brings extreme social scrutiny, and hypocrisy can very quickly annihilate moral standing.[92] Christianity preaches these lofty values, and we are expected to follow in the footsteps of the historically greatest moral exemplar: Jesus Christ. His commandment to love one's enemies will always sound counterintuitive. His teaching that forgiveness should be limitless will never stop being difficult. His instruction to forget about transient earthly pleasures will not stop being a challenge. Yet these are moral imperatives. Losing sight of them not only endangers ourselves but also risks isolating those who remain skeptical of their enduring relevance.

One final point worth considering is also one of the most important achievements of *The Abolition of Man*: unification under a single banner. Today, it has become far more common to highlight cross-cultural differences than to recognize what harmonizes them. Religious thought in fields like ethics is often brushed aside with the dismissive question, "Whose god is right?" In the spirit of Lewis, I believe this trend calls for a more unified front. Common ground can and should be consistently sought—not only among those who openly recognize the authority of the Tao, but also with those who lean toward subjectivism. Most of these individuals, when thoughtfully engaged, will reveal deeply held values that are themselves derived from the Tao. This common ground is substantial, as it demonstrates that the "beneficent obstinacy" Lewis describes still holds true.[93] However flawed, human beings remain tethered to a moral order they often claim to reject. This quiet allegiance to the Tao, whether acknowledged or not, remains our greatest source of unity and hope.

CONCLUSION

The dangers that C. S. Lewis points to in *The Abolition of Man* have not only materialized but have been amplified. The abandonment of objective value in favour of the flexible "Pick your Poison" moral approach has left individuals vulnerable to their own selfish rationalizations and ultimately to the

---

92. Monin and Merritt, "Moral Hypocrisy," 4.
93. Lewis, *Abolition of Man*, 31.

manipulation of corporations who will stop at nothing to shape desires in ways they deem profitable. This technological power grows daily, and the stakes are now higher than ever.

The need for students to be taught to recognize a binding, objective moral order is increasingly overlooked. Despite psychology's attempt to expose reason to being a mere servant of intuition and desire, students in the postmodern era are subtly led to believe that morality is what can be rationally explained. The result is not a flourishing individual but a fragmented one: a person whose chest has been hollowed out and whose mind is a court where every vice pleads its case, and every virtue is negotiable.

However dark things may appear, Lewis's insight points not only to the disease but to its cure. The cultivation of the chest— of trained sentiment aligned with objective value— remains the surest safeguard against manipulation and moral collapse. Those who endure the losses and sacrifices commanded in the Tao—the timeless source of objective value—are not only internally strengthened; they also serve as beacons in a morally murky world. Their lives testify that the Tao is not a relic of naivety, but a living guide to human flourishing. In this light, we can find unity that transcends time and culture where virtue is borne not out of preference or expediency but out of the pursuit of truth.

BIBLIOGRAPHY

Bai, Feng. "Beyond Dominance and Competence: A Moral Virtue Theory of Status Attainment." *Personality and Social Psychology Review* 21 (2017) 203–27.
Bandura, Albert. "Moral Disengagement in the Perpetration of Inhumanities." *Personality and Social Psychology Review* 3 (1999) 193–209.
Berry, Zachariah. "Explanations and Implications of the Fundamental Attribution Error: A Review and Proposal." *Journal of Integrated Social Sciences* 5 (2015) 44–57.
Blanken, Irene, et al. "A Meta-Analytic Review of Moral Licensing." *Personality and Social Psychology Bulletin* 41 (2015) 540–58.
Dawkins, Richard. *The Selfish Gene*. 30th anniv. ed. Oxford: Oxford University Press, 2006.
Epicurus. *Letter to Menoeceus*. Translated by Cyril Bailey. Oxford: Oxford University Press, 1926.
Goering, Marlon, et al. "Moral Identity in Relation to Emotional Well-Being: A Meta-Analysis." *Frontiers in Psychology* 15 (2024) 1–13.
Haidt, Jonathan. "The Emotional Dog and its Rational Tail: A Social Intuitionist Approach to Moral Judgment." In *The Cambridge Handbook of Thinking and Reasoning*, edited by Keith J. Holyoak and Robert G. Morrison, 1023–52. Cambridge: Cambridge University Press, 2005.
———. *The Righteous Mind: Why Good People Are Divided by Politics and Religion*. New York: Pantheon, 2012.

Part One: Apologetics and Philosophy

Hume, David. *A Treatise of Human Nature*. Edited by L. A. Selby-Bigge. Oxford: Clarendon, 1896.

Ivanhoe, Philip J., and Bryan W. Van Norden, eds. *Readings in Classical Chinese Philosophy*. 3rd ed. Indianapolis: Hackett, 2023.

Kant, Immanuel. "Groundwork for the Metaphysics of Morals." *Some Texts from Early Modern Philosophy* (2017). Translated by Jonathan Bennett, 1–52. Online: https://www.earlymoderntexts.com/assets/pdfs/kant1785.pdf.

Lewis, C. S. *The Abolition of Man: Or Reflections on Education with Special Reference to the Teaching of English in the Upper Forms of Schools*. 1947. Reprint, San Bernardino, CA: Samizdat, 2014.

———. *Mere Christianity*. 1952. Reprint, San Bernardino, CA: Samizdat, 2014.

Mazar, Nina, et al. "The Dishonesty of Honest People: A Theory of Self-Concept Maintenance." *Journal of Marketing* Research 45 (2008) 633–44.

Monin, Benoît, and Anna Merritt. "Moral Hypocrisy, Moral Inconsistency, and the Struggle for Moral Integrity." In *The Social Psychology of Morality: Exploring the Causes of Good and Evil*, edited by Mario Mikulincer and Phillip R. Shaver, 167–84. Washington, DC: American Psychological Association, 2010.

National Retail Federation. *The Impact of Retail Theft and Violence*. Washington, DC: National Retail Federation, 2024.

Nietzsche, Friedrich. *Beyond Good and Evil: Prelude to a Philosophy of the Future*. Translated and commented by Walter Kaufmann. New York: Vintage, 1989.

Plato. *The Dialogues of Plato*. Translated by David Horan. 2 vols. Kinsale: Gandon Editions, 2022.

Rachels, James, and Stuart Rachels. *The Elements of Moral Philosophy*. 7th ed. New York: McGraw-Hill, 2012.

Zuboff, Shoshana. *The Age of Surveillance Capitalism*. New York: PublicAffairs, 2019.

Zuckerman, Miron. "Attribution of Success and Failure Revisited, or: The Motivational Bias Is Alive and Well in Attribution Theory." *Journal of Personality* 47 (1979) 245–87.

Part Two

Fictional Worlds

Consider the Narnian Birds

Birdsong as Sacrament in C. S. Lewis's *The Chronicles of Narnia*

Paul Robinson

In *The Screwtape Letters*, C. S. Lewis's fantastical collection of infernal epistolary propaganda, the elder demon Screwtape warns his nephew Wormwood about the irresistible heavenly power that a fleeting experience of wonder can have on a human being. "Even if we contrive to keep them ignorant of explicit religion," Screwtape laments, "the incalculable winds of fantasy and music and poetry—the mere face of a girl, the song of a bird, or the sight of a horizon—are always blowing our whole structure away."[1] Screwtape is perplexed and infuriated by the affective power of such simple sensations. What is it about the simple *song of a bird* that can topple an old devil's infernal edifice? In this chapter, I seek to answer that question through a consideration of the sacramental role of music—and birdsong in particular—in another of Lewis's fantasies, *The Chronicles of Narnia*.

Before turning to the sacramental stage of Narnia, let us consider how Lewis understands the sacramentality of our own world. It is no secret that Lewis delighted in the natural world. But, as Kallistos Ware—who would himself occasionally bump into Lewis on his morning walks—points out, "While Lewis was sensitive to the beauty of the natural world, what mattered to him was not merely the external aesthetic appearance of nature around us. What mattered to him was that the world of nature has sacramental value. Through the world of nature we are brought into communion

---

1. Lewis, *Screwtape Letters*, 156.

with God."[2] By "sacramental value," Ware understands the natural world to be filled with signs which bear witness to and bear the weight of eternal glory.

In his sermon "Transposition," Lewis distinguishes between a symbolic relationship and a sacramental one. In a symbolic relationship the sign and that which it signifies are "not like one another, nor does the one cause the other to be. The one is simply a *sign* of the other and signifies it by convention."[3] We might call this "nominal" signification. A sacramental relationship, on the other hand, is "realist" signification. Lewis describes the relationship between a picture (sign) and the visible world (reality) as sacramental. He writes, "Pictures are part of the visible world themselves and represent it only by being a part of it. Their visibility has the same source ... It is a sign, but also something more than a sign, because in it the thing signified is *really in a certain mode present*. If I had to name the relation I should call it not symbolical but sacramental."[4] For Lewis the sacramental sign, whether a painting, the Blessed Sacrament (Eucharist), or—as we will see—the song of a bird, does not *develop* into the higher reality it points to, but the sign itself carries the higher reality—albeit often faintly, as an echo. "In a word," Lewis writes, "I think that real landscapes enter into pictures, not that pictures will one day sprout out into real trees and grass."[5]

But the quality of the sacramental sign—that it contains rather than becomes the higher reality—is not all that sacramental means. We must also discuss the effect that the sacramental sign has upon the individual. Lewis cautions against letting the sign take on more weight than it can bear. In other words, the sign must not become an idol. If the former could be called the *strong* sacramental sense, in which the reality signified is *contained* within the symbol, elsewhere Lewis describes a *weak* sacramental sense—that the reality signified is experienced through the sign only faintly, as an echo.

In another sermon, "The Weight of Glory," Lewis puts it this way: "These things ... are good images of what we really desire; but ... they are not the thing itself; they are only the scent of a flower we have not found, the echo of a tune we have not heard, news from a country we have never

---

2. Ware, "Sacramentalism," 53.
3. Lewis, "Transposition," 102.
4. Lewis, "Transposition," 102 (emphasis mine).
5. Lewis, "Transposition," 112.

yet visited."[6] Even more strongly, he writes, "If a transtemporal, transfinite good is our real destiny, then any other good on which our desire fixes must be in some degree fallacious, must bear at best only a symbolical relation to what will truly satisfy."[7] Here, with trepidation, I wonder if Lewis is contradicting himself. For every example that he gives—the scent of a flower, an echo of a tune, news from a far country—fits better within his own definition of sacramental than symbolical, that "in [the symbol] the thing signified is *really in a certain mode present*."[8] But while he perhaps misrepresents the sacramental nature of these things, this does not negate the necessity of the weak sacramental sense. Lewis writes, "The books or the music in which we thought the beauty was located will betray us if we trust in them; it was not in them, it only came through them."[9] Lewis's caution stands true for *all* signs, whether sacramental or symbolical: we must never allow the sign to usurp the reality. As Kallistos Ware writes, "Lewis valued [nature] . . . because of its transparency, because of the way in which the material world brings us to an apprehension of God."[10] Lewis was able to both delight in the reality within the sign and caution against misvaluing the sign as the reality itself.

For Lewis, the way in which the material world summons one toward God is through an experience he called "Joy"—that longing for more which comes to us through the transparency of the sign. In his autobiography *Surprised by Joy*, Lewis uses "Joy" in a technical sense, which must not be confused with mere happiness or pleasure.[11] Joy is an existential pang which may simultaneously hurt and delight because it is the foretaste of a feast which we cannot fully enjoy on this side of the sign. Lewis describes Joy as the experience of "an unsatisfied desire which is itself more desirable than any other satisfaction";[12] it is "the stab, the pang, the inconsolable longing" for the reality which is signified.[13] This is the effect that a sacramental world

---

6. Lewis, "Weight of Glory," 31.
7. Lewis, "Weight of Glory," 29.
8. Lewis, "Transposition," 102.
9. Lewis, "Weight of Glory," 30.
10. Ware, "Sacramentalism," 53.
11. Lewis, *Surprised by Joy*, 20 (the capitalization of the term "Joy" is original in Lewis).
12. Lewis, *Surprised by Joy*, 20.
13. Lewis, *Surprised by Joy*, 61.

has upon human beings, symbol-sensing and meaning-making creatures that we are.

We have seen that the sacramental world, for Lewis, has three qualities. First, the reality is truly present in the sign—the two are not merely similar by convention. Second, the sign is not to be mistaken for the reality which it signifies—it is an echo, a scent, a painting. Third, the sacramental sign—such as the natural world—evokes an insatiable sensation of longing for *more* than that the sign itself.[14] The same is true in Narnia. Narnia is written as a world *within* our universe, not an alternate one. Thus, the metaphysics of Narnia are real-world metaphysics.[15]

Music—notably, unaccompanied song—is a prominent sacramental sign throughout *The Chronicles of Narnia*. I do not wish to suggest that every musical reference is explicitly sacramental, simply that music is always *potentially* sacramental. That is, in Narnia, for those who have ears to hear, song is a sacramental sign of Aslan's country.

Narnia is musical from the very beginning. In *The Magician's Nephew*, Aslan creates Narnia with a song. The music is heard first by the cabby, the holy fool who would later be crowned the first king of Narnia: "'Hush!' said the cabby. They all listened . . . In the darkness something was happening at last. A voice had begun to sing. Sometimes it seemed to come from all directions at once."[16] The music is described as "beyond comparison, the most beautiful noise [Digory] had ever heard."[17] As Aslan makes his musical appearance in the void before Narnia, other things start to appear. First the sky is filled with singing stars, then winds and hills appear. As Aslan's song changes, fields spread out from his feet, followed by trees and flowers. Finally, all sorts of animals burst forth from the newly formed ground. That Lewis has Aslan sing Narnia into being is not incidental.

For Lewis, music was "a medium for meeting God."[18] Similarly, throughout the Chronicles music is presented as a medium for meeting Aslan. Music in Narnia is sacramental in each of the three sacramental

---

14. I do not mean to suggest, nor did Lewis, that nature, or any other sacramental sign, *always* evokes joy. Lewis is clear that it does not. But it ought to. The experience of joy, while subjective, is an objective power of the sacramental sign, even if it is not always sensed rightly.

15. As Digory Kirke remarks toward the end of *The Last Battle*, "It's all in Plato, all in Plato: Bless me, what do they teach them at these schools?" (Lewis, *Last Battle*, 216).

16. Lewis, *Magician's Nephew*, 116.

17. Lewis, *Magician's Nephew*, 116.

18. See MacInnis, "'Medium for Meeting God.'"

senses described above. First, it contains—not merely resembles—Aslan's song. The Lion's song of creation is a sort of *overture*—the initial setting of the theme which recurs throughout the performance. Second, the musical theme recurs faintly, as a transparent echo. And the echoes ought not be mistaken for the full chorus; Lewis only shows us the "reality" once, when Aslan sings creation. Third, music contains the power to evoke that pang of longing which Lewis called Joy.

Scholars have long understood Aslan's song of creation to be an imaginative description of the Pythagorean and classical concept of "the music of the spheres." Peter Schakel writes:

> By having the lion sing the song of creation, Lewis has quietly, unobtrusively put young readers in touch with an ancient tradition regarding the universe. In western culture music has long served as an image of the orderliness and harmony of the universe, particularly through the music of the spheres, which keeps the concentric hollow globes circling the earth in an orderly way.[19]

Michael Ward, in his monumental *Planet Narnia*, argues that the entirety of the *Chronicles* is an imaginative telling of the sevenfold planetary mythos and the music of the spheres, with each of the books representing one of the seven "wanderers"—that is, planets. The music of the spheres, Lewis wrote, "is the only sound which has never for one split second ceased in any part of the universe . . . [this] music which is too familiar to be heard enfolds us day and night and in all ages."[20] The music of the spheres is not heard *audibly* because it is never ceases. It is familiar in a deeper sense which cannot be fully described. It is, as Ward writes, "a pregnant silence, resonant with significance."[21] In Narnia, however, "the music of the spheres" is not an analogy; Aslan's song is not silent. It is a voice heard "deep enough to be the voice of the earth herself."[22]

Throughout the series, this song makes frequent *sacramental* appearances, sung by different voices and at different volumes. It not independent of the great Lion's theme. It is heard in all three sacramental senses. The strong sacramental sense is most evident in the voices of the stars. Shortly after Aslan's song is first heard in Narnia, "two wonders happened at the same moment":

19. Schakel, *Imagination and the Arts*, 104.
20. Lewis, "Imagination and Thought," 52.
21. Ward, *Planet Narnia*, 22.
22. Lewis, *Magician's Nephew*, 116.

> One was that the voice was suddenly joined by other voices; more voices than you could possibly count. They were in harmony with it, but far higher up the scale: cold, tingling, silvery voices. The second wonder was that the blackness overhead, all at once, was blazing with stars ... If you had seen and heard it, as Digory did, you would have felt quite certain that it was the stars themselves which were singing.[23]

And you would be right. In *The Voyage of the Dawn Treader*, the children and their Narnian companions meet Ramandu, "a retired star," and his daughter. At one point, "both of them held up their arms ... and turned to face the east. In that position they began to sing ... Lucy said afterwards that it was high, almost shrill, but very beautiful, 'A cold kind of song, an early morning kind of song.'"[24] Aslan creates the stars as singers in his cosmic choir. With the stars, Lewis makes explicit what elsewhere is only hinted at: it's all one song, or, at least, one performance. The stars do not sing for or by themselves. They sing for and with their creator. They bear the sacramental presence of Aslan's song; in the voices of the stars Aslan's song really is *in a certain mode present*.

Lewis's concern about idolatry is most clearly represented in *The Silver Chair*. *The Silver Chair* is, after all, a cautionary tale about the perils of mistaking the symbol for the reality. Underworld is a shadowy place, faintly reminiscent of the world above. But those who dwell there believe it to be all there is. They have, in Lewis's words, "mistaken [it] for the thing itself."[25] Only in *The Silver Chair* does music take on a largely negative role. When Eustace Scrubb and Jill Pole first encounter the Green Lady—the ruler of Underworld—she laughs "the richest and most musical laugh you can imagine."[26] Later, the witch—for that is what this lady turns out to be—enchants the children with a different sort of music than we have thus far encountered. "She took out a musical instrument rather like a mandolin. She began to play it with her fingers—a steady, monotonous thrumming that you didn't notice after a few minutes. But the less you noticed it, the more it got into your brain and your blood."[27] There are two qualities to this music which give it away. First, it is not song. While music in general is

---

23. Lewis, *Magician's Nephew*, 116.
24. Lewis, *Voyage*, 222.
25. Lewis, "Weight of Glory," 31.
26. Lewis, *Silver Chair*, 90.
27. Lewis, *Silver Chair*, 181–82.

significant throughout the *Chronicles*, it is singing which bears the nearest resemblance to Aslan's song. Second, the Green Lady's music is dull and flat, "a steady, monotonous thrumming."[28] Aslan's song, on the other hand, is expansive, complex, and life-giving. There is "harmony" and "scale," and the creatures join in.[29]

But the two forms of music are not *absolutely* unrelated. Later, when she has finally made her way out of Underworld, Jill Pole hears another kind of music: "wild music, intensely sweet and yet just the least bit eerie too, and full of good magic as the Witch's thrumming had been full of bad magic."[30] The witch, it turns out, is a sort of priestess of Underworld. Her music represents idolatry—that flowering of the *weak* sacramental sense—in full bloom. She does not mistake her music for that of Aslan's, she mistakes herself for God. Idolatry—worship of the sign rather than the reality—inevitably leads to such a perversion of perspective that one becomes the centre of their own universe. But as the witch's music reveals, it is a monotonous, "thrumming" universe, not the ordered harmony of Aslan's choir.

The witch's music is "bad magic," but it is still magic. In an essay entitled "God and Evil," Lewis articulates the difference between good and evil in this way: "A sound theory of value . . . demands that good should be original and evil a mere perversion . . . that good should be able to exist on its own while evil requires the good on which it is parasitic in order to continue its parasitic existence."[31] The Green Lady is unable to create her own evil. Even her powerful enchantment has something of Aslan's own magic in it, albeit in a disorderly way.

Finally, we turn to ask *how it is* that the sacrament of music draws one upward toward Aslan and eastward toward Aslan's country. We see that it is precisely by that affective power which Lewis calls "Joy." Like the Blessed Sacrament itself, music is both intensely satisfying and painfully incomplete. Music really is the sound of Aslan's country, but it is only an echo, a faint repetition of the grand theme. While the echo is at sometimes quite loud, at other times it is barely a whisper-song. Sometimes, as in *The Silver Chair*, it is nearly subverted altogether. In *The Voyage of the Dawn Treader*,

28. Lewis, *Silver Chair*, 182.
29. Lewis, *Magician's Nephew*, 116.
30. Lewis, *Silver Chair*, 230.
31. Lewis, "Evil and God," 23.

this theme is represented clearly in that book's most important character, the honourable mouse Reepicheep.

Shortly after the children are brought on board the Dawn Treader, they are told of the crew's mission to seek out seven lost lords of Narnia. Reepicheep, however, Caspian says, "has an even higher hope," to which Reepicheep responds, "As high as my spirit . . . Why should we not come to the very eastern end of the world? . . . I expect to find Aslan's own country."[32] Lucy is suspicious that Aslan's country could be arrived at in so natural a manner. Reepicheep himself shares this thought: "I do not know," he says, "But there is this. When I was in my cradle a wood woman, a Dryad, spoke this verse over me":

> Where sky and water meet,
> Where the waves grow sweet,
> Doubt not, Reepicheep,
> To find all you seek,
> There is the utter east.

"I do not know what it means," Reepicheep admits, "But the spell of it has been on me all my life."[33] That Reepicheep describes the song as a *spell* is a hint that we are here in the realm of that intense longing which Lewis terms "Joy." In "The Weight of Glory," shortly after describing the sacramental transparency of such things as books and music, Lewis asks, "Do you think that I am trying to weave a spell? Perhaps I am; but remember your fairy tales. Spells are useful for breaking enchantments as well as for inducing them."[34] We learn that Reepicheep who "never felt that the ship was getting on fast enough" made a habit of sitting at the very front of the Dawn Treader and "singing softly in his little chirruping voice the song the Dryad had made for him."[35] In *Mere Christianity*, Lewis defends the musical imagery of heaven in the Bible because "for many people (not all) music is the thing known in the present life which most strongly suggests ecstasy and infinity."[36] Perhaps this is the case for Reepicheep. However, as readers of *The Magician's Nephew*, we know that the suggestive power of Reepicheep's song lies not in the Dryad's verse itself, nor in Reepicheep's

---

32. Lewis, *Voyage*, 21.
33. Lewis, *Voyage*, 22.
34. Lewis, "Weight of Glory," 31.
35. Lewis, *Voyage*, 33.
36. Lewis, *Mere Christianity*, 137.

aesthetic sensibilities, but in the source of both—the "utter east" where both Reepicheep and the Dryad's song find their true home.

The entire eastward journey of the Dawn Treader—full of side-quests and island adventures as it may be—is a sacramental journey from sign to reality, from Reepicheep's lullaby to the grand song of Aslan's Country at the edge of the world. True, the Aslan we meet at the end of this book is the gentle Lamb who invites the children for breakfast. Here there is no singing lion or heavenly music. But this is easy to explain. While Reepicheep's journey may be the central theme of *The Voyage of the Dawn Treader*, the story is told from the perspective of the children from our world, and they do not join Reepicheep in Aslan's country. But, as they reach the very edge of the Narnian sea, "There came a breeze from the east . . . It lasted only a second or so but what it brought them in that second none of those three children will ever forget. It brought both a smell and a sound, a musical sound. Edmund and Eustace would never talk about it afterwards. Lucy could only say, 'It would break your heart.' 'Why,' said I, 'was it so sad?' 'Sad!! No,' said Lucy."[37] The narrator tells us no more, and I expect Lewis's hope was to leave the children—both the Pevensies and his readers—with a "pang" of longing of "Joy."

And it is on this note of longing that we turn, finally, to consider the Narnian birds. Here we begin where we have just ended, in *The Voyage of the Dawn Treader*, at the edge of the Eastern Sea. In *Planet Narnia*, Michael Ward begins by drawing attention to the etymology of the word "consider," which is cosmological. "Consider," Ward writes, "is formed from two Latin words: *con-*, meaning 'with,' and *sidus*, meaning 'star.' To consider something is, literally, '[to think] with the stars.'"[38] Ward then proceeds to masterfully draw out and expound upon the mythological planetary imagery and symbolism throughout the *Chronicles*. He argues that *consideration*—(to think) with the stars—is the key to understanding Narnia's deeper meaning as a cosmological Christian mythology. Ward supplies the verb "to think" in his etymological assessment, though "thinking" need not be the only way of (doing something) "with the stars." What if we instead supply the verb "to sing"? Lewis, I believe, would be quite pleased with the notion of "singing with the stars," as his fondness for the music of the spheres attests. This is how I would like to *consider* bird song in Narnia. That is, the birds are

---

37. Lewis, *Voyage*, 265.
38. Ward, *Planet Narnia*, xiii.

members of the same divine and cosmological choir as the stars—singing the song of Aslan.

Before attending to the birds, allow me to make one final remark about Lewis's sacramentalism. While sacramental signification is always *realist* in that it truly shares something real with that which it signifies, the mechanism of the signification is, for Lewis, beside the point. Lewis writes of the sacramental presence of Christ in the Eucharist, "I don't know and can't imagine what the disciples understood our Lord to mean . . . Yet I find no difficulty in believing that the veil between the worlds . . . is nowhere else so thin and permeable to divine operation . . . Here is big medicine and strong magic . . . the command, after all, was Take, eat: not Take, understand."[39] Accordingly, to explain *how* birdsong is sacramental is not my purpose. I merely wish to hold out for observation the myriad ways Lewis uses birdsong in a sacramental manner throughout *The Chronicles of Narnia*.

Recall towards the end of *The Voyage of the Dawn Treader*, when Ramandu, the star, and his daughter, turn to face the east and sing toward the sun—toward Aslan. Shortly after, Lewis tells us, "The air became full of voices—voices which took up the same song that the Lady and her Father were singing, but in far wilder tones and in a language which no one knew. And soon after that the owners of these voices could be seen. They were birds, large and white."[40] Here, at "the beginning of the end of the world," we encounter birds who literally *sing with the stars*. These are no ordinary birds. These are birds of the edge of the world, who can fly to the sun and back every morning. They sing with the stars, it seems, for no particular reason. Their song is not a message, nor an artform, it is simply what these birds do. Here birdsong is both divine and disinterested. It does not appear to serve a *purpose*. Elsewhere, birds sing a song which is a fainter echo of Aslan's theme and which bears more evidently a message or meaning—even though that meaning may not be explained or understood.

Let us next turn to the beginning pages of *The Silver Chair*. When Jill and Eustace find themselves whisked out of England and away from Experiment House, the first thing they notice is a "very different sort of sound":

> It came from those bright things overhead, which now turned out to be birds. They were making a riotous noise, but it was much more like music—rather advanced music which you don't quite

---

39. Lewis, *Letters to Malcolm*, 136.
40. Lewis, *Voyage*, 223.

take in at the first hearing—than birds' songs ever are in our world. Yet, in spite of the singing, there was a sort of background of immense silence. That silence, combined with the freshness of the air, made Jill think they must be on the top of a very high mountain.[41]

There is much contained in this short passage. For Lewis, the complementary interplay of song and silence is a chief characteristic of heaven. In *The Screwtape Letters*, Screwtape expresses his diabolic preference: "Music and silence—how I detest them both!"[42] The demon would rather have Noise, "Noise, the grand dynamism, the audible expression of all that is exultant, ruthless, and virile."[43] In *The Silver Chair*, Jill and Eustace begin their journey on top of a mountain *in* Aslan's country, where the song of birds and the accompaniment of silence fills the air. As we have seen, their journey takes them, however, all the way to Underworld, where the music of the witch is scarcely music at all. It is endless "thrumming" which never breathes a moment's silence, lest her evil enchantment be broken.

In *The Silver Chair*, music marks the journey from Aslan's country to Underworld and back again. But this first music sets the stage. These birds of Aslan's country—could they be the same birds who fly to and from the sun in *The Voyage of the Dawn Treader?*—sing a song that is "rather advanced music which you don't quite take in at the first hearing."[44] This is birdsong which must be studied and learned over considerable time and not without considerable effort. In *An Experiment in Criticism*, Lewis expressed concerns about the ways in which "the many" *use* music rather than *receive* it.[45] The many cling to a catchy tune and make no effort to do the work of deeper listening that is musical education. Most, if a musical piece is too difficult—containing no tune which can easily be "used"—simply discard or ignore the music altogether. At the beginning of *The Silver Chair*, Lewis subtly informs readers that wonder is not simply the spontaneous pleasure of a melody. Sacramental participation—enjoying and even joining the song of the stars—can be cultivated. Alternatively, as we learn later in *The Silver Chair*, it can be suppressed, even lost entirely. Jill and Eustace do not disdain the birds' heavenly song, but they do not yet understand it. They have been thrust to the edge of heaven, bypassing the sacramental

---

41. Lewis, *Silver Chair*, 12.
42. Lewis, *Screwtape Letters*, 44.
43. Lewis, *Screwtape Letters*, 4.
44. Lewis, *Silver Chair*, 12.
45. Lewis, *Experiment in Criticism*, 25–26 (emphasis mine).

formation that is necessary to fully delight in the magic of the birds' sacred music. In Narnia itself, we will see, birdsong is not the "advanced music" of Aslan's country. Nor is it the "wilder tones" of the birds at the edge of the Eastern Sea. Most often, it is ordinary birdsong, just as we know it in our own world. But its source is the same as these birds of the utter east and its sacramental power is that same sacramental pull that draws one "further up and further in."[46]

The world of nature is not always perceived as sacramental. That it *is* sacramental is not something we can empirically learn from this side of the sign. The same is true of birdsong in Narnia. In Narnia, one may *sense* that birdsong is sacramental—through the experience of "Joy." But in order to see—or hear—"through" the sacrament, we must know something of the higher reality to which it points. This is why we have considered the birds in Aslan's country and at the edge of the Eastern Sea before entering Narnia itself.

In *The Lion, the Witch, and the Wardrobe*, birdsong functions *evangelically*. That is, the song of birds is an announcement of good news; it is a declaration of royal victory. We ought not, however, sharply distinguish evangelical from sacramental.[47] To do so would be to say, in Narnian terms, that the good news is something other than Aslan himself.

There are two notable instances of birdsong in *The Lion, the Witch, and the Wardrobe*. The first occurs as winter is fading and signs of spring are quickening. Edmund observes flowers blooming and snow melting and then

> came a sound even more delicious than the sound of the water. Close beside the path they were following a bird suddenly chirped from the branch of a tree. It was answered by the chuckle of another bird a little further off. And then, as if that had been a signal, there was chattering and chirruping in every direction, and then a moment of full song, and within five minutes the whole wood was ringing with birds' music.[48]

On the surface, the scene represents the acceleration of winter's fall and spring's arrival as "Aslan is on the move." The whole chorus of spring

---

46. "Further Up and Further In" is the title of the fifteenth chapter of *The Last Battle*.

47. That is, apart from designated ritual (liturgical) function. Even then, however, the proclamation of the gospel (preaching) is sacramental, and the sacrament of communion is evangelical.

48. Lewis, *Lion, the Witch, and the Wardrobe*, 132.

birdsong, which usually appears in fits and starts, bursts forth in the forest all at once. Edmund notices the sudden change, but it is the Witch and the dwarf who know what is really happening: "This is no thaw," the dwarf says, "This is Spring . . . This is Aslan's doing."[49] The dwarf recognizes, and fears, not the *signs* of spring, but its source. In Lewis's poem, "What the Bird Said Early in the Year," the sacramentality of spring is similarly on full display:

> I heard in Addison's Walk a bird sing clear
> This year the summer will come true. This year. This year.
> . . .
> This year, this year, as all these flowers foretell,
> We shall escape the circle and undo the spell.[50]

The signs of spring—notably the singing birds—is an announcement of summer yet to come. As an announcement, the birdsong has an *evangelical* function. But the announcement is also a *sign*—of the full bloom of summer and the harvest of autumn. It is, in Lewis's terms, a *sacramental* sign, truly bearing that which it points towards.

Later in *The Lion, the Witch, and the Wardrobe*, as the sun rises on the morning following Aslan's unexpected execution, birdsong makes another appearance. Susan and Lucy are shaken with grief and attending to the great lion's lifeless body when suddenly, "In the wood behind them a bird gave a chuckling sound. It had been so still for hours and hours that it startled them. Then another bird answered it. Soon there were birds singing over the place."[51] Shortly after, the stone table cracks, and Aslan reappears with the rising sun. Again, the birds *announce* the presence of Aslan. No sacramental connection is explicitly given; we know it from elsewhere in the *Chronicles*. In Narnia, the ordinary singing of birds is, as Lewis describes in "The Weight of Glory," "the echo of a tune we have not heard, news from a country we have never yet visited."[52] In *The Lion, the Witch, and the Wardrobe*, no particular sacramental sense is explicitly represented through birdsong, but those who are attending to Lewis's novels for a second or third time will *receive* the simple tune of a bird as an instance of that singular theme which finds its full display only in *The Magician's Nephew*. The whole of the *Chronicles* turns out to be "music" of a "rather advanced sort," full of sacramental depths, of which birdsong is only but one instance.

49. Lewis, *Lion, the Witch, and the Wardrobe*, 133.
50. Lewis, "What the Bird Said," lines 1–2, 9–10.
51. Lewis, *Lion, the Witch, and the Wardrobe*, 176.
52. Lewis, "Weight of Glory," 31.

Part Two: Fictional Worlds

In *Prince Caspian*, there is a particularly notable scene which symbolically gathers much of what we have considered. Lucy, unable to sleep, "opens her eyes" and drifts into a liminal, dream-like state:

> with a thrill of memory, she saw again, after all those years, the bright Narnian stars . . . And now she began to feel that the whole forest was coming awake like herself . . . Somewhere close by she heard the twitter of a nightingale beginning to sing, then stopping, then beginning again. It was a little lighter ahead. She went towards the light and came to a place where there were fewer trees, and whole patches or pools of moonlight, but the moonlight and the shadows so mixed that you could hardly be sure where anything was or what it was. At the same moment the nightingale, satisfied at last with his tuning up, burst into full song.[53]

The first-time reader, like Lucy, will be overwhelmed by the symbolic power of the scene. Like Lucy, she may also feel halfway between wakefulness and sleep, light and shadow, uncertain of the meaning of it all. Here there is a deep sense of *longing* for a world which has faded. Lucy whispers, "Oh, Trees, wake, wake, wake. Don't you remember it? Don't you remember me? Dryads and Hamadryads, come out, come to me."[54] Lucy does not know it, but she is echoing the first words which were spoken by Aslan when Narnia was newly formed: "Narnia, Narnia, Narnia, awake. Love. Think. Speak. Be walking trees. Be talking beasts. Be divine waters."[55] The reader, presuming they read in order of publication (beginning with *The Lion, the Witch, and the Wardrobe*), also does not recognize Aslan's voice in Lucy's words—but that does not mean it is not there. The singing nightingale and the bright Narnian stars evoke Lewisian "Joy" in Lucy and the reader, existential longing which cannot be fully explained, only sensed. As the scene ends, Lucy "had the feeling (as you sometimes have when you are trying to remember a name or a date and almost get it, but it vanishes before you really do) that she had just missed something."[56] Soon after, the reader discovers that Aslan has been near all along. The symbolism of this scene represents a mystical experience of Aslan's sacramental presence in the stars, the stream, the trees, and the nightingale's song.

---

53. Lewis, *Prince Caspian*, 120–22.
54. Lewis, *Prince Caspian*, 123.
55. Lewis, *Magician's Nephew*, 138.
56. Lewis, *Prince Caspian*, 123–24.

That Lucy hears a nightingale is not accidental. Lewis would have been aware of the prominence of the nightingale in English poetry. It is quite possible that he had Keats's "Ode to a Nightingale" directly in mind while penning this scene. In Keats's poem, the nightingale, that "light-winged Dryad of the trees . . . Singest of summer in full-throated ease."[57] The nightingale is a sacramental bird *par excellence*. She is the "immortal Bird" whose song is the same as that heard "In ancient days by emperor and clown," "Through the sad heart of Ruth," and "in faery lands forlorn."[58] The nightingale symbolizes both beauty—which is eternal—and poetry, upon whose "viewless wings" the poet himself hopes to fly away.[59] At the end, the poet wonders, like Lucy in her own liminal state, "Was it a vision, or a waking dream? / Fled is that music:—Do I wake or sleep?"[60] Lucy's nightingale, like Keats's, sings an immortal song. Lucy hears it—as she also sees the stars and stream—but the whole experience is fleeting, and she is not sure what to make of it. But we know the *desire* that it evokes in her: "Oh, Trees, wake, wake, wake."

A sacrament, we recall, bears a resemblance to that which it signifies not as something which the sign is *becoming*, but as a true embodiment of the reality in signified form. One might say that the *whole* (Aslan's song) is expressed in the *part* (the birdsong). If we read the novels in the order in which they were published, the sacramental reality of music and birdsong unfolds only gradually and suggestively. Alternatively, if we begin with *The Magician's Nephew*, we know the source of the song from the outset.[61] The entire world of Narnia is sacramental, of course; all of Aslan's world sings creation's song: "cawing, cooing, crowing, braying, neighing, baying, barking, lowing, bleating, and trumpeting."[62] Birdsong is not *more* sacramental than the voices of the other animals, but it is unlike the others in that Lewis chooses to use birdsong as a unique sacramental sign throughout the *Chronicles*. It is birds who sing *with* the stars. It is birds who sing *in* Aslan's country. In Narnia birdsong is simple and suggestive, flighty and

---

57. Keats, "Ode to a Nightingale," lines 7, 10.
58. Keats, "Ode to a Nightingale," lines 61, 64, 66, 70.
59. Keats, "Ode to a Nightingale," line 33.
60. Keats, "Ode to a Nightingale," lines 79–80.
61. If it is not clear, I must here announce my unshakeable preference for reading (at least one's first reading) in the order of publication, beginning with *The Lion, the Witch, and the Wardrobe* (1950).
62. Lewis, *Magician's Nephew*, 135.

unassuming, as it is so often in our own world. But for those who have ears to hear, in the nightingale's simple song is an echo of a far more marvelous performance, an occasion for awe and wonder.

From the very beginning, we are made privy to the two alternative responses to Aslan's song. The cabby, who is a sort of childlike "holy fool," responds with increasing wonder, from, "Hush!" to "Gawd! Ain't it lovely?" to "Glory be!" to "'Old your noise, everyone . . . I want to listen to the moosic."[63] He goes from curiosity, to delight, to praise, to peace. Uncle Andrew, on the other hand, "was not liking the Voice. If he could have got away from it by creeping into a rat's hole, he would have done so."[64] And, in fact, he gets his wish: "He soon did hear nothing but roaring in Aslan's song . . . he didn't hear any words: he heard only a snarl."[65] The cabby and Uncle Andrew encounter, not the sacramental form of Aslan's song, but the reality itself. In one, it leads to wonder and peace, in the other, resentment, ignorance, and an inability to experience reality. The same invitation to wonder is present in the simple call of a bird's song. It is the invitation to *sing with the stars*, to "consider" the birds' song as it was meant to be, a divine sacrament.

BIBLIOGRAPHY

Keats, John. "Ode to a Nightingale." In *Keats's Poetry and Prose*, edited by Jeffrey N. Cox, 457–60. Norton Critical Edition. New York: Norton, 2009.
Lewis, C. S. "Evil and God." In *God in the Dock: Essays on Theology and Ethics*, edited by Walter Hooper, 21–24. Grand Rapids: Eerdmans, 1978.
———. *An Experiment in Criticism*. Cambridge: Cambridge University Press, 1961.
———. "Imagination and Thought in the Middle Ages." In *Studies in Medieval and Renaissance Literature*, edited by Walter Hooper, 41–63. Cambridge: Cambridge University Press, 1966.
———. *The Last Battle*. 1956. Reprint, New York: HarperTrophy, 2005.
———. *Letters to Malcolm: Chiefly on Prayer*. London: Geoffrey Bles, 1964.
———. *The Lion, the Witch, and the Wardrobe*. 1950. Reprint, New York: HarperTrophy, 2005.
———. *The Magician's Nephew*. 1955. Reprint, New York: HarperTrophy, 2005.
———. *The Mere Christianity*. 1952. Reprint, New York: HarperCollins, 2004.
———. *Prince Caspian*. 1951. Reprint, New York: HarperTrophy, 2005.
———. *The Screwtape Letters*. 1950. Reprint, San Francisco: HarperCollins, 2001.
———. *The Silver Chair*. 1953. Reprint, New York: HarperTrophy, 2005.

63. Lewis, *Magician's Nephew*, 116–17, 121.
64. Lewis, *Magician's Nephew*, 118.
65. Lewis, *Magician's Nephew*, 150.

———. *Surprised by Joy: The Shape of My Early Life*. 1955. Reprint, C. S. Lewis Signature Classics. London: HarperCollins, 2002.

———. "Transposition." In *The Weight of Glory*, 91–115. 1949. Reprint, New York: HarperCollins, 2015.

———. *The Voyage of the Dawn Treader*. 1952. Reprint, New York: HarperTrophy, 2005.

———. "The Weight of Glory." In *The Weight of Glory*, 25–46. 1949. Reprint, New York: HarperCollins, 2015.

———. "What the Bird Said Early in the Year." In *Poems*, edited by Walter Hooper, 71. San Diego: Harcourt Brace Jovanovich, 1964.

MacInnis, John. "'A Medium for Meeting God': C. S. Lewis and Music." *Christian Scholar's Review* 49 (2019) 25–41.

Schakel, Peter J. *Imagination and the Arts in C. S. Lewis: Journeying to Narnia and Other Worlds*. Columbia: University of Missouri Press, 2002.

Ward, Michael. *Planet Narnia: The Seven Heavens in the Imagination of C. S. Lewis*. Oxford: Oxford University Press, 2008.

Ware, Kallistos. "Sacramentalism in C. S. Lewis and Charles Williams." In *C. S. Lewis and his Circle: Essays and Memoirs from the Oxford C. S. Lewis Society*, edited by Roger White et al., 53–64. New York: Oxford University Press, 2015.

Playing with a Lion

(Christian) Leadership According to *The Chronicles of Narnia*

Seán M. W. McGuire

INTRODUCTION

For pastors the world over, questions of what kinds of methods or strategies bring positive outcomes are legion. Strategies whose results are negative are avoided—with results generally being tied to numerical growth; a strange metric for a vocation focused on the slow work of cultivating souls. In so much as an approach to ministry is deemed personally useful, it is valuable, and if not immediately useful it is ignored. Such is the pragmatic approach many pastoral leaders have adopted, often unreflectively, in their contemporary ministry practice.

In *The Chronicles of Narnia* series, C. S. Lewis develops notions of pragmatism related to leadership that act as a rebuke to this way of thinking and being as leaders.[1] Lewis develops a tension in this series between practicality and playfulness that is instructive for the church and her leaders today. Examples of both can be found throughout the series and are often found in juxtapositions. While both practicality and play have been given some limited reflection in the saga to varying degrees, the tension between

---

1. When my wife and I were first married, she was shocked that I had never read (or watched) *The Chronicles of Narnia* series. It became our habit that she would read the books to me in the evenings, which was my first introduction to the series. Suffice it to say that, without her interest, expertise, and work re-reading the series, developing and correcting notes, and editing, this would be a much worse chapter. Thank you, Jessica!

the two seems to have so far gone unexplored. Yet, in their juxtaposition, Lewis builds a vision for leadership, particularly for leaders who follow the King above high kings, who are marked not by a pragmatic mentality but by a playfulness that gives rise to virtue.

CULTIVATING IMAGINATION AND VIRTUE

Besides some of the more obvious examples of play in the series, which I will talk about momentarily, this chapter was birthed out of reflecting on Lewis's dedication to his goddaughter Lucy in *The Lion, the Witch, and the Wardrobe*. He says, "My Dear Lucy, I wrote this story for you, but when I began it, I had not realized that girls grow quicker than books. As a result, you are already too old for fairy tales, and by the time it is printed and bound you will be older still. But some day you will be old enough to start reading fairy tales again."[2] This raised some questions for me: Who and what are fairy tales for, and why would Lewis describe these books as fairy tales rather than fantasy? The fantasy genre was well known at the time of the book's publication, and the series seems to have been put into this genre-category very quickly. Yet Lewis specifies fairy tales as a more specific, perhaps better, genre description.

This observation is important to note from the outset because the Narnia series is sometimes mistaken for an allegory. While there are debatable allegorical elements (although I think Lewis would disagree, to some extent, with such characterizations), developing an allegory was not Lewis's intent. Instead, Lewis thought of the Narnia stories as mythology. Lewis described the difference between allegory and myth while reflecting on the work of his friend J. R. R. Tolkien, saying "My view wd. [sic] be that a good myth (i.e., a story out of which every varying meaning will grow for different readers and in different ages) is a higher thing than an allegory (into which one meaning has been put). Into an allegory a man can put only what he already knows; in a myth he puts what he does not yet know and cd. [sic] not come by in any other way."[3] Reflecting on his works of fantasy, including *The Chronicles of Narnia*, Lewis makes clear that he did not set out to develop allegories but, instead, he imagined creatures of various sorts, and from these creatures a mythical story developed. "Everything began with images," he wrote reflecting on the Narnia series, "a faun carrying

---

2. Lewis, *Lion, the Witch, and the Wardrobe*, 5.
3. Lewis, *Collected Letters*, 789.

an umbrella, a queen on a sledge, a magnificent lion. At first there wasn't even anything Christian about them; that element pushed itself in of its own accord."[4] This is why *The Chronicles of Narnia* are a fairy tale, because myths—including fairy tales—invite the imaginative participation of the reader in the story that broadens their understanding. Lewis sees all stories as inviting imaginative participation but recognized that only fairy tales are regularly charged with encouraging escapism. Yet these stories are no less imaginative than other stories one might describe as being more "grounded in reality." As Lewis says:

> In a sense a child does not long for fairy land as a boy longs to be the hero of the first eleven. Does anyone suppose that he really and prosaically longs for all the dangers and discomforts of a fairy tale?—really wants dragons in contemporary England? It is not so. It would be much truer to say that fairy land arouses a longing for he knows not what. It stirs and troubles him (to his life-long enrichment) with the dim sense of something beyond his reach and, far from dulling or emptying the actual world, gives it a new dimension of depth.[5]

Indeed, "at its best," Lewis says elsewhere, "[the fantastic or mythical] can give us experiences we have never had and thus, instead of 'commenting on life', can add to it."[6] It is this quality that makes fairy tales a genre that is *explicitly* playful in a hermeneutical sense.

Play and Imagination

According to my current favourite dead German, Hans-Georg Gadamer, play is the fundamental element of human life and understanding.[7] More than just as in a game, play describes a phenomenon of "to-and-fro movement"[8] marked by a number of characteristics: play is serious; play occurs for play's sake; as an *infinite* movement of to-and-fro, play therefore has infinite potential; play's outcome is unknown; play has its own rules, regulations, and field of play; and participation in play is to be played (that is, the game takes priority over the individual).[9] Gadamer views all of life

---

4. Lewis, "Sometimes," 36.
5. Lewis, "On Three Ways," 29.
6. Lewis, "Sometimes," 36.
7. Gadamer, *Relevance*, 22–23.
8. Gadamer, *Truth and Method*, 107.
9. See Kosma, "Gadamer's Hermeneutic Universality," 10–12; Judd, *Playing with*

through this concept of play, including and especially understanding (that is, hermeneutics), such that by reading something like a fairy tale—which is to play an artistic language game—the reader is ushered into experiencing a "wholly transformed world."[10] Discussing Tolkien's thoughts on the topic of fairytales, Lewis argues that such stories allow one to become a "subcreator . . . making, so far as possible, a subordinate world of his own."[11] By naming the saga's genre outright as a fairy tale, Lewis sets the rules and field of play for the game he invites readers/subcreators to participate in—one that is serious, as it is a battle of good versus evil; one that has an unclear outcome; one that has rules of magic and mystery that elude us, and which represents the truth in a way that is as expansively wonderous as it is wonderful (particularly as relates to its allegorical-mythical characteristics).

Yet it is not just the genre itself that is play-filled; the books are filled with examples of play we might intuit as being more than *just* play. While play occurs for play's sake, there is still a kind of outcome to play related to formation. Because play is infinitely recursive, its outcome is tentative and continual; in the same way that formation is an ongoing recursive process, especially as regards one's transformation in Christ. One is formed "more and more" into the image of Christ, and one does so through a dialogical process of play whereby one's understanding is constantly developed (cf. 2 Cor 3:18; Eph 4:15; Phil 1:9–11). As Andrew Judd summarizes, play "provides a testing not only of prowess but also of the player's moral quality, for the challenge is to achieve an uncertain goal without cheating."[12] Fairy tales are particularly effective for this testing, as the genre is honest about inviting readers to imagine new worlds and the possibilities given their experience within the imagined field of play, and by doing so invites them to come to a better understanding of how best to live in the world.

To put this another way, fairy tales are tales of vice and virtue, good and evil, that help people discern, through use of their imagination, how to live the good.[13] Play is what makes this discernment possible, as it is through the infinite recursiveness of play that understanding is shaped as one is drawn into the world of a piece of art—whether a painting, play, or well written fairy tale. The shaping of understanding is formative in the

---

Scripture, 68–70.

10. Gadamer, *Truth and Method*, 117.
11. Lewis, "On Three Ways," 27.
12. Judd, *Playing with Scripture*, 46.
13. Davis, *Becoming by Beholding*, 160, 245.

sense that formation requires, as Evan Howard argues, "the continuous process" of "coming to be, changing, [and] ceasing to be."[14] Howard goes on to describe formation in a way that echoes Gadamer, whereby the one being formed and that which is forming them are entangled in a back-and-forth dance, and for Christians such back-and-forth is done in the context of community (in front of a participating audience, so to speak). Gadamer describes this in terms of the relationships between a player and a game and the player and an audience, which Gadamer argues must "play along with" the player and thus participate vicariously in the game being played.[15] "The spectator is manifestly more than just an observer who sees what is happening in front of him, but rather one who is a part of it insofar as he literally 'takes part.'"[16] As such, both player and spectator are formed by play—including imaginative play.

Imagination and Formation

In the field of play of fairy tales, reality is mixed with imagination such that you can get so lost in imaginative play that reality becomes indistinguishable from that which is imagined. And in some sense, this is the goal. In the words of Lewis, reflecting in *Mere Christianity* on how children "play" adulthood, "they are hardening their muscles and sharpening their wits so that the pretense of being grown up helps them grow up in earnest."[17] The same is true of the use of imagination in general; imagination helps give shape to who we are becoming, whether positively or negatively. As Karen Swallow Prior argues, "The imagination shapes us and our world more than any other human power or ability."[18]

While reflecting on the Narnia series, we may be tempted to think of all this in terms of children's formation, but fairy tales were initially meant for adults, or at least a mixed-age audience, not children only.[19] In fact, Lewis bemoaned the fact that the Narnia series was pushed by publishers as a children's story because "a book only worth reading in childhood is not worth reading even then."[20] This, along with the tension between play

14. Howard, *Guide to Christian Spiritual Formation*, 21.
15. Gadamer, *Relevance*, 24.
16. Gadamer, *Relevance*, 24.
17. Lewis, *Mere Christianity*, 188.
18. Prior, *Evangelical Imagination*, 7.
19. Lewis, "On Three Ways," 26.
20. Lewis, "Sometimes," 38.

and practicality in the saga, may help reveal why Lewis expected his goddaughter would pick the Narnia series up again at some point, because these books are meant to be imaginative encounters that cultivate the virtues elucidated in the fairy tale—and virtue is something every age needs.

Because the central character of the Narnia story, the Lion, is an imaginative representation of Christ, we might say the virtues which the Narnia story cultivates are Christian virtues, and that the imaginative encounter the story promotes is one centred on God. By making the Christ-like Aslan the central character of the story, Lewis orients the readers' imagination towards the good embodied by Aslan, offering a personification of virtue that invites imitation, at least in a limited sense, while also pointing beyond that personification to that which cannot be imitated but must, instead, be experienced in a personal, transformative way.[21]

The virtues this saga cultivates have been written about at length. Mark Pike claims they are the four cardinal virtues of wisdom, fortitude or perseverance, self-control, and justice, as well as love and integrity.[22] In essence, through playful participation in the story through imagination, virtues begin to furnish the mind of the reader and eventually move from habits of mind to habits of being. But how does this come about? Through play—in the text, and in our understanding. Play is the ground from which these habits of virtue grow, and in the inverse it is where practicality reigns that vice gains a chokehold. Indeed, practicality, what we might otherwise call pragmatism, was described by the unfortunately named American philosopher C. I. Lewis as regarding "meaning as limited by reference to what could make a difference for some active intent."[23] A practical person is concerned with relevance above all other considerations, particularly relevance to their own interest and a wanted end, such that they pay little concern to possibility in the hermeneutically playful sense. As such, they are restricted by "relevance" in a fundamental way.

Such a restriction is not only a restriction on play but on the very possibility of formation, because restricting play frustrates the to-and-fro nature that informs the development of understanding (and formation). This is a serious issue for Christians, and particularly Christian leaders, for the self-imposed limitation on play that a focus on practical output brings is one that limits formation by limiting renewed understanding—or at least

---

21. Davis, *Becoming by Beholding*, 214.
22. Pike, *Narnian Virtues*, 80.
23. C. I. Lewis, "Logical Positivism and Pragmatism," 94.

limits renewed understanding to within a very narrow, focused area of personal concern. The narrow focus of practicality ultimately disallows insight from outside one's present concern to widen and deepen the horizons of their understanding. Moreover, a narrow focus on the practical limits one's capacity to be confronted and, in this limitation, to thus be changed—as, for Gadamer, confrontation (in the sense of coming to know that you do not know) is the precondition and catalyst of understanding and thus (trans)formation. In Christianity, such a precondition/catalyst finds correlation in the biblical confession that even as we do not know, God does—for "his understanding is beyond measure" (Ps 147:5b) and "unsearchable" (Isa 40:28b), he "is perfect in knowledge" (Job 37:16) and knew us even before we were born (Ps 139:13–16; Isa 44:2; Eph 2:10). It is, in fact, the very knowledge of God in Christ that confronts us, as well as the declaration of the kingdom that has come near whose King reigns forever. Thus, while we may not know much, Christians can be confident in their knowledge of God, not simply because God has graciously revealed God's self in a knowable way, but because Scripture declares "whoever loves God is known by God" (1 Cor 8:3). And, as we will see shortly, C. S. Lewis invites readers of the Narnia series to imagine the confrontation of being known by a wild and living God in distinctly play-filled terms.

The above is, in many ways, surprising, not least within my discipline of practical theology—particularly given the work of Don Browning.[24] In his influential book *A Fundamental Practical Theology*, Browning brought Gadamerian hermeneutics and the philosophy of pragmatism together to form a vision of practical theology as an activity of *phronēsis* or practical reason.[25] Browning contrasts this with theoretical reason (*theoria*), which asks the question "What is the nature of things?", and technical reason (*technē*), which Browning says asks, "What are the most effective means to

---

24. Another scholar of note is Richard Osmer, who suggests practical theology has a "pragmatic task." That is, Osmer argues that practical theologians must, at some point, ask "what then should we do [in a given situation]?" (*Practical Theology*, 9). While oriented towards *doing*, I do not consider this question pragmatic or necessarily practical, as generally understood, and, as I will argue below, think it better understood to mean "what is our faithful response [in a given situation]?"

25. Browning cast a vision for practical theology as what Andrew Root summarizes as "a kind of pragmatically engaged ethics" (*Christopraxis*, 26), and in doing so fails to recognize the role play has in Gadamerian hermeneutics and thus its implications. I consider this a significant weakness of his project, as it seems to leave Browning unable to robustly recognize the interplay of divine and human action(s) that would be made possible by integrating Gadamer's notion of play into his project.

a given end?"[26] Instead, practical wisdom asks "What should we do? and How should we live?" [27] For Browning, "the modern experiment has been dedicated to the improvement of human life through the increase of objective scientific knowledge (*theoria*) that is then applied to the solution of human problems (*technē*)."[28] Yet, rather than pragmatism, practical wisdom is, in a critical sense, oriented towards *response*, or what is otherwise colloquially termed "application" in North American ecclesial circles. That is, practical wisdom does not necessarily seek to find a solution to a problem; instead, practical wisdom is concerned with response(s) to situations. Such a concern means that the mode of response is left open for discernment, as practical wisdom shapes the contours of the response—especially so in one's dealings with God, the response to whom must be a *faithful* response.

As such, I suggest that when most think about practicality and pragmatism, especially in the evangelical church today, they are not concerned with faithful response but are instead thinking about *theoria* leading to *technē*; how the theoretical might lead to techniques that bring about a particular end. Insomuch as this is the case, "practicality" and "pragmatism," as I am using these terms, are postures towards practice whereby one seeks relevance (including applicability to a desired end; most regularly today, numeric church growth) above all other considerations.[29] In contrast, practical wisdom seeks faithful response regardless of perceived outcome, for the response is deemed good insomuch as it is deemed faithful.[30] Certainly, this helps clarify the tension between play and practicality in the Narnia series, as shall soon be seen.

---

26. Browning, *Fundamental Practical Theology*, 10.

27. Browning, *Fundamental Practical Theology*, 10.

28. Browning, *Fundamental Practical Theology*, 34.

29. Robert Dean ("Heresy of Relevance," 80) quotes Bonhoeffer's reflection on this point in relation to the practice of preaching in German churches, which had begun taking "practical application" as preaching's highest end: "Whatever the question of contemporizing is *taken as the theme of theology*, however, we can be sure that the substance has already been betrayed and sold away."

30. This understanding is in line with that of Swinton and Mowat, who have argued against a pragmatic view of practical theology: "The key thing in this understanding is not that the practice brings particular benefits to individuals or communities (although it may do). The important thing is that the practice bears faithful witness to the God from whom the practice emerges, and whom it reflects, and that it enables individuals and communities to participate faithfully in Christ's redemptive mission" (Swinton and Mowat, *Practical Theology*, 22).

Part Two: Fictional Worlds

LEWIS'S JUXTAPOSITION OF PLAY AND PRACTICALITY

In *The Chronicles of Narnia*, the juxtapositions between play and practicality, between virtue and vice, are found most explicitly in those we might consider leaders in the story. Characters such as Aslan, the Pevensie children, Caspian, and Eustace versus Uncle Andrew, Jadis (the White Witch), the Lady of the Green Kirtle, King Miraz, Rishda Tarkaan, and Tash. The former are largely described in terms of playfulness and transformation, while the latter are described in terms of pragmatism and a grotesqueness matching their moral character. This juxtaposition implies a vision of leadership, centred in focus on following the Lion of Narnia, that invites readers of the series to consider whether the focus of their leadership is on following the Lion as well—and if not, whether one's practicality is making them grotesque. In the following subsections I will give attention to critical moments where this tension between play and practicality is explicitly revealed and/or reflected on. My intention is not to review every example of each in the saga, but instead to provide a robust enough picture of these themes that their interplay can be recognized as an element in the background of the Narnia series.

The (Practical) Magician's Nephew

Some of the best-known examples of both pragmatism and playfulness are found in *The Magician's Nephew*. This is, in no small part, because of how Lewis made both very obvious, as if to allow a child to understand and to develop a theme that readers would find throughout the *Chronicles* series (*The Magician's Nephew* being a later entry to the saga). For example, Jadis—and all witches—are described as being "not interested in things or people unless they can use them; they are terribly practical."[31] Uncle Andrew is similarly described. Throughout the book, practical relevance in relation to their wants and aims become the focus of both Jadis and Uncle Andrew. For Jadis, anyone who is not helping her is quickly ignored—a fact noted by Polly and Digory after Jadis's arrival in London.

While we might consider Jadis a more extreme version of this, Uncle Andrew's behaviour is more instructive, as he is—seemingly—more ordinary, more grounded in the world as we know it. We can imagine an older adult tinkering with something in their attic, and in fact can imagine that we may be that person one day. But what was he doing? We only find out

---

31. Lewis, *Magician's Nephew*, 97.

once he gives a ring to a child, and Polly is sent to another realm as part of a twisted magical experiment. The experiment a seeming success, the ever-practical Uncle Andrew makes Digory feel guilty so that he will go after his friend—for why would he put himself in harm's way? As Digory proclaims, "If you [Uncle Andrew] had any honour and all that, you'd be going yourself. But I know you won't. All right. I see I've got to go. But you *are* a beast."[32] For both Uncle Andrew and Jadis, practicality gives way to cruelty—including and especially cruelty to children.

Uncle Andrew's pragmatism is further highlighted, perhaps most starkly, when Aslan sings Narnia into existence. The song of creation is set up as a playful act, with playful song being a focus of the previous chapters, and the playful song of creation is followed by Aslan playfully cracking jokes. But as Aslan sings, Uncle Andrew notices a lamppost thrown by Jadis that had grown into a whole new lampstand, and his first thought is: I could use this place to become a millionaire. And at this point Uncle Andrew is described like Jadis: "he was dreadfully practical."[33] For Uncle Andrew and the Witch, the focus that practicality gives is ultimately a focus on the self, and relevance a question of personal utility rather than sacrificial service, such that the kind of playfulness that marks Aslan's world is neither welcomed nor even recognized, let alone participated in.

In a sense, Uncle Andrew and Jadis do not understand the game they are playing, because it is Aslan who sets the rules of play in Narnia, not them. This sheds light on the tension at the end of the book, when the Witch tries to convince Digory that he needs to bring an apple from Narnia to his mother rather than give it to Aslan, because it is more practical to help your own than help the Lion who just sang a world into being. Offended by the Witch, Digory responds, "Look here; where do *you* come into all this? Why are *you* so precious fond of my Mother all of a sudden? What's it got to do with you? What's your game?"[34] In Gadamerian terms, play is the ontological structure of reality, even in Narnia, and pragmatism is evidence of a disordered structure and, therefore, of disordered play.

The theme of singing in the Narnia saga, elucidated by Paul Robinson elsewhere in this volume, holds play and practicality in tension in an interesting way. Song throughout the Narnia series is connected to the use of magic, with playful songs bringing wonderous miracles, and pragmatic

---

32. Lewis, *Magician's Nephew*, 37 (italics original).
33. Lewis, *Magician's Nephew*, 162.
34. Lewis, *Magician's Nephew*, 210 (italics original).

song—songs sung for a self-serving purpose—being tied to dark magic. The former is most clearly seen during the aforementioned creation scene; Aslan's play-filled song brings a play-filled world to life. In contrast, the White Witch is said to have destroyed an entire world with just a single word.[35] Likewise, in *The Silver Chair*, the Lady of the Green Kirtle uses songs as a medium for enchantment, by which those who hear are lulled towards denying reality and entering servitude.[36] Likewise, in *The Magician's Nephew*, Polly hears Uncle Andrew's rings humming, and it would be by these rings that she and Digory would be transported to another realm—an invitation to play in a sense, but used (by Uncle Andrew) to a practical end.[37]

The Horse and His Boy versus Prince Caspian

The books *The Horse and His Boy* and *Prince Caspian* open with conflicting visions of leadership related to play and practicality. In *The Horse and His Boy*, Arshesh tells Shasta, whom he had found as a baby and taken in as his own child, that he should not "be distracted by idle questions, for . . . application to business is the root to prosperity but those who ask questions that do not concern them are steering the ship a folly toward the rock of indigence."[38] In other words, if you want to prosper, be practical. But the irony of this is that Arshesh is abysmally poor—in money, and in imagination. Again, Lewis points out that Arshesh has "a very practical mind"[39]—a mind that leads him to mocking, beating, and generally abusing Shasta. In light of the core theme of the book, freedom, I think there is a suggestion that pragmatism itself is something one must be set free from in order to flourish.

This opening scene is quite different from that of *Prince Caspian*, where the Pevensie children find themselves back in Narnia. And what do they immediately do? Start playing in some water on a beach, "splashing

---

35. Lewis, *Magician's Nephew*, 82–83.

36. This scene, which plays out in chapter 12 of *The Silver Chair*, is noteworthy as an example of what would now be called gaslighting, whereby the Queen relentlessly pushes her victims to question what they know to be true. The Lady of the Green Kirtle, it would seem, uses both music and words to ensnare victims whom she wishes to use in service of her purposes.

37. Lewis, *Magician's Nephew*, 25.

38. Lewis, *Horse and His Boy*, 11.

39. Lewis, *Horse and His Boy*, 11.

and looking for shrimps and crabs."⁴⁰ This sort of playful behaviour is what the Kings and Queens of Narnia, as well as their subjects, are known for throughout the series. For example, in *The Horse and his Boy*, Narnians are described as walking "with a swing . . . [they] let their arms and shoulders go free . . . [they] chatted and laughed [and whistled] . . . ready to be friends with anyone who was friendly."⁴¹

Yet there is one Narnian Queen who is missing by the end of the series: Susan. Susan is described as practical in *Prince Caspian*,⁴² and her siblings go on to reflect on her eventual inability to return to Narnia:

> "My sister . . . is no longer a friend of Narnia." "Yes," said Eustace, "and whenever you've tried to get her to come and talk about Narnia or do anything about Narnia, she says 'What wonderful memories you have! Fancy your still thinking about all those funny games we used to play when we were children . . . She always was a jolly sight too keen on being grown-up . . . She wasted all her school time wanting to be the age she is now, and she'll waste all the rest of her life trying to stay that age. Her whole idea is to race on to the silliest time of one's life as quick as she can and then stop there as long as she can."⁴³

This description of vanity is not a surprise for Susan, as she regularly lagged behind the other siblings as they sought to follow Aslan—though especially Lucy, whom Susan shows a general mistrust of even from the start of *The Lion, the Witch, and the Wardrobe*. Susan's pragmatism ultimately shuts her out of Narnia, though it is certainly a slow process that begins in Narnia as she is repeatedly unable to see or recognize Aslan even as Lucy and her siblings *are* able to do so. Susan's decisions are regularly marked by a self-centred pragmatism whereby her needs trump what others—especially Lucy—see. For example, in *Prince Caspian*, when Lucy sees Aslan and wants to follow him, Susan's protest against her sister can be summarized as her being tired and refusing to believe that Lucy saw Aslan as she says she did. Even when Edmund argues that Lucy has always been the first one to see the Lion of Narnia at work and thus should be trusted, Susan stands

40. Lewis, *Prince Caspian*, 13.
41. Lewis, *Horse and His Boy*, 71.
42. Lewis, *Prince Caspian*, 141.
43. Lewis, *Last Battle*, 176–77.

her ground—and in doing so, convinces the others not to follow Lucy's lead (and thus, also, the lead of Aslan).[44]

While Susan is held to be a practical person whose pragmatic mind causes her to be shut off from Narnia, Prince Caspian is shown to be an imaginative person whose playful imagination is evidence of a good heart. He uses the stories of Old Narnia as a guide, especially as those stories are confirmed—first through the Narnian remnant, then through the Pevensie children's arrival, and finally through the arrival of Aslan himself. Yet before these things, Caspian had to choose whether he would believe the stories and even imagine himself within them so as to learn a better way to live or reject them. Other characters, such as Nikabrik, share a similar knowledge of Narnia and Aslan but choose to reject them. Nikabrik even goes so far as to want to attempt to defeat Miraz by resurrecting the White Witch—a plan that takes quite the imagination to conjure and is conjured explicitly because of the practicality of the Witch's power manifested in a one-hundred-year reign of winter.[45]

Catching the Playful Lion

Perhaps the most famous example of play in *The Chronicles of Narnia* belongs to Aslan himself, though it should be noted that the book begins with play—the Pevensie children happen on Narnia during a game of hide and seek, after all. But I digress. After his resurrection in *The Lion, the Witch, and the Wardrobe*, Aslan approaches Susan and Lucy and, after some conversation, gives them an unexpected instruction: "Catch me if you can!"[46] And suddenly, the scene transitions from one of hopeful trepidation to unbridled joy as Susan and Lucy attempt, with all their might, to catch Aslan. Aslan's invitation here may well be the central call of the saga, as character after character is invited to follow him in strange, unexpected, and playful ways. Aslan's playfulness becomes a marked characteristic of his people—a playfulness that is not meaningless but, consistently, faith testing, as one must regularly decide whether to play according to Aslan's rules in order to flourish in both understanding and joy.

Telling the story of following Aslan is also marked by playfulness. In *The Horse and His Boy*, Lucy tells the story of how she and her siblings

---

44. Lewis, *Prince Caspian*, 147–58.
45. Lewis, *Prince Caspian*, 192–94.
46. Lewis, *Lion, the Witch, and the Wardrobe*, 176.

became Kings and Queens of Narnia in the midst of "a grand feast" filled with good drink and music.[47] And in *The Voyage of the Dawn Treader*, Eustace, having heard the Pevensies speak of Narnia before, repeatedly refers to their stories as a game.[48] While he does not believe them at first, calling his emergence into Narnia via the painting a "silly trick,"[49] Eustace eventually does believe in Narnia and even comes to love this magical land.

In contrast, in *The Last Battle*, the story of Aslan is perverted for practical ends through the otherwise playful means of dress-up. An ape named Shift and donkey named Puzzle find a lion's skin that they use to create a lion costume for Puzzle to wear. After seeing Puzzle in the costume for the first time, Shift and Puzzle have a conversation that sets the plot of the book into motion:

> "You look wonderful, wonderful," said the Ape. "If anyone saw you now, they'd think you were Aslan, the Great Lion, himself."
> "That would be dreadful," said Puzzle.
> "No it wouldn't," said Shift. "Everyone would do whatever you told them."
> "But I don't want to tell them anything."
> "But think of the good we could do!" said Shift. "You'd have me to advise you, you know. I'd think of sensible orders for you to give. And everyone would have to obey us, even the King himself. We would set everything right in Narnia."[50]

Settled on their course of action, Puzzle will "pretend to be Aslan" and Shift will tell Puzzle what to say, and in doing so practical ends corrupt play such that Aslan is replaced by an imposter—Tashlan, the "new angry Aslan"—through whom those who would otherwise follow Aslan's lead can be deceived into unfaithfulness.[51] This scene progresses as a distortion of (faithful) play and imagination, offering a glimpse of what non-Narnia play and use of imagination looks like and the kinds of "virtue"—which is to say, vice—that these develop: lying, manipulation, greed, apathy, vanity, and pride.

---

47. Lewis, *Horse and His Boy*, 250–51.
48. Lewis, *Voyage*, 13–14.
49. Lewis, *Voyage*, 16.
50. Lewis, *Last Battle*, 20–21.
51. Lewis, *Last Battle*, 21, 125, 134.

Part Two: Fictional Worlds

IMPLICATIONS FOR FOLLOWERS OF THE LION OF JUDAH

I would be remiss not to mention one key example in the saga of a leader being redeemed from pragmatism. In *The Voyage of the Dawn Treader*, Eustace is described as "practical" in a way that is similar to Susan in *Prince Caspian*.[52] Yet, by the end of *The Last Battle*, Eustace is as playful as Peter and Lucy—although still, we are told, a bit of a know it all. Eustace's character development suggests something about play that Gadamer recognized, which is that play transforms. In *The Chronicles of Narnia*, the game being played may best be described as "follow the Lion." And so it is too for Christians today. Following Jesus is not a matter of practicality and application in the sense of "applying" theology to bring about certain practical (procedural) outcomes; it is, instead, about faithfulness to the one being followed.

Moreover, the language of application is increasingly contested in the field of practical theology, in part because practical theologians do not view the development of "tips and tricks" for applying theologies or concepts all that helpful for cultivating Christians who are flourishing in their faith. On the contrary, the pragmatic approach to Christianity and Christian ministry has done untold damage to churches in the West, especially as these approaches have risen in tandem with the rise of secularism.[53] As Andrew Root notes, secularism fundamentally redefined the pastoral vocation towards hyper-pragmatism in service to material prosperity (broadly described). Root writes, "After all, the pastor's job was not to take people into sacred time or uphold the sacredness of ordinary life but to help people flourish, and it appeared that the new secular disciplines of psychology and sociology were much more helpful in this vein."[54] Thus, "what works" became more important than meeting the living God face to face, and this practical bent towards ministry especially short-circuited discipleship.

When practicality becomes one's abiding concern, one will inevitably mistake the game they are playing, and thus hinder themselves from transformation—namely, for Christians, a focus on practicality will invariably hinder us from following Christ, because Christ is regularly *impractical*. Indeed, Christian doctrines—such as the Trinity—have practical implications to be sure, but many are not practical in a pragmatic sense. Rather, the focus of theology is not on practicality but reality—is what we are saying in the presence of God true of God? And one's theology will shape their living.

---

52. Lewis, *Voyage*, 233.
53. Newton, "Pastor and Church Growth," 266.
54. Root, *Pastor in a Secular Age*, 12.

To be leaders in the Narnian sense, and in a Christian sense, Christian leaders such as pastors, deacons, worship leaders, and others must follow the Lion, not knowing where the Lion will lead, but knowing that their following is a faithful response, it is serious, and it has rules of faith, obedience, prayer, and miracles that regularly elude us, and that the playful response of following itself represents the truth of who God is in a way that is as wonderous as it is wonderful. And as they follow, these leaders, like Lucy throughout the Chronicles series, must invite others to join them on the mysterious journey of obedient faith (Cf. 1 Cor 11:1; Phil 3:17; Heb 13:7; 2 Thess 3:9).

Yet, what happens if a church leader invites others to follow along, but their invitation is, in fact, an exercise in pragmatism? Some leaders may not be obviously pragmatic but may subtly use people by asking them to fulfill a vision that that leader "received from on high," thus making their invitation to obedient faith an invitation to obedience to the leader themselves. Uncle Andrew does this in a previously mentioned scene in *The Magician's Nephew*, when he manipulates Polly through flattery to test his magic rings.[55] Throughout the scene, Uncle Andrew very clearly has a hidden purpose for trying to have Polly or Digory put the rings on, but what that purpose was exactly is kept hidden from view—especially due to his flattery. While Polly is unable to see the manipulation for what it is, Digory discerns that *something* is amiss: "Polly, don't be a fool! . . . Don't touch them."[56] Yet Polly does touch them, and Digory eventually touches one as well, having been manipulated by his Uncle into going after his friend.

The above touches on an important element of application for this essay, what we might call a "take away." That element is the importance of wise discernment in leadership. Throughout the Narnia series, leaders are invited not just to playfully follow Aslan but to discern good from evil and even to discern the truth of Aslan so that they might decide whether to place their faith in him. This is starkly the case in the final two books of the series. In *The Silver Chair*, Eustace, Jill, and Puddlegum must discern the stories of Narnia under pressure of the denial of their existence from the Lady of the Green Kirtle. And in *The Last Battle*, various characters must discern the truth about Tashlan. In each case, the characters have to discern Aslan's presence (or lack thereof) in order to live according to the Narnian vision of life that Aslan offers. Moreover, there is a repeated theme

---

55. Lewis, *Magician's Nephew*, 23–25.
56. Lewis, *Magician's Nephew*, 25.

throughout the series of characters seeing Aslan at a distance and having to choose whether or not they will follow him, his presence often seeming like a dream—so much so that when Aslan saves Shasta in *The Horse and His Boy*, Shasta comments that he "must have dreamed" the cat at his feet was a Lion.[57] To choose to follow is a decision of both wisdom and faith—weighing the evidence and trusting that following Aslan is the best way forward.

Yet following Aslan does not guarantee what each character might consider the best outcome that will (immediately) come to pass. While Aslan certainly offers protection, as in the case of Shasta, he also leads people towards difficulty, even battles, requiring greater faith and the exercise of all the Narnian virtues to get through. Furthermore, no one expects Aslan's death to be the most effective means for defeating the White Witch. Such is the case of the wisdom of Aslan and the wisdom of Jesus; it is wisdom that is not pragmatic and, in fact, can lead to ends that one would retreat from in any other scenario. But why is this? It is because faithful action does not depend on humans but God, or in the case of Narnia on Aslan. In other words, the most important element of faithful action is not the action itself but God's action amid human action, which is what brings about a given end. This entails thinking about human action in light of divine action such that the ends of following God are not caused by humans but by God, even as humans participate in a given action. Indeed, the strange characteristic of wisdom undergirding this—that wisdom can be applicable but not practical—is seen throughout Scripture, but especially in Proverbs. Reflecting on the first chapters of this book of Scripture, John Goldingay remarks,

> While there is a built-in linkage between action and result, so that doing the wise thing that is also the right thing issues in good results, this process entails Yahweh's involvement too. Yahweh is the one who makes things work this way. So someone who repudiates Yahweh but tries in other respects to operate in a skillful and shrewd way (maybe even in a way that expresses faithfulness to other people) may find that the expected linkage between action and result fails. And someone who operates on the basis of trust in and submission to Yahweh but who is not very shrewd or skilled may find that things nevertheless work out.[58]

The above fundamentally summarizes many of the story beats in *The Chronicles of Narnia*: when the characters trust Aslan and seek to follow

---

57. Lewis, *Horse and His Boy*, 105.
58. Goldingay, *Proverbs*, 5–6.

where Aslan is leading, even if they are unskilled, dimwitted, or simply foolish, things still work out for them in the end. Conversely, for those who are *expertly* (and otherworldly) skilled, their skill does not necessarily match the outcome of their plans. For while they have goals in mind, their goals are routinely frustrated by Aslan and his followers, even as their plans may seem to work for a time or season. Yet every season changes, winter always turns to spring, and the plans of the practical often come to ruin when made against the plans of the playful Son of the Emperor-Over-the-Sea.

CONCLUSION

I think it appropriate to conclude with Puddlegum's famous speech from *The Silver Chair*, given in response to the Witch as she tries to convince the story's protagonists that Narnia and Aslan do not exist:

> Suppose we have only dreamed or made up all those things, trees and grass and sun and moon and stars and Aslan himself, suppose we have? Then all I can say is that, in that case, the made up things seem a good deal more important than the real ones. Suppose this black pit of a kingdom of yours is the only world? Well it strikes me as a pretty poor one. And that's the funny thing when you come to think of it, we're just babies making up a game if you're right, but four babies playing a game can make a play world which licks your real world hollow! That's why I'm going to stand by the play world! I'm on Aslan's side even if there isn't any Aslan to lead it! I'm going to live as like a Narnian as I can, even if there isn't any Narnia![59]

There may not be a Narnia, nor an Aslan as such, but the Lion of the tribe of Judah has triumphed and his kingdom has come near. And everyone, including leaders, is invited to repent, believe, and chase the Lion who is beckoning them to follow, and especially for leaders to bring along others in faithful response—a beckoning that is, in a phrase, an invitation to play.

BIBLIOGRAPHY

Browning, Don. *A Fundamental Practical Theology: Descriptive and Strategic Proposals*. Minneapolis: Fortress, 1996.
Davis, Lanta. *Becoming by Beholding: The Power of Imagination in Spiritual Formation*. Grand Rapids: Baker Academic, 2024.
Dean, Robert J. "The Heresy of Relevance: Bonhoeffer's Warning to Preachers." *Pro Ecclesia: A Journal of Catholic and Evangelical Theology* 31 (2022) 73–93.

---

59. Lewis, *Silver Chair*, 212–13.

Part Two: Fictional Worlds

Gadamer, Hans-Georg. *The Relevance of the Beautiful and Other Essays*. Translated by Nicholas Walker. Cambridge: Cambridge University Press, 1986.

———. *Truth and Method*. Translated by Joel Weinsheimer and Donald G. Marshall. London: Bloomsbury Academic, 2013.

Goldingay, John. *Proverbs*. Commentaries for Christian Formation. Grand Rapids: Eerdmans, 2023.

Howard, Evan B. *A Guide to Christian Spiritual Formation: How Scripture, Spirit, Community, and Mission Shape our Souls*. Grand Rapids: Baker Academic, 2018.

Judd, Andrew. *Playing with Scripture: Reading Contested Biblical Texts with Gadamer and Genre Theory*. London: Routledge, 2024.

Kosma, Maria. "Gadamer's Hermeneutic Universality of Play: The Greatest Form of Human Play Is Art and its Signification to Movement Education." *Athens Journal of Sports* 11 (2024) 9–20.

Lewis, C. I. "Logical Positivism and Pragmatism." In *Collected Papers of C. I. Lewis*, edited by John D. Goheen and John L. Mothershead Jr., 92–112. Stanford, CA: Stanford University Press, 1970.

Lewis, C. S. *The Collected Letters of C. S. Lewis: Narnia, Cambridge, and Joy, 1950–1963—Volume III*. Edited by Walter Hooper. HarperSanFrancisco, 2007.

———. *The Horse and His Boy*. 1954. Reprint, London: Arcturus, 2018.

———. *The Last Battle*. 1956. Reprint, London: Arcturus, 2018.

———. *The Lion, the Witch, and the Wardrobe*. 1950. Reprint, London: Arcturus, 2018.

———. *The Magician's Nephew*. 1955. Reprint, London: Arcturus, 2018.

———. *Mere Christianity*. 1952. Reprint, Toronto: HarperOne, 2005.

———. "On Three Ways of Writing for Children." In *Of Other Worlds: Essays and Stories*, edited by Walter Hooper, 22–34. New York: Harcourt Brace Jovanovich, 1966.

———. *Prince Caspian*. 1951. Reprint, London: Arcturus, 2018.

———. *The Silver Chair*. 1953. Reprint, London: Arcturus, 2018.

———. "Sometimes Fairy Stories May Say Best What's to be Said." In *Of Other Worlds: Essays and Stories*, edited by Walter Hooper, 35–38. New York: Harcourt Brace Jovanovich, 1966.

———. *The Voyage of the Dawn Treader*. 1952. Reprint, London: Arcturus, 2018.

Newton, Phil A. "The Pastor and Church Growth: How to Deal with the Modern Problem of Pragmatism." In *Reforming Pastoral Ministry: Challenges for Ministry in Postmodern Times*, edited by John H. Armstrong, 263–80. Wheaton, IL: Crossway, 2001.

Osmer, Richard R. *Practical Theology: An Introduction*. Grand Rapids: Eerdmans, 2008.

Pike, Mark A. *Narnia Virtues: Building Good Character through the Stories and Wisdom of C. S. Lewis*. Cambridge: Lutterworth, 2021.

Prior, Karen Swallow. *The Evangelical Imagination: How Stories, Images, and Metaphors Created a Culture in Crisis*. Grand Rapids: Brazos, 2023.

Root, Andrew. *Christopraxis: A Practical Theology of the Cross*. Minneapolis: Fortress, 2014.

———. *The Pastor in a Secular Age*. Grand Rapids: Baker Academic, 2019.

Swinton John, and Harriet Mowat. *Practical Theology and Qualitative Research*. 2nd ed. London: SCM, 2006.

Regarding *Screwtape*

David I. Yoon

INTRODUCTION

I FIRST READ C. S. Lewis's *The Screwtape Letters* in college and recently decided to reread it. I probably lacked the maturity to properly digest the book then, compared to more recently, with life experience in hand (or so I tell myself). I try to have one non-academic book in my rotation, so in the summer of 2024, I decided I would revisit ol' *Screwtape*. As I read it again, I was, for one, surprised that a book some eighty years old was still relevant for today and addressed issues that we continue to experience. Perhaps there is nothing really new under the sun. But second, I wondered about what an angelic counterpart world might look like. Here we have an experienced devil, Screwtape, giving his lesser experienced nephew, Wormwood, advice on how to properly tempt people and lead them astray. Of course, this book is fiction, and there is no basis to think that devils have uncle-nephew relationships with each other; but Lewis created this "world" as a means of providing insight into the human condition and identify ways in which humanity can succumb, and often does succumb, to failure in life under God. So, *what would a conversation between angels look like as they navigate serving and ministering to humans?* I wondered. *Perhaps someone should write a counterpart to it.* Incidentally, soon after I had finished reading it, McMaster Divinity College (where I obtained my PhD and was a research fellow) had announced that it would host a gathering—not quite a conference but more than an informal meeting—called "Faith, Fantasy, and Philosophy: An Afternoon of C. S. Lewis," which was held on December 4, 2024. It ended up being more like a conference, as there were about eighty people gathered for the afternoon. However, I had made travel plans, where I would be arriving back in the Hamilton, Ontario, area on the morning of the conference, so I thought the timing would be too tight, and I would not submit a paper proposal. But it just seemed too coincidental to me that at the same time I read Lewis in a long while and subsequently had a related book idea in mind, that there was also a conference to which I could submit a paper presentation on this topic. This could be a helpful venue to test out my idea and get some helpful feedback. In addition, I was chatting with Dr. Stanley Porter, the organizer of the conference and casually mentioned my book idea. He thought a preliminary paper on that topic would be appropriate and interesting for the conference. Thus, I submitted a presentation entitled "Letters to Bradus" and proceeded to draft a few letters. So, on the morning of the conference, I arrived at the Buffalo–Niagara airport from an overnight flight from California (on which I slept very little), drove across the border fueled by coffee, picked up my dogs who had stayed with a good friend, unpacked and settled in, showered, and headed over to McMaster Divinity College for the conference, just in time for the ending of the first session.

The conference presentation included a brief explanation of my project, the reading of a few of the initial letters, and a subsequent discussion with attendees. The discussion proved to be thoughtful and helpful, with many insightful questions posed from the audience. I have since been thinking more about their comments and how to proceed. This chapter, which you are reading now, is a reflection on *Screwtape* in anticipation of *Letters to Bradus*, the tentative title of my forthcoming book.

REFLECTING ON *SCREWTAPE*

Lewis was—to state the obvious—not only an insightful thinker, as evinced in his books like *Mere Christianity* and *The Abolition of Man*, but a brilliant creator.[1] He created whole worlds such as in *The Chronicles of Narnia*, the Space Trilogy, and *The Great Divorce*, which both children and adults continue to refer to in both academic settings and casual conversations. This, in part, is due to his imaginative—one might even call it playful—mind, where the boundary between pretend and real often blurs in his fictional writings.

---

1. Since Lewis's books have been published by a number of different publishers in various editions, I will feel free not to list any bibliographic information of these works.

An apt example of Lewis's imagination is the first sentence of the preface to *Screwtape*, in which he writes, "I have no intention of explaining how the correspondence which I now offer to the public fell into my hands."[2] The correspondence, of course, is the collection of letters by Screwtape, a creation of Lewis, the actual writer of these letters by the fictional senior devil. Or perhaps, a devil named Screwtape actually does exist, and Lewis was fortunate to come across these letters somehow. The mere invocation of the mystery of the letters' origins is a playful invitation by Lewis to imagine that these are real letters from the demonic realm and to read them as such.

Lewis makes two other points in the preface. First, he states that two extremes ("errors") should be avoided, to either pay *no* attention to the existence of devils or to pay *too much* attention to them ("an excessive and unhealthy interest"). He calls the person on the one extreme a materialist and the other a magician—both delights to the devils. Materialists pay no attention to the devil and his influence in the world, as if a life of faith in Christ was simply about one's own personal relationship with him. Magicians, on the other hand, are so preoccupied with the devils that they may be spiritually paralyzed or pay less attention to Christ himself. Second, he states that the devil is a liar and that not everything Screwtape says is *true*, even from his own vantage point. The brilliance of Lewis is reflected throughout this book, as he uses satire to reveal how the devil works in people. Thus, it is crucial to seek a healthy, balanced, and sober understanding of the demonic realm and its influences for our Christian lives.

I offer some reflections on some major themes in *Screwtape*, in which Lewis, implicitly, explicitly, or ironically, highlights how people can recognize and guard against demonic influences and temptations in their lives.

Subtlety and Complacency

In his correspondence with his nephew, Screwtape advises him that the easiest road to hell is a subtle or gradual slope. It is not the grand, audacious decisions that lead a person to hell, although sometimes this may be the case, but the incremental and seemingly innocuous compromises that lead a person away from God. Creating an immediate separation of 1,000 miles from a point is drastic, but incremental distances of a mile a day, after 1,000 days, can make one oblivious to the fact that they are now 1,000 miles removed from the point of origin. "Slow and steady wins the race,"

2. Lewis, *Screwtape Letters*, ix (Originally written in 1942, with the preface written in 1961).

it is often axiomatically said, and this applies to the realm of evil influence as well. There are several letters I wish to highlight in which subtlety and complacency are thematized.

Letter 9 builds on the previous Letter 8, which discusses how the law of undulation works in humans (see section further below). This law describes the normality of human life as consisting of ups and downs, what Screwtape calls "peaks" and "troughs"; it is a natural part of this earthly life. While Letter 8 is instructive for Wormwood on how this law works, and how God uses the troughs to draw his people closer to him, Screwtape in this next letter provides insight into how troughs can be properly exploited by the devils. He begins by stating that the trough provides an excellent opportunity to invoke sensual temptations, especially sexual ones, since there is less energy during the trough periods to resist. But he also states a more effective focus on exploiting the trough, to let the Patient think that this trough is permanent. If the Patient is a pessimist, he can further be tempted by convincing him to try to get out of the trough by sheer willpower. If the Patient is an optimist, he can be tempted by convincing him that the trough is not so bad and that "moderation" is the key to life. "If you can once get him to the point of thinking that 'religion is all very well up to a point,'" Screwtape writes, "you can feel quite happy about his soul. A moderated religion is as good for us as no religion at all—and more amusing."[3] Moderation, or in another word, complacency, in the case of one's faith and spiritual life, reflects a lukewarm approach to life, and Lewis depicts the devils being satisfied with that outcome for the humans during the trough.

In Letter 12, Screwtape praises Wormwood for his work and notes how pleased he is that the Patient is still a regular churchgoer. He writes, "As long as he retains externally the habits of a Christian he can still be made to think of himself as one who has adopted a few new friends and amusements but whose spiritual state is much the same as it was six weeks ago."[4] As long as the Christian does the "Christian things," Screwtape says, he does not tend to find himself concerned about the state of his spiritual life. As another instance of subtle complacency, Screwtape cautions his nephew from seeking out only "spectacular wickedness" from his Patient and to remember that accumulating small sins can be even more effective to bring the Patient far from God. He concludes the letter by stating, "Indeed the safest road to Hell is the gradual one—the gentle slope, soft underfoot,

---

3. Lewis, *Screwtape Letters*, 46.
4. Lewis, *Screwtape Letters*, 58.

without sudden turnings, without milestones, without sign posts."[5] He does not state it outright, but the spectacular sins usually do not lead a person away from God so much as a gradual walking away, with perhaps a spectacular sin occurring when the person has gone too far away to realize that it is even sin.

In the next letter, Letter 13, Screwtape begins by chastising his nephew for allowing the Patient to repent and be renewed to experience a "second conversion," which apparently occurs between Letters 12 and 13. The mistake that Wormwood made, according to Screwtape, was that the Patient experienced two "real positive Pleasures," enjoying a good book and taking a solitary walk in the countryside with a cup of tea, which lifted him up from the lull that he was in. The implication here is that the simple pleasures of life can be used, for the Christian, to bring them out of spiritual dryness. It is subtle but effective, nonetheless. Screwtape writes, "The man who truly and disinterestedly enjoys any one thing in the world, for its own sake, and without caring two-pence what other people say about it, is by that very fact forearmed against some of our subtlest modes of attack."[6] Enjoying the simple pleasures of life for their own sakes, rather than for other secondary motives, is a gift of God that can be used to draw closer to him. The application of this is that the Christian would do well to find a few simple things he or she finds pleasure in, for the sake of the things themselves, and regularly participate in them as a spiritual exercise. Lewis uses a quiet walk in the countryside with tea, or reading a good book, as examples. For others, it could be going to a concert or symphony, engaging in physical exercise, or enjoying a quiet cup of coffee in the yard while listening to the orchestra of the birds. The subtlety of life applies for both realms, both heaven and hell. In this letter, Lewis identifies a subtle joy that contributes to one's spiritual health.

In Letter 25, Screwtape identifies what he calls "the horror of the Same Old Thing."[7] In short, it is a fear of doing the same old thing and a pursuit of constant novelty. Just as God created seasons, he also created in humans a balance of both change and permanence, calling their union Rhythm. The imbalance, then, is to focus on the change and to constantly seek it out. And although Lewis does not explicitly comment on the converse, its counter-imbalance would be to focus on the permanence and fear of any

5. Lewis, *Screwtape Letters*, 61.
6. Lewis, *Screwtape Letters*, 66.
7. Lewis, *Screwtape Letters*, 137.

sort of change (perhaps a form of neuroticism). But to exploit the horror of the Same Old Thing, Screwtape advises Wormwood to combine Christianity with something else: "'Christianity And.' You know—Christianity and the Crisis, Christianity and the New Psychology, Christianity and the New Order, Christianity and Faith Healing, Christianity and Psychical Research, Christianity and Vegetarianism, Christianity and Spelling Reform."[8] Regardless of whether or not one agrees with this particular list, the point is that it is not Christianity alone but joined with something else, with the something else always being replaced every so often like a filter or battery. This relates to the section below on distractions as well, but it relates to subtlety in the sense that there are subtle shifts to the main thing that distract a Christian from God. Instead of focusing on the main thing, the side thing becomes the main thing in the name of the main thing, so much so that the main thing remains no longer the main thing—and this is usually done unwittingly. And the horror of the Same Old Thing is the means by which this shift occurs. Screwtape states, "For the descriptive adjective 'unchanged' we have substituted the emotional adjective 'stagnant.'"[9] The subtle word "and" tacked onto Christianity is subtle but effective to lead a Christian astray from the fundamentals of his faith.

The subtlety of temptation and the complacency of one's faith—mirror opposites of contentment—are often the most powerful tools of the devil to lead a Christian away from God. Take, for example, the disqualified Christian leader who has stepped down from ministry—which unfortunately happens much too often—usually involving sexual, financial, or abusive misconduct. In most of these cases, it is not one spectacular sin that disqualifies the leader, but there is a pattern of years (sometimes decades) that eventually result in the public exposure of the sin. In some of these cases, one might say that the leader was a deliberate sociopath who preyed on people within his domain and took advantage of his authoritative position. But in other cases, the leader probably started with the subtle steps, or compromises, that led to greater and greater compromises, that led to carelessness and finally exposure. Screwtape as a cunning mentor urges his nephew to exploit this opportunity to draw Christians as far away from God as possible—slowly and subtly—because it works.

---

8. Lewis, *Screwtape Letters*, 135.
9. Lewis, *Screwtape Letters*, 139.

Pride and Self-Deception

Another topic that Screwtape emphasizes is pride, along with its partner, self-deception. Numerous teachings in Scripture warn against pride as one of the most prominent sins, namely because it results in self-reliance and independence from God. In turn, pride is the result of self-deception, the broader category, whereby one's pride is the result of one being deceived into thinking that one is independent and fully autonomous. I want to highlight four of Screwtape's letters in which Lewis refers to the themes of pride and self-deception.

In Letter 10, the Patient has made some new friends, described as a "middle-aged married couple . . . just the sort of people we want him to know—rich, smart, superficially intellectual, and brightly sceptical about everything in the world."[10] The joy of Screwtape stems from the fact that these friends represent the values that are opposed to the Patient's faith, but the Patient is either not aware of it or in denial of it. With the help of pride, among other qualities, Wormwood should be able to defer the Patient's acknowledgment that his new friends' opinions and ideologies are in direct opposition to his Christian faith. One of the ways in which Screwtape advises his nephew to accomplish this is by tempting the Patient to take pleasure in the inconsistencies of the two sides of his life, one that reflects his Christian faith and the other his worldly friends. He writes:

> This is done by exploiting his vanity. He can be taught to enjoy kneeling beside the grocer [i.e., an ordinary man] on Sunday just because he remembers that the grocer could not possibly understand the urbane and mocking world which he inhabited on Saturday evening; and contrariwise, to enjoy the bawdy and blasphemy over the coffee with these admirable friends all the more because he is aware of a "deeper," "spiritual" world within him which they cannot understand.[11]

Lewis, I believe, is not critiquing having both Christian and non-Christian friends, both ordinary and extraordinary friends, in general. He seems to be identifying the Christian who seeks to please both worlds but in doing so is self-deceived; that is, his revelry in his new friends is for "a greater cause" in which these friends fulfill some sort of worldly pleasure.

---

10. Lewis, *Screwtape Letters*, 49.
11. Lewis, *Screwtape Letters*, 51.

Referring to Letter 13 again, the situational context is that the Patient has experienced Pleasures—noble pleasures in and of themselves—which apparently have brought him out of the trough. Screwtape chastises Wormwood for letting this happen without any intervention. Towards the end of the letter, Screwtape advises, "You should always try to make the patient abandon the people or food or books he really likes in favour of the 'best' people, the 'right' food, the 'important' book."[12] The quotation marks signify the best and right and important *according to popular consensus*—which may not be the best and right and important according to the individual. There is a subtle address of pride in this advice that the casual reader of the letter may miss. Pride is essentially an over-focus on oneself that may manifest itself as preoccupation with *appearances*—a preoccupation with oneself in relation to outward perception. Sometimes, pride is outwardly manifested due to insecurities about oneself—a compensation or an overcompensation, so to speak. So, the advice to tempt the Patient is to abandon security and surety in oneself, to abandon true confidence, by tempting the Patient to be attracted to the popular consensus. Now arrogance, a relative of pride but distinct in its orientation, is usually manifested by disdain for others, using it to elevate oneself. Thus, in this case, an arrogant Patient would favor what he really likes and let his whole world know this, and thereby overtly put down the popular consensus. But pride is more subtle than arrogance in its elevation of oneself by not requiring the disdain for others. One who is proud elevates himself in this case by identifying with the "best of the best" in every category, because he wants to be identified with the "best"; this may also arise from subconscious insecurities about himself in who he is. But in doing this, the Patient suppresses what he really enjoys and finds pleasure in it. And in this way, the Patient is being dishonest with himself, being self-deceived. The lesson: to be honest with oneself and find noble pleasures regardless of popular opinion. And when found, enjoy them without condemnation.

The next letter, Letter 14, changes course and depicts the humility of the Patient. Screwtape expresses his disappointment—questioning whether Wormwood is even doing his job—that the Patient is no longer making the overconfident commitments that he made early on in his new life. He is instead resolved to live day to day by the grace of God. This, Screwtape identifies, is *humility*, and it "is very bad."[13] Wormwood fails to guide his Patient

---

12. Lewis, *Screwtape Letters*, 66.
13. Lewis, *Screwtape Letters*, 69.

towards hell, and instead his Patient is back on track towards heaven. But Screwtape offers an immediate solution: to tempt the Patient to take *pride* in his *humility*. How ironic, yet pervasive, the potentially co-dependent relationship between pride and humility! The tactic that Screwtape advises his nephew to take is to go with humility but let it become a source of self-focus. He writes, "You must therefore conceal from the Patient the true end of Humility. Let him think of it not as self-forgetfulness but as a certain kind of opinion (namely, a low opinion) of his own talents and character."[14] Screwtape continues, "Fix in his mind the idea that humility consists in trying to believe those talents to be less valuable than he believes them to be ... The great thing is to make him value an opinion for some quality other than truth, thus introducing an element of dishonesty and make-believe into the heart of what otherwise threatens to become a virtue."[15] If humility is best described as less of self and more of God and others (cf. Phil 2:3–4), Screwtape says essentially that even humility can be quickly whipped into its polar opposite, if done well. Screwtape writes, "But always and by all methods the Enemy's [i.e., God's] aim will be to get the patient's mind off such questions, and yours will be to fix it on them. Even of his sins, the Enemy [God] does not want him to think too much: once they are repented, the sooner the man turns his attention outward, the better the Enemy [i.e., God] is pleased."[16] Lewis identifies pride as an overfocus on oneself, and he sees that the devils work to exploit humility—probably better stated as *false humility*—in Christians to cross over to pride.

Letter 24 addresses one of the most insidious temptations for Christians: spiritual pride. In the previous letter (see the next section on distraction), Screwtape notes that the Patient has a new love in his life, a Christian girl who has become a "bad" influence on him (bad for the devils, good for Christians). But he notes in this letter that she has a "chink in her armour," which means that she views outsiders who do not share in her Christian faith as stupid and ridiculous. Screwtape states, "It is always the novice who exaggerates. The man who has risen in society is over-refined, the young scholar is pedantic. In this new circle your patient is a novice ... Can you get him to imitate this *defect* in his mistress and to exaggerate it until what was venial in her becomes in him the strongest and most beautiful of the

---

14. Lewis, *Screwtape Letters*, 70.
15. Lewis, *Screwtape Letters*, 70.
16. Lewis, *Screwtape Letters*, 72–73.

vices—Spiritual Pride?"[17] The angle of spiritual pride that Screwtape advocates for this Patient is tribalism—although this term is not used by Lewis. Tribalism is the phenomenon in which people strongly identify and show loyalty to a particular group, usually to the exclusion and detriment of outsiders. Tribalism and pride almost always go hand-in-hand. One feels like he *belongs* to a superior group, and thus he feels superior, and that is pride, subtly manifested. Screwtape writes, "The idea of belonging to an inner ring, of being in a secret, is a very sweet to him. Play on that nerve."[18] Thus, belonging to a spiritually "elite" group often results in spiritual pride, often without the person being aware of it. In our current society, this happens with certain mega-churches and networks of churches, where the group in question becomes the fount of all truth and knowledge, and an air of superiority is palpable among its members, especially since God is "blessing" this organization through growth and expansion. Lewis's focus was on Christians versus non-Christians, the particular tribe being Christianity, but I think in our North American society—and probably other Western societies that operate on Judeo-Christian principles—tribalism exists in a different, narrower domain among the varieties of Christianity that exist today. *Our way of doing Christianity is the best way, and others who are not a part of us are lesser Christians.* This is spiritual pride and is used by the Enemy (not Screwtape's Enemy but the real Enemy) to distract Christians from the true and ultimate goal.

In these letters, Lewis identifies the subtlety of pride and self-deception as hindering one's spiritual growth, and that even humility can be carefully used to activate pride in a person. The most insidious form of pride is spiritual pride, where the boundary between spiritual maturity and spiritual pride can easily be blurred: being proud about being humble.

Distraction

Another cunning tactic of the devil is to distract Christians, usually with tangentially related things, things that may be noble in and of themselves but ultimately detract from closeness to God. Instead of maintaining focus on what a Christian should focus on, the devils resort to distracting them with not overtly incompatible leisures but subtle pleasures that move a Patient away from God incrementally.

---

17. Lewis, *Screwtape Letters*, 130.
18. Lewis, *Screwtape Letters*, 132.

Letter 6 addresses the potential for the Patient to go into military service; this is significant because of the situational context of *Screwtape* during World War II. Screwtape states how he would use this opportunity to distract the Patient: "We want him to be in the maximum uncertainty, so that his mind will be filled with contradictory pictures of the future, every one of which arouses hope or fear. There is nothing like suspense and anxiety for barricading a human's mind against the Enemy [i.e., God]."[19] Screwtape continues and states that God's will for humans is to focus on what they *do*; Screwtape's will is for humans to be preoccupied about what will happen to them. The proper response to such a situation, for a Christian, is to trust in God's sovereign will and live life in the present moment, day to day. Screwtape's tactic is to distract the Christian by trying to get him to be overly concerned about the immutable future. He also advises Wormwood to distract the Patient by making the focus of his prayers not on God directly but on his own attitudes and thoughts about God and then to divert his focus from the thing feared to the emotion of fear itself. Thus, the tactic is a continual distraction from the main focus, as Screwtape writes towards the end of this letter:

> Think of your man as a series of concentric circles, his will being the innermost, his intellect coming next, and finally his fantasy. You can hardly hope, at once, to exclude from all the circles everything that smells of the Enemy: but you must keep on shoving all the virtues outward till they are finally located in the circle of fantasy, and all the desirable qualities inward into the Will."[20]

The "desirable" qualities, of course, are desirable according to Screwtape, but undesirable to God. Lewis identifies what Christians continue to struggle with, perhaps even unwittingly succumb to, being preoccupied with peripheral issues so that they cease to grow and mature in their faith and intimacy with God.

Screwtape begins the next letter, Letter 7, by addressing the question of whether it is beneficial for the devils to remain concealed or revealed but moves to another question of whether the Patient should be made to be an extreme patriot or extreme pacificist. (At this point, he states, this is concealed.) Screwtape states, "All extremes, except extreme devotion to the Enemy [i.e., God], are to be encouraged."[21] He nuances this by stat-

19. Lewis, *Screwtape Letters*, 25.
20. Lewis, *Screwtape Letters*, 28.
21. Lewis, *Screwtape Letters*, 32.

ing that some periods in history are characterized by lukewarmness and complacency, in which extremism is to be avoided and complacency encouraged. But in the present age of *Screwtape*—Lewis's 1940s England—characterized by imbalance and factions, increasing extremism is "beneficial" (for the devils). But whichever extreme is adopted, patriotism or pacificism, Screwtape advises that it must be a part of the Patient's religion and then regarded as the central part of his religion. Then as patriotism or pacifism becomes central, the Christian faith becomes important in so far as it helps either cause. The value of Christianity eventually lies in its strong arguments for that cause. Screwtape writes, "Once you have made the World an end, and faith a means, you have almost won your man, and it makes very little difference what kind of worldly end he is pursuing."[22] Lewis labels patriotism and pacifism as worldly, not in the sense of sinful but in the sense of *belonging to the world*. While they may be oppositional counterparts, with each view containing both valid and invalid arguments, even from a Christian worldview, these are distractions to a Christian's primary calling to follow Christ. Screwtape continues, "Provided that meetings, pamphlets, policies, movements, causes, and crusades, matter more to him than prayers and sacraments and charity, he is ours—and the more 'religious' (on those terms) the more securely ours."[23] Were this statement written today, it would include social media, blogs, podcasts, Instagram reels, and TikTok videos as replacements for . . . prayers, sacraments, and charity—the same foundational activities involved in devotion to God. The point that Lewis makes here is not that patriotism and pacifism are wrong in and of themselves, but that one can easily make them the focus, resulting in a neglect of true devotion to God. Any extreme, except extreme devotion to God, can serve as a distraction to the main thing.

Letter 15 begins by addressing the War again, but this time because humans are experiencing a lull. Screwtape asks: Should they promote this lull or keep him worried about the future? He answers his own question: "Tortured fear and stupid confidence are both desirable states of mind."[24] (Did not Lewis have a trenchant way of putting things? Brilliant.) Which is the better, continued lull or projected worry? Screwtape describes what God wants: for humans to focus on eternity and the present, since the present is the point in time which touches eternity. Being concerned with

---

22. Lewis, *Screwtape Letters*, 34.
23. Lewis, *Screwtape Letters*, 34.
24. Lewis, *Screwtape Letters*, 75.

eternity means being concerned with him; being concerned with the present means being fully engaged and active, since the present is the only point in time in which humans can experience what eternity offers, freedom and actuality. The past and the future offer no such things. Thus, the task is to distract Christians from the present or eternity by tempting them to live in the past, to relish what has been. The good ol' days. But focusing on the past is not as strong a temptation, since there is a real knowledge of the past, and it has some semblance of eternity. So, it is a better temptation to have them focus on the future. The future is where both fear and hope reside. Screwtape further explains, "Hence nearly all vices are rooted in the future. Gratitude looks to the past and love to the present; fear, avarice, lust, and ambition look ahead."[25] So a tactic of the devil to tempt Christians is to distract them with either the past or the future, so that they may ignore the present life they are to be living and enjoying in God's will.

In Letter 23, Screwtape finds the Patient in a new relationship with a Christian girl who comes from a Christian family. He fears that this pervading influence in his life will make it impossible to *remove* spirituality from his life, so Screwtape suggests another tactic: *Corrupt* it. And the best way to corrupt the Patient's spirituality is to conflate it with politics. On the one hand, Screwtape warns, allowing Christianity to pervade areas of politics, such as social justice (a term, interestingly, that was used eight decades ago by Lewis), is a danger; but on the other hand, that could be used to make Christianity only a means of social justice, and not the end itself. Thus, while not denying his Christian faith, the Patient can be distracted by "good" things like social justice, or any other cause or goal that may be good in and of itself but has the potential to cause a Christian to forget about his faith. The bulk of the letter, however, is a discussion of the then-trending—and presently-lingering—historical Jesus studies. One might wonder if Screwtape himself becomes distracted in this letter by expounding on a tangential topic. What is the connection between his tactic to distract the Patient with a political focus and the historical Jesus? As Screwtape explains to Wormwood, historical Jesus studies have been and can be used to distract people from true devotion to the Jesus presented in the Gospels by focusing merely on ethics and social justice issues. A strong devotional life with God is replaced with something else that seems good.

Through these letters, Lewis focuses on the temptation to be distracted, sometimes by seemingly good and noble things. One is the future, or

---

25. Lewis, *Screwtape Letters*, 76.

fear of the future, which may seem to be proper to think about, especially in the context of preparing for the future and being a responsible planner. Another is religion and politics, where one goal is conflated with the other, so much so that religion is displaced with politics, only to occupy a handmaiden's role to it. However, Lewis sees these potentially harmless occupations to be used by the devil to distract Christians from what they ought to be focused on, the truly important and central task of living for God in the present moment.

Suffering and Trials

The final theme in *Screwtape* that I will focus on is suffering and trials. In *Screwtape*, Lewis addresses the theme of suffering and trials in the human experience from various perspectives, and he imagines how the devils use this to deter Christians away from God, to lead them closer to hell.

The situational context in Letter 5 is the inception of the Second World War. Screwtape is less than pleased that Wormwood is overjoyed at the Patient's fear and anxiety about the War. So the Patient had a bad night's sleep. *Big deal*, states Screwtape in so many words. The real victory (for the devils) is to capture a person's soul, not simply enjoy their torture. He states, "So do not allow any temporary excitement to distract you from the real business of undermining faith and preventing the formation of virtues."[26] He does, however, admit to being entertained by watching humans express fear and anxiety: "The immediate fear and suffering of the humans is a legitimate and pleasing refreshment for our myriads of toiling workers [i.e., the demons]. But what permanent good does it do us unless we make use of it for bringing souls to Our Father Below?"[27] Wormwood must focus on the greater task of capturing the Patient's soul, not simply revel in the Patient's frivolous mood. However, in this letter, Screwtape does not offer any advice to Wormwood on exploiting this situation; instead, he complains that this kind of long-term suffering often strengthens Christians. He writes towards the end of the letter, "The Enemy's [i.e., God's] human partisans have all been plainly told by Him that suffering is an essential part of what He calls Redemption; so that a faith which is destroyed by a war or a pestilence cannot really have been worth the trouble of destroying."[28] In other words, if a

---

26. Lewis, *Screwtape Letters*, 22.
27. Lewis, *Screwtape Letters*, 22.
28. Lewis, *Screwtape Letters*, 24.

person leaves the Christian faith due to such sources of suffering like war or pestilence, it was not a strong enough faith for the devils to even bother with. It is within the Christian experience to expect suffering and trials. Thus, Lewis highlights the axiom that trials and suffering are an expected part of the Christian life and that Christians should not be surprised when experiencing this.

In Letter 8, Lewis introduces (and later popularizes) the law of undulation. Screwtape reminds his nephew that humans are half spirit and half animal, whereby the spirit side is directed towards spiritual things, and the animal side is subject to continual change, due to the changing nature of the flesh, passions, and imaginations. Thus, there is *undulation*, which orients the human back to the level from which they fall, "a series of troughs and peaks,"[29] lows and highs, valleys and mountains. But this law of undulation, Screwtape advises, should be used to do the opposite of what the Enemy (i.e., God) does with it, and he observes that God surprisingly uses the troughs more than the peaks to orient the human to himself. Screwtape states that both God and the devils have the same purpose—both wish to obtain the obedience of humans—but he identifies the crucial difference in how they achieve this. The method of devils is to devour and consume humans so that they would become one with them at the expense of their own human identities. Obedience for the devils is achieved by absorbing their wills into their own wills: total capture. The method of God for obedience, on the other hand, is to use to troughs, periods of lowness, even pain and suffering, to draw humans to himself: voluntary devotion. Screwtape explains: God does not devour, God does not consume, God does not force, but desires humans to freely come to him, not merely as servants but as sons and daughters. Lewis writes, "It is during such trough periods, much more than during the peak periods, that it is growing into the sort of creature He wants it to be. Hence the prayers offered in the state of dryness are those which please Him best."[30] Thus, Screwtape warns that their cause is essentially lost when a person looks around the world, wonders why he has been forsaken (an allusion to Jesus' very words on the cross), and yet continues to remain devoted to God. He also states that "some of His special favourites have gone through longer and deeper troughs than anyone else."[31] Perhaps Lewis is drawing on his own experience, but also certain

---

29. Lewis, *Screwtape Letters*, 37.
30. Lewis, *Screwtape Letters*, 40.
31. Lewis, *Screwtape Letters*, 38.

characters in the Bible who can be described as God's "favourites," those who are depicted as close to God but have experienced significant troughs in their lives (e.g., Abraham, Moses, David, Job, Ruth, Esther, the Prophets, Paul, and of course even Jesus bar Joseph himself). Screwtape ends the letter with a glimpse of how they can still exploit these periods of trough but points out several important points regarding pain and suffering: (1) pain and suffering—or periods of dryness—are a normal part of the human experience; (2) God often uses pain and suffering to draw his people closer to him, and the devil uses it to distract; and (3) God does not compel or force obedience, but gives opportunity for closer obedience through pain and suffering. Thus, the Christian would do well to accept periods of both highs and lows in his life and to capitalize on the periods of lowness by strengthening his faith in God.

Letter 21 approaches pain and suffering from an indirect angle. Screwtape writes, "Men are not angered by mere misfortune but by misfortune *conceived as injury*. And the sense of injury depends on the feeling that a legitimate claim has been denied. The more claims on life, therefore, that your patient can be induced to make, the more often he will feel injured and, as a result, ill-tempered."[32] The difference between misfortune and misfortune-conceived-as-injury is subtle but significant. Screwtape gives an example of a man who has reserved a period of time for himself, which is taken away by an unexpected visitor; or when he wants to spend time conversing with his friend to catch up on things, but his friend's wife shows up with him and dominates the conversation. Thus, Screwtape advises increasing these *claims on life* to maximize misfortune-conceived-as-injury. This can be done by confusing the use of possessive pronouns, such as "my": my time, my boots, my house, my car, my wife, my country, even my God, may all be used to refer to ownership, a claim. Screwtape writes, "The sense of ownership in general is always to be encouraged. The humans are always putting up claims to ownership which sound equally funny in Heaven and in Hell and we must keep them doing so."[33] Even the devils know that humans do not really own anything, although Screwtape is mistaken about the implication that both heaven and hell equally possess ownership of things. So, from this angle, pain and suffering are viewed in terms of perceived robbery (e.g., of time) or frustrations (e.g., of unmet expectations or thwarted plans). In this case, the pain and suffering stem

---

32. Lewis, *Screwtape Letters*, 111 (emphasis mine).
33. Lewis, *Screwtape Letters*, 113.

from one's misconceived notions of ownership, with the implication that it is really God who owns all things—although Screwtape may never admit this directly. Left unchecked, as Screwtape encourages Wormwood to capitalize on this and increase the Patient's sense of ownership, pride and selfishness can grow and flourish.

Letter 26 explores another domain of suffering and trials, relational ones, as Screwtape addresses the situation of the Patient in the early stages of dating or courtship. He advises that this early period is prime for sowing seeds that in ten years will turn into domestic hatred. These seeds, he notes, involve several confusions. First is to confuse the meaning of "love" to the neglect of charity. He states that humans often in the name of love simply avoid or postpone a conflict that needs to be addressed. Second is to promote "unselfishness" in place of charity. The way in which unselfishness can be exploited is to sacrifice one's advantages, not for the sake of benefitting others, but so that one can simply claim unselfishness for oneself. Another way this can be accomplished is to exploit the different understandings of unselfishness by the sexes. Screwtape observes that men define unselfishness by not being trouble for others and women by taking on trouble for others. In exploiting this difference, men may see women as selfish and women may see men as selfish, for not doing what they each define as unselfish. In this vein, Lewis describes the passive-aggressive nature of humans in relationships, where instead of open and honest communication, there linger assumptions and expectations that should be clear to all. Screwtape writes:

> If each side had been frankly contending for its own real wish, they would all have kept within the bounds of reasons and courtesy; but just because the contention is reversed and each side is fighting the other side's battle, all the bitterness which really flows from thwarted self-righteousness and obstinacy and the accumulated grudges of the last ten years is concealed from them by the nominal or official 'Unselfishness' of what they are doing or, at least, held to be excused by it.[34]

Lewis implies that honest communication of one's needs and desires, rather than a feigned pretense of unselfishness, paves the way for true love to flourish, in both romantic and platonic relationships.

Finally, the situational context of Letter 29 is the continuing War, where the Patient's town is expected to be bombed. Screwtape wonders

---

34. Lewis, *Screwtape Letters*, 144.

what the best way to exploit this situation might be: (1) cowardice; (2) courage which may lead to pride; or (3) hatred. He states that courage is useless, as the devils have no way of producing any such virtue. Courage, or any other virtue, must be supplied by God, but at least they can manipulate the virtue to their own malevolence. Hatred, on the other hand, can be used if wielded properly. Hatred is best when combined with fear. Fear alone, cowardice alone, is shameful for humans, but when compensated with hatred, a person is assuaged by the pain of cowardice. Screwtape writes, "The more he fears, the more he will hate. And Hatred is also a great anodyne for shame. To make a deep wound in his charity, you should therefore first defeat his courage."[35] To achieve this, Screwtape suggests keeping the Patient preoccupied with future possibilities and liabilities, so that he might avoid any potential trial or hardship in his life. And then, when after copious planning for the prevention of any trial the trial happens, the Patient may act upon his fear. He concludes, "For remember, the *act* of cowardice is all that matters; the emotion of fear is, in itself, no sin and, though we enjoy it, does us no good."[36] The emotion of fear is not to be avoided; it is the action that follows the fear that makes a difference. Furthermore, it is not the presence of trials and suffering in our lives that matter, for these are a part of human life on earth; it is the human response to these trials and suffering that bring about deeper spiritual maturity and closeness with God. The devils wish to increase fear and cowardice through trials; God wishes deeper dependence and courage that can be found in him.

CONCLUSION

Lewis used the playfully imagined character of Screwtape, as well as a further removed Wormwood, to provide insights not only into how the devils may tempt humans, but also into the human condition itself. Some of the prominent, recurring themes in *Screwtape* which I have outlined include: (1) subtlety and complacency; (2) pride and self-deception; (3) distraction; and (4) suffering and trials. These are also some of the themes that will be explored in my *Letters to Bradus*, but from an angelic perspective. The temptations identified by Lewis eight decades ago are the same types of temptations that humans encounter today. This illustrates the fact that while the world is certainly developing in many ways, the human condition

---

35. Lewis, *Screwtape Letters*, 160.
36. Lewis, *Screwtape Letters*, 163.

remains the same, and there is nothing really new under the sun in this regard.

Lewis warned us against two extremes in thinking about the demonic realm, either not to think about it at all or to think about it too much; either to dismiss the power of the devil in our lives or to obsess over its power. I hope this essay and my forthcoming book provide some help for us to find a healthy balance between either extreme and that the only extreme we succumb to is extreme devotion to Our Father Above.

BIBLIOGRAPHY

Lewis, C. S. *The Screwtape Letters: With Screwtape Proposes a Toast*. Reprint, New York: HarperCollins, 2001.

Part Three

Literature and Criticism

What Kind of Scholar Was C. S. Lewis?

STANLEY E. PORTER

INTRODUCTION

THE QUESTION OF WHAT kind of scholar C. S. Lewis was invites a host of answers. Some might answer that he was an Irish scholar, and indeed he was. He was born and reared in Belfast before making his educational journey to England to be educated.[1] He was an English literature scholar, and he was that also, one who studied English literature from the medieval to the modern periods. He was a medievalist and Renaissance scholar, and he was that, too. He concentrated upon the medieval and Renaissance periods of not just English literature but the literature of many different languages during that time. He was a literary historian, and indeed he was that as well. During a time of growing emphasis upon the New Criticism in English-speaking circles, Lewis persisted as a literary historian in writing one of the most important volumes on literary history of the last century. He was a literary critic and theorist, and indeed he finally was that also. Besides being a literary historian, Lewis was a literary critic and theorist, by which I mean that he did not just chronicle the history of English literature, but he offered critical comments upon its authors and theorized about literature, how one should read it and interpret it and how one should enjoy it. Lewis was all these things, and probably many more besides.

In this chapter, I wish to survey and then assess the major works of literary history and criticism that Lewis wrote, that is, the book-length

---

1. For more information on Lewis and his life, see one or more of the several biographies. Among others, see Duriez, *Lewis* and McGrath, *Lewis*. For some of my previous thoughts on Lewis as a Christian thinker, see Porter, "C. S. Lewis's Worldview."

treatments. After all, even though Lewis is well-known as a Christian apologist, writer of children's literature, author of science fiction, and lay theologian, he made his living for nearly forty years as a literary scholar at the universities of Oxford and Cambridge. During that time, he wrote books of literary scholarship, numerous articles within the field, and engaged with other literary scholars on important literary topics of the day. Lewis had opinions on such matters, whether they were on selected authors or the broad sweeps of literary and secular history, and he did not hesitate to express those opinions. He expressed them in various ways, but often in trenchant articles and books that provided compelling, even if not always convincing, arguments regarding the authors, movements, and texts involved.

THE MAJOR LITERARY WORKS OF C. S. LEWIS

It may come as a surprise to know that Lewis only published seven books of literary scholarship during his lifetime, along with three volumes of collected essays and probably around thirty critical essays. These were posthumously followed by two more scholarly work and many volumes of collected essays. In this section, I will focus upon the published books, only mentioning articles and chapters as they are relevant.

The Allegory of Love (1936)

The Allegory of Love, published by Lewis in 1936, was his first book of literary scholarship, and it in many ways served to define his scholarly career, or at least the major components of that career, especially as a medievalist.[2] First of all, it is a complex work about how love, as evidenced in particular in courtly love, was conceptualized in the medieval world—he focuses upon the medieval notion of courtly love, as found in such authors as *The Romance of the Rose*, Chaucer (excluding *The Canterbury Tales*), John Gower's *Confessio Amantis*, Thomas Usk, and ultimately Edmund Spenser's *The Faerie Queen*—and expressed most clearly and well through allegory. He differentiates allegory from symbol—a point on which he has divided subsequent scholarship and been soundly criticized over the years[3]—because of

---

2. Lewis, *Allegory of Love* (reprinted several times since). On how Lewis became a medievalist, in the context of his major works on the topic, including *The Allegory of Love* and *The Discarded Image* (see below), see Yandell, "*Allegory of Love*."

3. See Adey, *Lewis*, 41. For critical response on other topics in *The Allegory of Love*, see esp. pp. 43–48.

his desire to identify and then describe the material and immaterial worlds. I will return to this worldview below. This work, secondly, defines Lewis because it is a book that draws upon a range of primary literature written in medieval English, Latin, Italian, Old French, besides scholarly literature in various languages. Lewis saw himself from the start and throughout his career as a medievalist—and had distinct views on the Middle Ages that I will mention further below—and his use of the variety of literature of the time meant that he drew upon more than simply one language's literature but the literature pertinent to an entire mindset and worldview. A third feature of this work is that it is highly textual. Lewis was, above all and throughout his career, a close reader of texts, even if he did not explicitly identify with the movement that identified itself with close readings, the so-called British practical criticism or American New Criticism.[4] Nevertheless, Lewis throughout the book meticulously examines texts that address his notion of the conception of love in the Middle Ages. A fourth feature—and one that would appear to be at odds with the previous one but is not—is that Lewis has a theme that he is developing in this work, as in all his works. Lewis's theme in *The Allegory of Love* is that conceptions of love in the Middle Ages, most dominantly expressed through allegory, provide the best means of describing the values and virtues, as well as shortcomings, of medieval human life. Lewis is an advocate for the notion of courtly love, not because of its features of adultery or similar, but because it captures a view of how love should be conceived and enacted and how these actions reflect its values of fidelity, devotion, courage, virtue, and the like.

This brings us almost immediately to one of the most important dimensions of Lewis's scholarship. Lewis is well known for his view regarding the relationship of the Middle Ages to the Renaissance. This view may come as a surprise when one learns that he was appointed to a personal chair in Medieval and Renaissance Literature at Cambridge University in 1954, the position he held until just before his death in 1963. Before that time, although he wrote and taught on a wide range of subjects in English literature, Lewis was known as a medievalist. In fact, he was known as a medievalist who had serious doubts about the Renaissance, certainly as a defining turning point in Western history and culture, the standard view in literature and history. What does Lewis mean by disputing the significance or even occurrence of the Renaissance, at least as usually conceived? In his

---

4. The literature on this approach to reading is voluminous. For a handy guide, see Stevens, *Literary Theory and Criticism*, 157–61.

later writing, Lewis refers to what he calls "the Model." The Model is the way that, he believes, medieval life (and later) was organized, not just as a social structure, but as much more than that, as an entire view of the universe, a cosmology, including God, humanity, and nature. In other words, Lewis subscribed to a form of what is often referred to as the "Great Chain of Being."[5] The Great Chain of Being—the title of a book also published in 1936—is a cosmological model that entwines, or enchains, everything within an appropriate hierarchy within the world. God stands at the top of the hierarchy, and within the hierarchy each element has its own hierarchy. This is where we get the idea that the lion is the king of the beasts and the eagle is the king of the birds, and of course the king is the first of the humans (origin of the notion of the divine right of kings) as a surrogate for God. This great chaining and intertwining is what establishes beliefs, order, and values in the cosmos. Lewis's argument is essentially that when the so-called Renaissance occurred, there were inevitably some changes that occurred, especially in such things as increase in knowledge of Greek, greater exploration and adventure, and the like. However, Lewis asserts that the major view of the universe—the medieval Model—remained virtually intact and unchanged (until the Enlightenment). Lewis apparently became convinced of this cosmological model and its persistence early in his career—and returned to it often—and was unmoved in his belief in it throughout the rest of his life.

This view of the Middle Ages is found in the first scholarly article that Lewis published. This article became very well-known and is still often anthologized and discussed by medievalists. The title of the article is, "What Chaucer Really Did to *Il Filostrato*" (1932).[6] This article was my introduction to Lewis the scholar. One of my undergraduate professors had intended to do his PhD under Lewis, but Lewis had the temerity to die before my teacher was able to commence his studies, so he studied elsewhere in the UK. My teacher was a fierce advocate for Lewis and offered a course in his creative literature. I did not take that course with that professor, but did take his course in literary criticism, which I enjoyed immensely. When I was doing my MA in English, my Chaucer professor was a medievalist who had known both Tolkien and Lewis. Despite being a secular Jew, my professor only spoke highly of Lewis and Tolkien. I was assigned to lead

---

5. Lovejoy, *Great Chain of Being*. The author claims this is the first intellectual history of the concept that dominated human thought from the ancients to the moderns.

6. Lewis, "What Chaucer Really Did to *Il Filostrato*."

the seminar in discussion of Lewis's article on *Il Filostrato*. *Il Filostrato* was written by the Italian Renaissance author Giovanni Boccacio in the fourteenth century based upon an earlier account from the thirteenth century by Benoit de Sainte-Maure, entitled *Le Roman de Troie*, and provided the inspiration for Chaucer's arguably best work, *Troilus and Criseyde*.[7] This is the story of two lovers from the city of Troy who were separated from each other over the division between the Greeks and the Trojans, and it provided inspiration for Shakespeare's play of the tragedy of *Troilus and Cressida*. The Troilus and Cressida story—now virtually unknown except perhaps by students of English literature—is one of the important stories of ancient life that has been transformed into medieval and Renaissance versions. This is what Lewis studied in his article, particularly the use of the story made by Chaucer of Boccaccio's version. Lewis argues, in effect, that Chaucer has medievalized the account and by doing so has enshrined within the version those features of the Model that are so important, including the nature of courtly love as virtue-filled and triumphing over human circumstance in its fidelity to genuine love. Lewis also saw this as a triumph of medievalism over Renaissance thought, with Chaucer's medieval account in his eyes challenging Boccaccio's. As some scholars have pointed out, however, there is an interesting chronological and conceptual lag between the two accounts based upon the relationship between the medieval and Renaissance periods and where they occurred. The Italian Renaissance occurred much earlier than the English Renaissance, with most pointing to the thirteenth century as the beginning of the Italian Renaissance and the fifteenth century for the British Renaissance. Boccaccio, along with such writers as Petrarch and Machiavelli, was a major writer of the Italian Renaissance that had already re-interpreted the conventions of medievalism within the new context of an increasingly secular state that rivaled the church. Chaucer, however, represented medieval Britain, with its religious and social conventions still firmly dominated by the church and courtly love firmly entrenched.[8] In that sense, it was not so much that Chaucer had improved upon the Renaissance in his re-medievalization—certainly he did not stop the Italian Renaissance—so much as he had retreated from it and attempted to reintroduce what had passed away within a society that had already moved beyond medieval conventions.

---

7. These versions, as well as Robert Henryson's *The Testament of Cresseid*, are found in Gordon, trans. and ed., *Story of Troilus*.

8. See Adey, *Lewis*, 51.

Part Three: Literature and Criticism

The Allegory of Love apparently won a prize awarded by the British Academy for the best work in early English literature, thus starting Lewis's career off on a positive note.[9]

The Personal Heresy with E. M. W. Tillyard (1939)

In 1939, Lewis published a book with the Cambridge English scholar E. M. W. Tillyard, entitled *The Personal Heresy*, expanding upon an exchange of articles from 1934 to 1936.[10] Tillyard was one of the most important scholars in English studies of his time, the first half of the twentieth century, and was an important scholar on Renaissance literature, including Shakespeare and John Milton.[11] In the history of literary criticism, there has been a long-standing debate about the centre of interpretive authority, that is, the basis of our understanding of literature. There are various ways that this debate has been chronicled. Much literary criticism, such as it was, from the ancient Greeks and Romans until the eighteenth century was mimetic. That is, works of literature were to be imitative of life, and one looked to the world either to confirm or deny the picture of reality presented. However, in the Enlightenment and especially beginning with Schleiermacher, Romantic criticism (sometimes referred to as Romantic-humanist criticism) highlighted the importance of the author, to the point that Schleiermacher argued that the purpose of interpretation was to know the mind of the author better than the author knew it themselves.[12] In the twentieth century, with the rise of practical criticism and the New Criticism, there was a shift to emphasis upon the text itself as the centre of authority. Then in the later twentieth century there was a further shift to emphasis upon the reader, with the rise of such things as reader-response criticism, bolstered in many ways by post-structuralism and what has often been called deconstruction.[13]

---

9. See McGrath, *Lewis*, 186.

10. Tillyard and Lewis, *Personal Heresy*, with the first three essays (two by Lewis and one by Tillyard) having appeared in *Essays and Studies* 19 (1934), 20 (1935), and 21 (1936).

11. His most well-known work is Tillyard, *Elizabethan World Picture*. This book is Tillyard's own take on the Great Chain of Being as described in Renaissance literature by such authors as Shakespeare, Donne, and Milton, among others. Cf. Adey, *Lewis*, 53, who notes that "Lewis's disbelief in the Renaissance seems less eccentric now than it did in 1954." As already noted, there were already many who, even if they did not dispute the Renaissance, saw strong lines of continuity with the Middle Ages.

12. Schleiermacher, *Hermeneutics and Criticism*, 23.

13. See my brief survey of these movements in Porter, "Literary Approaches," esp.

This linear view of the development of criticism is helpful, so far as it goes, but it fails to note that interpretation of texts has always been much more complex than that. This complexity is reflected in the dispute between Lewis and Tillyard. The dispute is over what was labelled by Lewis as the personal heresy. The personal heresy was a growing trend Lewis identified in the early part of the twentieth century that focused upon knowledge of the author, in terms of the author's characteristics, especially his personality, and even his psychology, as the locus of interpretive authority. The term "mental pattern" is sometimes used in the essays. This Romantic view was held by Tillyard. Lewis, on the other hand, held a view that did not believe that knowledge of the author as a person or as a personality was the basis of authority but that the text itself, in particular Milton's *Paradise Lost* (the inciting topic of discussion, although they ranged over a wide array of literature), was the locus of interpretation. In a series of articles, first published in a journal and then supplemented by further articles that went back and forth, Tillyard and Lewis presented and then refuted their differing views. By all accounts, Lewis prevailed in his arguments, although the engagement seemed to be done in good spirits and the two scholars seem to have retained their scholarly respect for each other. Lewis eventually joined Tillyard in Cambridge, although Tillyard fully retired not too many years later.

We notice several important factors present in Lewis's objective position. The first is its similarity to the New Criticism, with its view of the text as artefact.[14] For the New Criticism, the text is treated as an integral literary whole that sets the parameters for interpretation. Even though Lewis never overtly identified with such a position, we see that he held to a somewhat similar view very early in his career (apparently as early as his student days) and expresses it in this book with Tillyard. The second factor is that the personal heresy was associated with the question of the relation of the poet to his or her poetry, and as a result, was a view that exalted the view of the poet. Tillyard therefore took a view that judged poetry based upon the poet and believed that the poet was an extraordinary person with special gifts and abilities that commanded such response. Lewis, on the other hand, did not believe that one needed to know about who the poet was but that one

---

88–92.

14. See Calin, *Twentieth-Century Humanist Critics*, 92. Calin uses this and Lewis's views in *An Experiment in Criticism* (see below) for his defense of Lewis as a literary theorist, despite how Lewis would have wanted to see himself.

was to judge the poem based upon the poem itself to arrive at a view of its meaning.[15] Lewis took a view that left poetry open to the common person who did not have specialized knowledge of the author. A third factor is that Lewis recognized that within a poem there was an authorial voice but that this authorial voice was not necessarily to be equated with the poet. Thus, one can tell the differences between poems by differing authors, but this is through the presentation within the text, not through knowledge of the personality of the author. In this, Lewis clearly anticipates what later writers such as Wayne Booth and other narratological views would identify as the implied author and narrative voice as separate from the author him- or herself.[16]

Lewis seems to have held to this position of rejecting the influence of personality and related background issues and placing emphasis upon a more objective view of the text for the rest of his critical career (and in his theology), as similar viewpoints are reflected in other of his writings throughout his career.[17]

A Preface to Paradise Lost (1942)

Lewis's two favourite authors that he wrote on were Edmund Spenser and John Milton.[18] This may come as a surprise to some, especially since Lewis was a medievalist who looked down upon the notion of a Renaissance in discontinuity with the preceding period. Lewis's love for Spenser is predicated upon his seeing Spenser as an author who attempts to embody the allegory of love within his writings, which are enactments of the medieval mind and values, especially those of various virtues by means of pageantry representing various levels of thought from the mundane to the theological. Lewis's love for Milton is based upon the fact that Milton confronts some of the most important questions of human existence, especially questions that find their origins and home within the medieval world of belief and

---

15. This view is evidenced in Lewis's examination of Christopher Marlowe and George Chapman's *Hero and Leander*, a work with two authors and hence problematic for those who argue for interpretation based upon the author's personality. See Lewis, "Hero and Leander."

16. Booth, *Rhetoric of Fiction*, 71 and elsewhere.

17. See, e.g., Lewis, "Christianity and Culture" (1940); "Psycho-Analysis" (1941); "Poison of Subjectivism" (1943); "Parthenon" (1944); "Historicism" (1950); "Modern Theology" (1959); and "On Criticism" (1966), esp. 134–35. See also further discussion of other book-length literary critical works.

18. See Calin, *Twentieth-Century Humanist Critics*, 86 and n. 13.

thought, and then depicts them in representations that capture such virtues in characters that also reflect his allegorical view of life.

A Preface to Paradise Lost began as a series of lectures that Lewis delivered at the University College of North Wales in 1941 and was published in 1942.[19] In many ways, Lewis continues his discussion of the personal heresy in his treatment of Milton's *Paradise Lost* in that he argues against those who would claim that understanding *Paradise Lost* is contingent upon knowing and understanding the personality of Milton. Instead, Lewis argues for a non-personal, even objective, view that discusses a range of topics. Seven of the first eight chapters are concerned with the notion of epic and its appropriate style, especially as used by Milton. He raises the question of why Milton chose to write an epic, as opposed to, say, a tragedy or a lyric poem. He then distinguishes between primary and secondary epic, with primary epic including those of Homer. Secondary epic consists of those works that are fashioned after primary epics, such as Vergil's *Aeneid* or Milton's *Paradise Lost*. The two types of epic have differing styles that Lewis outlines, before defending Milton's use of the style that he does. Lewis then treats a variety of other topics in a series of brief chapters. These include many well-known topics from discussion of Milton, including his view of the human heart, his support of Milton's enchantment with a hierarchical view of the world, the theology of *Paradise Lost*, Satan and his followers, angels, and finally Adam and Eve, sexuality, and the fall. Perhaps most interesting are his discussions of the purpose of the work and of Satan. As he also indicates in *The Personal Heresy*, Lewis does not believe that Satan is the hero of the work, as have argued some others both before (notably Dryden)[20] and after Lewis. Milton's Satan may be a well-defined character, but he is ultimately a limited and evil figure to be resisted. This brings us to chapter 2 of the book, "Is Criticism Possible?" which is oddly placed in the midst of discussion of epic. This chapter is clearly addressed to T. S. Eliot's belief that only a poet can judge a poem, a view expressed in an essay Eliot published in 1936 that Lewis rejects. This chapter is clearly an attack on the Cambridge school of English, in particular, the views held by Eliot and developed further by F. R. Leavis, who did not have a high regard for Milton, at least at this time.

---

19. Lewis, *Preface to Paradise Lost*. See also Lewis, "Note on Comus."

20. Lewis is clearly not a fan of Dryden. See Lewis, "Shelley, Dryden and Mr. Eliot," where he also responds to Eliot's views in promoting Shelley over Dryden.

Lewis had a much higher regard for Milton than did Leavis and Eliot, although Eliot later lessened his criticism of Milton.[21]

The Abolition of Man (1947)

Lewis's book *The Abolition of Man* is not a work of literary history or criticism in the same way as his other books but considered by most to be a work of popular philosophy.[22] This book too is based on a series of lectures that he gave at the University of Durham, but it is devoted to the education system and the teaching of English, which merits its inclusion here. Lewis directly responds to a book that was widely used in English sixth-form colleges to teach English. In that book, the authors contend that value judgments are all merely personal judgments. Lewis responds to this by contending that such determinations lead to moral and ethical relativism and ultimately society's destruction (he along the way also attacks I. A. Richards's attempt to create a hierarchy of relative values).[23] Lewis instead claims that there are objective values, including in literary texts. In other words, this book too is part of his rejection of the personal heresy and an

---

21. See Adey, *Lewis*, 79–80, citing Eliot, *On Poetry and Poets*, reprinting two essays on Milton (1936, 1947), with the latter revising the views of the former (pp. 138–45, 146–61); and Leavis, *Revaluation*, 43–44. See Adey, *Lewis*, 81–84 for other criticism, especially by some New Critics. Cf. Barbour, "Lewis and Cambridge." Barbour's emphasis throughout is the opposition between Lewis and the Oxford approach to teaching English and Leavis and the Cambridge approach. There are many places where Lewis refers to scholars associated with Cambridge English, such as Richards, Leavis, and Empson (and to a limited extent Eliot). However, Calin (*Twentieth-Century Humanist Critics*, 98) is probably right that the situation was more complex than Barbour reflects, since there were boundaries crossed and mixed allegiances (e.g., Tillyard was not part of the Cambridge group, Eliot and Leavis had disagreements, and Leavis himself had many enemies in Cambridge). Another way to look at it is that Lewis took a stance opposed to those scholars and their positions who were associated with the New Criticism (although Lewis did have some similar beliefs) especially when they opposed the authors that he favoured (in particular Milton), and many of those happened to be associated with Cambridge, a very dynamic centre of English studies in Britain at the time. If a strong case is to be made for such antagonism, it was probably more pronounced in the period from 1934–1944 (see Barbour, "Lewis and Cambridge," 444–59) rather than from 1954 on. As Barbour points out, Lewis and Leavis did not have any personal animosity even when Lewis was a professor in Cambridge, but Lewis seems to have done everything he could to support Leavis (470–72).

22. Lewis, *Abolition of Man*. For a paper dealing with similar themes, see Lewis, "On Ethics" (see also the editor Hooper's note [47n1] regarding the relationship).

23. Richards, *Principles*. Richards is probably better known for and elsewhere challenged for his *Practical Criticism*.

argument on behalf of objective interpretation, in which judgments may be made of literature not based upon personal criteria or simply in relation to the author. For Lewis, literature has a capacity to convey and represent objective morality and ethics and not simply represent the personal values of the author. However, that is not Lewis's emphasis in this book. He instead appeals to the Confucian notion of the Tao or the laws by which humans should live, found not just in Confucius but in other thinkers as well (laid out in a lengthy appendix to the book). Lewis notes that even those who argue a subjective view must appeal to something as the basis of their thought, and he argues that outside of the Tao there is no basis for such a claim. Throughout his career—and this is something that Lewis especially develops in his Christian theology—he was an objectivist. That means that he believed in absolute values and that these values were able to be represented and conveyed through literature. He argues for such an objectivist view in his Christian apologetics and depicts the same in his fiction. In *The Abolition of Men*, one of the images that Lewis uses as a point of critique is what he calls "men without chests." In other words, he argues that men without chests are those without real character and strong beliefs and who do not uphold objective truths. He believes that literature is one of the ways in which these values are conveyed and that readers of texts should seek to discern these values.

English Literature in the Sixteenth Century (1954)

In the late 1930s, Lewis was asked to contribute a volume to the Oxford University Press History of English Literature. Lewis is often and rightly depicted as a literary historian, rather than a theoretician—although as we have seen, Lewis held a theoretical position that he developed early on and that he returned to in several of his writings regarding objectivism as opposed to personalism. The Oxford History of English Literature (OHEL) was a multi-volume work (twelve were originally envisioned, with fifteen in the final set) designed to provide an authoritative history of English literature from the medieval to the modern period. The project took much longer than envisioned and added volumes along the way. Lewis originally gladly accepted the offer to write on the literature of the sixteenth century excluding the drama (drama being one of the most important forms of literature of this time), since he often lectured on this literature, but the project dragged on much longer than he had hoped. The project took him over fifteen years to complete and along the way he wrote several letters in which he complained about the task and wished at times that the publisher would cancel his contract.[24] On more than one occasion, Lewis referred to the book project as OHEL. Based upon and a great expansion of lectures that Lewis originally gave in 1944 at Trinity College, Cambridge, Lewis nevertheless threw himself wholeheartedly into the project. To write it, he reportedly read everything written in the sixteenth century apart from drama that was held in the Oxford University Bodleian Library as the basis for his volume, which was finally completed and published in 1954.[25] This is the same year that he received his personal chair in Medieval and Renaissance Literature at Cambridge University. To mark the occasion of his assuming the chair, he delivered his inaugural lecture entitled "*De Descriptione Temporum.*"[26] This talk is Lewis's attempt to justify his receiving a chair in both medieval and Renaissance literature, especially since he disputes the notion of the Renaissance. He takes the occasion to contemplate aloud where he would draw the big divides in the epochs of history and concludes that virtually all of the lines of division have been arbitrarily and incorrectly drawn, and that the only one that can be drawn is one that separates the earlier and later periods at the nineteenth century.[27] In other words, according to Lewis, Jane Austen and Walter Scott have more in common with Shakespeare and even Homer, than we have with them.

Lewis's volume, entitled *English Literature in the Sixteenth Century Excluding Drama*, is one of the most enduring works of literary history and has stood the test of time for the last seventy years, even though it is in many ways a highly contentious and opinionated work.[28] It has been re-issued in several forms by Oxford University Press. Lewis provides a thorough and complete study of the major and minor works of the sixteenth century, in which he offers critical comments upon well-known

---

24. See the letter of January 25, 1938, in Hooper, *Lewis*, 477, written to F. P. Wilson, one of the series editors, during the volume's writing (476–82), used for the historical information above.

25. Lewis, *English Literature*. The work has now been re-titled in the Oxford History of English Literature series as *Poetry and Prose in the Sixteenth Century* (1990).

26. Lewis, "*De Descriptione Temporum.*"

27. A differentiation at around this time, especially the rise of Romanticism, seems to be one that is commonly held by those who argue for the importance of the concept of the Great Chain of Being.

28. Calin (*Twentieth-Century Humanist Critics*, 87) believes that Lewis's *English Literature* (1954) did more for Renaissance studies than it did for medieval studies, despite Lewis's efforts or beliefs.

authors and positively presents several lesser-known authors in new light. Not surprisingly, Lewis was not afraid to express his views about authors and literature. His sixty-five pages introduction is framed in terms of what he calls "new learning" and "new ignorance," which are categories he uses to trace developments within the sixteenth century. He essentially argues that much of what is called new learning or new science is exaggerated in its influence and effects, especially upon literature, and is countered by contrary developments. One of his major arguments is that there is not an opposition between puritans and humanists (if we define the terms as they were used then) but that often they were the same people. The humanists were marked by their use of Latin, with Greek learning not becoming significant until the nineteenth century. He ends up disputing the notion that we can differentiate an old and new age during the sixteenth century. We must keep in mind that this volume describes an important literary period within the framework in which Lewis disputes the Renaissance as occurring as a separate period from the Middle Ages. As a result, he divides the century into three periods: the Late Medieval period, the Drab Age, and the Golden Age. The first part is concerned with the late medieval period, first in Scotland (to which he devotes more space especially to poetry) and then England (upon which he has very little good to say of its poetry and less of its prose). The next two parts divide the bulk of sixteenth-century literature into those he calls Drab and those he calls Golden, terms that have been repeatedly discussed by critics since.[29] These are less time periods than kinds of literature. By this terminology, he does not necessarily mean bad or good writing but that which excels in finding right and new ways of expressing meaning in language. Lewis thought highly of many of the early Scottish writers but less so of many of the English authors of the time. He gives much more credence to Thomas More, William Tyndale, and Hugh Latimer as major English authors than had previous literary historians, although he says that the Book of Common Prayer is "the one glory of the Drab Age."[30] However, those who emerge as the most significant in Lewis's mind are Philip Sidney (whom he calls "dazzling")[31] and Edmund Spenser (on whom I say more below). He commends these authors as those who were the leaders of the Golden Age. Despite his tendency to favour the

---

29. For a discussion of critical response to Lewis's *English Literature*, as well as a defense of his terminology, see Williams, "*English Literature*," esp. 151–57.

30. Lewis, *English Literature*, 204.

31. Lewis, *English Literature*, 324.

Golden Age, Lewis does not hesitate to criticize when warranted. For example, he states that "William Webbe is in a class by himself, uniquely bad" and "display[s] an ignorance even then hardly credible."[32] Nevertheless, of Shakespeare he states that his "sonnets are the very heart of the Golden Age, the highest and purest achievement of the Golden way of writing."[33]

It is hard to know how to respond to a work such as this. Lewis is clearly encyclopedic in his knowledge of the period and does not hesitate to organize the writers within it according to his own unique scheme, in which he does not hesitate to offer evaluation of them and the importance of their writings.

Studies in Words (1960)

Studies in Words is the only of Lewis's books of literary criticism that went to two editions; all the others were only published in one edition.[34] This may surprise those of us who are used to reading many later reprints or editions of Lewis's works of fiction or apologetics, which, if not in multiple editions, are certainly in many reprints. What makes *Studies in Words* even more surprising is the kind of book that it is. This book is, as the title says, a collection of a few studies of different words. For those of us in disciplines such as biblical studies familiar with the problems of word studies as pointed out in the classic work by James Barr, *The Semantics of Biblical Language*, published soon afterwards, Lewis's work will raise many questions, and indeed it should.[35]

In this volume, Lewis identifies several words—perhaps better a collection of English words under which are treated a selection of other words, including Greek, Latin, and related—that represent related concepts. Lewis makes clear from the outset of this work that he is not writing a work of what he calls "higher linguistics."[36] For those who know the field of linguistics, one might somewhat cynically say that he is not writing a work

---

32. Lewis, *English Literature*, 429.

33. Lewis, *English Literature*, 502. Note that Lewis says, "In certain senses of the word 'love', Shakespeare is not so much our best as our only love poet" (505). Lewis was excluded by mandate from treating drama in his volume. For his view of Shakespeare's *Hamlet*, see Lewis, "Variation"; and Lewis, "Hamlet," where he offers an expansive reading of the play.

34. Lewis, *Studies in Words*.

35. Barr, *Semantics of Biblical Language*.

36. Lewis, *Studies in Words*, vii.

of lower linguistics either. In other words, his study of words is not the kind of study that one might find in most works within the field of lexical semantics as part of the wider field of linguistics. Such studies are typically characterized as being either conceptual studies focused upon semantic domains or semantic fields, within which the different semantically related lexemes are categorized and discussed in relation to each other (such as synonymy, antonymy, etc.); or lexical studies of the behaviour of individual lexemes, their collocations, and their resultant meaning or meanings.

Instead, Lewis's treatments are diachronic studies that are concerned to establish the history of a concept and how it is expressed in a variety of words in different languages throughout the course of its development as an aid to reading of books, especially older ones.[37] This means, for example, that when Lewis studies "Nature," as his first entry, he begins by discussing the Greek word *physis* and then the Latin *natura*, before moving to other, related words, such as "kind" and its relationship to such words as *genos*. In effect, Lewis provides extended entries that one might find in a highly expansive conceptual dictionary constructed along the lines of the Oxford English Dictionary, which had been produced from 1884 to 1928, but reaching much further back than the earliest forms of English to the etymological and historical roots of each word and then tracing how these concepts and their related words are used especially in the English language. Lewis provides etymological reconstructions that he admits may surprise his readers as they discover that the "meaning" of a word that they think they know well may originate in a different semantic environment that appears, at least at first glance, to be unrelated to the later usage. Lewis provides discussions of such word/concepts as "Nature" with *physis*, kind, and physical, "Sad" with *gravis*, "Wit" with *ingenium*, "Free" with *eleutherios*, liberal, frank, "Sense" with sentence, sensibility, and sensible, "Simple," and "Consciences and Conscious" in the first edition, later expanded with "World," "Life," "I Dare Say," and "At the Fringe of Language," with the last chapter clarifying his purpose. One of Lewis's recurring objects of criticism is William Empson, who he believes went too far in his own attempt to deal with words.[38]

As in his previous work, Lewis is concerned, not with the personal heresy, but with objectification in language. There is no success in an author simply asserting that a word or line or phrase is emotive. Such a state of

---

37. See Calhoun, "C. S. Lewis," esp. 93.
38. Empson, *Structure of Complex Words*. See Adey, *Lewis*, 101–2.

emotion must be objectively depicted in the written work.[39] Lewis's goal is to provide the kind of objective knowledge of words that allows authors (and readers) to understand how to convey genuine emotion within their work without it being dependent upon the author.

An Experiment in Criticism (1961)

This final volume written and published by Lewis during his lifetime, *An Experiment in Criticism*,[40] is his longest and most provocative statement about reading and is arguably his major, perhaps his only, work of literary theory.[41] In some ways, his approach to reading is very similar to his earlier statements about objective readings, a theme that he developed early and apparently maintained throughout his academic career. However, this work also departs from his previous approach to reading by making a much stronger case for the role of the reader in interpretation, despite an overt distancing of his approach from what he calls the therapeutic approach of I. A. Richards and presumably other New Critics.[42] In fact, the major focus of this work is upon the reader and the reader's relationship to the literary text. Lewis differentiates two kinds of readers in this book. The one kind of reader is the one who enjoys popular writings and reads them once and for whom reading is not a habit or a preference and does not change their life. The other kind of reader is one who reads—and has read—the serious works of literature from a young age and who not just reads them once but reads them again and again and whose life is transformed by such literary works, to the point that they live lives in which they are transfixedly immersed in such literature. The first kind of reader abounds but the second is in a clear minority.

There are several observations to make about Lewis's *Experiment in Criticism*. The first is that he integrates the notion of objectivity in

---

39. Lewis, *Studies in Words*, 317–18.

40. Lewis, *Experiment in Criticism*.

41. See Edwards and Edwards, "'Everyman's Tutor,'" esp. 166; see 166–73, where the authors place *An Experiment in Criticism* in relation to Lewis's other major potentially theoretical works and the New Criticism.

42. See Calin, *Twentieth-Century Humanist Critics*, 93, where he sees Lewis as anticipating reader-response theory (Wolfgang Iser), sociology of literature (Raymond Williams), and reception theory (Hans Robert Jauss), but with some reservations (96–100). As Calin notes, not all scholars see such an emphasis in Lewis at this point. For example, see Edwards, "Deconstruction and Rehabilitation." Edwards's opposition to the New Criticism is clear. See Adey, *Lewis*, 92–94.

interpretation into objectivity of experience of the reader. Lewis's characterization may appear to be a highly subjective one simply regarding tastes. However, for Lewis, the kinds of tastes and likes and dislikes reflected in the two different kinds of readers are a world apart. What it means for most readers to like a literary work is categorically different from what it means for the minority to like a literary work. The difference is found in their relationship to literature. The second observation is that Lewis takes an essentialist view of literature. By this, I mean that he believes that there is such a thing as literature that is not simply the result of social convention or community assent. Even though most readers might read individual works in particular ways, it does not, for Lewis, indicate that these readers are readers of literature. To the contrary, literature belongs to a class of undefined but relatively easily knowable texts that are savoured by the minority, regardless of what the majority might do. This view of literature is consistent with Lewis's view of objective interpretation. That a scene is depicted as beautiful in a work of literature is not simply the product of the author's personal desire to convey beauty but is to be found within the text by the reader, and it conveys an objective sense of beauty. The same holds true for a literary work—it has an objective status as literature regardless of social conventions that may or may not reflect the same beliefs regarding it within the wider public as are held by the literary minority and it reveals what Lewis characterizes as "truths of life."[43]

The Discarded Image (1964 posthumous)

The Discarded Image was finished by Lewis in July 1962, according to the preface. However, the book did not appear in print until 1964, making it thus the first of his posthumously published works of literary thought and criticism.[44] *The Discarded Image* reflects lectures that Lewis made over the course of much of his career, and hence some of his material dates back to ideas that he had lectured on from the beginning of his teaching career concerning medieval and Renaissance literature.[45] Whereas *The Allegory of Love* assumes the medieval cosmology and Lewis develops this further in subsequent works, in *The Discarded Image*, he focuses upon the major elements of the medieval cosmology or the Model. This remains Lewis's

43. Lewis, *Experiment in Criticism*, 130.
44. Lewis, *Discarded Image*.
45. This makes it surprising that he elicited such strong response from some scholars of the time. See Adey, *Lewis*, 62–64.

fullest and most developed statement on what the Model entailed and how it relates to the literature of that time.[46]

Lewis believed that the medieval situation was unique and unparalleled. This provided a unique and ripe situation in the twelfth century or so for the emergence of medievalism. In an early section, Lewis speaks of the uniqueness of the Middle Ages as being an age of unity and distinction. He traces the roots of this age to the late classical age, especially the early days of Christianity, such as the third to the fifth centuries. These centuries established the ways in which humanity chose to live. There is a sense in which Lewis is an Aristotelian with his emphasis upon organization and hierarchy.

The second major part of the book is on major writers who helped to define the period. These include Chalcidius, Macrobius, Pseudo-Dionysius, and Boethius. The traits of human life are informally paired with features of the heavens. As Lewis states, "In medieval science the fundamental concept was that of certain sympathies, antipathies, and strivings inherent in matter itself. Everything has its right place, its home, the region that suits it, and, if not forcibly restrained, moves thither by a sort of homing instinct."[47] Out of these pairings comes the so-called four humours by which matter is defined. As noted above, what Lewis is referring to in his cosmological model is what was elsewhere labeled the Great Chain of Being (by Lovejoy and Tillyard, among others). This means that all originates with God as the prime mover who causes the planets to rotate by means of their love of God. The universe is motivated by both God's love and its love of God, so that love and God are identified with the cosmos.

The inhabitants of earth also participate in the divinely ordered cosmos, to the point of there being a terrestrial intelligence, what Lewis calls Fortune. This intelligence is what determines the rise and fall of nations. The medieval person believed that the earth was round—an idea not displaced until later—but that Jerusalem was its centre, as reflected in maps of the time. The human being is a creature who contains a mix of heavenly beings and earthly beings, that is, angels and animals, combining rationality and physicality. Rationality is related to the intellect, while the physical side of the body reflects the four humours. The human is thus a kind of microcosm.

---

46. Lewis provides a summary of the same view as in *The Discarded Image* in Lewis, "Imagination and Thought," and to a lesser degree, in Lewis, "*De Audiendis Poetis.*"

47. Lewis, *Discarded Image*, 92.

Lewis sees this model as being in place from ancient times until long past what is called the Renaissance. Whatever may have happened in the Renaissance, the cosmological model was not displaced until long after, as is evidenced in such Renaissance authors as Milton. Lewis includes here a discussion of the liberal arts because of their relevance for understanding the literature that undergirds this model. These consist of the trivium and the quadrivium. These seven liberal arts were not just considered the basis of education, much like our current curricula, with their general education courses or majors, etc. For the medieval mind, the liberal arts were immutable as they were the foundation of all knowledge. The trivium consisted of grammar, dialectic, and rhetoric. Lewis believes that these three liberal arts are much more than just the basis of a classical or humanist education but even more fundamental, in that grammar stood for language itself, dialectic for logic or thought, and rhetoric for the practical art of application that came to represent the study of literature. The quadrivium consisted of arithmetic, music, geometry, and astronomy. Lewis somewhat surprisingly passes over these quickly as they have little to do with literature. However, a moment's thought will reveal that they are integral to the cosmological model that Lewis outlines—a model that is arithmetically balanced, resounds with the music of the spheres, is geometrically well-fashioned, and only fully perceived by means of astronomy.

Lewis is not so narrow in his focus as to herald the cosmological model as without fault. He recognizes that it had its day—even if that day was a much longer day than most have realized—and that it had its limitations. It did not provide the kind of imagination as did a William Wordsworth, whom Lewis characterizes as having a "transforming imagination," or a Shakespeare, whom Lewis characterizes as having a "penetrative imagination." But it did have a "realising imagination," that is, an imagination that was embraced by those who lived within it.[48] It had a structure and a form that reflected "the wisdom and goodness that created it,"[49] but it does so in such a way that is transparent in the best literature of its age in that one sees the world through it but without seeing it. When comparing it with the modern age—which Lewis sees as being behaviouristic and subject-centred, to the point that "we only think that we think"—Lewis sees the

---

48. Lewis, *Discarded Image*, 206.
49. Lewis, *Discarded Image*, 204.

contemporary result as self-consuming and envisions, by contrast, a dark future.[50]

Lewis concludes with an interesting epilogue. He says that he admits that he was attracted to the cosmological model because of its grandeur and orderliness. However, he also admits that it was not true. However, he then notes that nineteenth- and twentieth-century (and now twenty-first-century) discoveries are beginning to look more and more like the medieval cosmological model as we are able to envision mental models of worlds unseen, mathematical means of recreation that give insights into imaginative worlds, and conceptions of a universe that has shapes and forms that resemble the kind of world conceived of by the medieval mind. His point is not that he wishes to return to the old model, but that our models influence how we see things but are also always fashioned according to our age, and that many of the patterns that we may be tempted to see as new to us have in fact been envisioned before.

Spenser's Images of Life (1967 posthumous)

The final work, also posthumous, is on Edmund Spenser. Along with Milton, Spenser was the author that Lewis thought and wrote most about.[51] He apparently intended to write a book on Spenser and had lectured on him but died with only the notes of such lectures. These were turned into a book of literary criticism by the English scholar Alastair Fowler, who took Lewis's notes and expanded them into a relatively brief and concise treatment of Spenser entitled *Spenser's Images of Life*, focusing upon *The Fairie Queene*.[52] Spenser is not most people's favourite author these days, and he was not most people's favourite in Lewis's lifetime, either. Lewis begins by acknowledging the difficulties. They reside in the fact that Spenser's writings exist on two levels—they are a complex allegory. The story itself, though incomplete and divided into parts, is relatively straightforward, if one can make it through the often-complex poetry, and it appeals to those with romantic inclinations. However, the allegory also exists on other levels, and this is where the difficulty lies. This second level makes great use of a variety of means to convey its symbolism. Lewis refers to this as Pageantry, which

---

50. Lewis, *Discarded Image*, 215.

51. For example, apart from sections in his previous books, see Lewis, "Edmund Spenser" (1941); "On Reading *The Faerie Queene*" (1941); "Spenser's Cruel Cupid"; and "Genius and Genius" (1936).

52. Lewis, *Spenser's Images of Life*.

can be found in numerous forms, including the kind of pageantry found in the fifteenth-century court, tournament pageantry, masque, traditional images of gods that range over a variety of traditions (not just classical), hieroglyphs and other emblems, and philosophical icons. Lewis believes that the readers of Spenser would have been familiar with much of this pageantry. However, to be familiar with it means that one is drawn into a complex world of theology, philosophy, politics, and more.

Lewis attempts to lay out many of the images that Spenser treats and to explicate them. He discusses the False Cupid and its antitypes; Belphoebe, Amoret, and the garden of Adonis; evil; mutability; the image of good; the dream of Britomart; faceless knights; Florimell; and the Arthurian story. The Arthurian story may be the most familiar to contemporary readers, although it is complex with pagan and Christian symbolism, not untypical of Spenser. On many occasions, Lewis delves into a scene only to reveal the complexity of the layers of allegory and symbolism that Spenser uses.

COMMENTS AND CRITIQUE

The question that has been raised by various scholars is what kind of literary scholar Lewis was. There have been several studies of Lewis's literary history and criticism. Lionel Adey, for example, emphasizes the psychological elements of Lewis's work,[53] while William Calin places Lewis within the panoply of twentieth-century humanist scholars, such as Leo Spitzer, Ernst Robert Curtius, Erich Auerbach, Albert Béguin, Jean Sousset, F. O. Matthiesssen, and Northrop Frye—those scholars who resisted the interpretive and critical hegemony of the New Criticism (although we have seen that Lewis is not too far removed from their interests in some instances). Lewis is anthologized alongside a variety of scholars in various collections of critical comments on individual authors, many of them New Critics, but that is perhaps because the age was dominated by New Critics, even if Lewis was sometimes an outlier.[54]

Calin is probably right in placing Lewis within what we might call humanist critics for several reasons. The first is his emphasis upon literary history. Lewis was a writer of literary history as much as he was anything

---

53. Adey, *Lewis*, 40–106.

54. For examples from near the time of Lewis's living and writing, see Lewis, "What Chaucer Really Did to *Il Filostrata*" (cited above); "Addison" (1945); "Donne and Love Poetry" (1938); and "Style of Secondary Epic" (1942) excerpted from his *Preface to Paradise Lost*.

else. His major work on the sixteenth century was a work in literary history that still commands respect, even if most scholars would want to move beyond his characterization of authors as drab or golden. Lewis's *Allegory of Love* is an exercise in literary history as well. The second is that Lewis is not just concerned to offer critical readings of authors—although he does that often, regularly, and well[55]—but he is also concerned to place these authors within the world in which they wrote. From first to last work, Lewis is concerned to see his authors as those who reflected and influenced the age in which they lived. A third reason is that Lewis invested his greatest literary efforts in defining a cosmological model and arguing for its continuing relevance from the Middle Ages to the Renaissance, to the point that its perseverance called into question the independence of the Renaissance as a separate and unique period of literary history. This is what Lewis is probably still best remembered for. Many of his major works, from *The Allegory of Love* to *English Literature in the Sixteenth Century* to especially *The Discarded Image*, are driven by his favourable view of the medieval cosmology into which he places those authors that he favours most, especially Spenser and Milton.

Having said that, I still believe it is worth noting Lewis's literary critical contribution. Although he was not a New Critic, he shared some of the New Critical inclinations. Whereas the New Criticism reflected analytic philosophy, in particular logical positivism, and its attempt to identify empirical facts in the form of literary facts, Lewis rejected personalist views of interpretation as part of a romantic view of interpretation and argued for interpretive objectivism. His notion of objectivism moved away from the idea of the author as the locus of interpretive authority and toward the text. For Lewis, however, he moved to the text but went deeper to a reality that he believed underlay the text itself.[56] Whereas the New Critics gave the text ontological status, Lewis believed that there were deeper truths, even divine ones. His objectivism was not focused upon just the structure or form or artifactual integrity of a literary text, but an actual object of concrete existence upon which one could establish meanings apart from authors and their personal beliefs or even interpreters and their subjective responses. In that regard, Lewis was an objectivist New Critic who for the most part—although not entirely—rejected the move to the reader as

---

55. Calin, *Twentieth-Century Humanist Critics*, 90, who regards Lewis as an excellent practical critic.

56. See Adey, *Lewis*, 92–93.

interpretive authority. Nevertheless, Lewis wished to differentiate types of readers, and he placed higher value on those readers who savoured and re-read texts and whose lives were affected by them. But for Lewis, these were readers who focused upon texts that had essentialist properties of literary quality that demanded and rewarded such focused attention.

The final question to ask is how Lewis will be judged in the long term as a literary historian and critic. Insofar as his literary history is concerned, I think the judgment is mixed although generally favourable. Lewis was clearly a historian of strong opinions, especially regarding the rejection of personalism and the embrace of objectivism, and this had a strong effect on his thinking. However, he was not afraid to make literary judgments, by which he elevated authors who perhaps had been overlooked while not simply accepting and lauding authors that he did not believe merited such attention. However, his major contribution to literary history is his strong advocacy for the cosmological model that he traced from ancient times even to the present, with its high point in the Middle Ages and Renaissance. This cosmological model is directly reflective of what might be called a Christian epoch, and this perhaps accounts for at least part of Lewis's favour toward it, although it is also entirely possible that this model had an even stronger influence on Lewis's seeing the hand of God in the cosmos and how this empowered humans in their literary endeavours.

As far as literary criticism or theory is concerned, I think that Lewis does not fare so well. Whereas his dispute with Tillyard over the personal heresy was an important one at the time, and he continued to promote his objective views in his later work, the kinds of issues that Lewis and Tillyard raised are not nearly as current as others within literary criticism. The kinds of philosophical, ideological, and literary critical models that are currently discussed are not confined to the romantic-versus-objective paradigm that Lewis debated. However, with the rise of the New Historicism there are points of contact with Lewis as a historical critic who wishes to recognize the place of authors within their literary contexts as important for interpretation.[57] Insofar as the New Historicism is influenced by Marxism, however, Lewis would part company with them as he rejected such a Marxist influence and viewpoint as important for literary creation and interpretation. In his final major work of literary criticism, his *An Experiment in Criticism*, Lewis is clearly at odds with most literary criticism in his return to a kind of common sense and essentialist criticism. Even though

---

57. See Stevens, *Literary Theory*, 180–85.

he emphasizes the reader, the reader is here not the creator of meaning so much as the consumer, even devourer, of meaning, especially good literature. This ties in well with Lewis's advocacy of the trivium and quadrivium as fundamental to the liberal arts, and perhaps says all we need to know about Lewis and his view of the reader within the wider world.

CONCLUSION

C. S. Lewis was a masterful writer, a keen thinker, an imaginative literary historian, and a competent literary critic. Even though he is far less well known in most circles today for his literary history and criticism than he is for his works of children's literature, fantasy, science fiction, and Christian apologetics, his body of literary related work still merits consideration. Even though some of his ideas are now out of favour, so far as mainstream criticism is concerned, many of his ideas are still worth considering as providing important interpretive frameworks for assessing the English and related literary tradition. In any case, Lewis remains a major figure in literary history and interpretation whose works reward close attention as they offer insights into many of the major figures in the English literary tradition.

BIBLIOGRAPHY

Adey, Lionel. *C. S. Lewis: Writer, Dreamer, and Mentor*. Grand Rapids: Eerdmans, 1998.
Barbour, Brian. "Lewis and Cambridge." *Modern Philology* 96 (1999) 439–84.
Barr, James. *The Semantics of Biblical Language*. Oxford: Oxford University Press, 1961.
Booth, Wayne C. *The Rhetoric of Fiction*. Chicago: University of Chicago Press, 1961.
Calhoun, Scott. "C. S. Lewis as Philologist: Studies in Words." In *C. S. Lewis: Life, Works, and Legacy, Volume 4*, edited by Bruce L. Edwards, 81–98. Westport, CT: Praeger, 2007.
Calin, William. *The Twentieth-Century Humanist Critics: From Spitzer to Frye*. Toronto: University of Toronto Press, 2007.
Duriez, Colin. *C. S. Lewis: A Biography of Friendship*. Oxford: Lion, 2013.
Edwards, Bruce L., Jr. "Deconstruction and Rehabilitation: C. S. Lewis' Defense of Western Textuality." *Journal of the Evangelical Theological Society* 29 (1986) 205–14.
Edwards, Michael I., and Bruce L. Edwards. "'Everyman's Tutor': C. S. Lewis on Reading and Criticism." In *C. S. Lewis: Life, Works, and Legacy, Volume 4*, edited by Bruce L. Edwards, 163–94. Westport, CT: Praeger, 2007.
Eliot, T. S. *On Poetry and Poets*. London: Faber and Faber, 1957.
Empson, William. *The Structure of Complex Words*. 1951. Reprint, London: Hogarth, 1985.
Gordon, R. K., trans. and ed. *The Story of Troilus*. 1934. Reprint, Toronto: University of Toronto Press, 1978.
Hooper, Walter. *C. S. Lewis: A Companion and Guide*. San Francisco: HarperSanFrancisco, 1996.

Leavis, F. R. *Revaluation: Tradition and Development in English Poetry*. London: Penguin, 1936.

Lewis, C. S. *The Abolition of Man: Or Reflections on Education with Special Reference to the Teaching of English in the Upper Forms of Schools*. New York: Macmillan, 1947.

———. "Addison." In *Eighteenth Century English Literature: Modern Essays in Criticism*, edited by James L. Clifford, 144–57. New York: Oxford University Press, 1959.

———. *The Allegory of Love: A Study in Medieval Tradition*. Oxford: Oxford University Press, 1936.

———. "Christianity and Culture." In *Christian Reflections*, edited by Walter Hooper, 12–36. Grand Rapids: Eerdmans, 1967.

———. "De Audiendis Poetis." In *Studies in Medieval and Renaissance Literature*, edited by Walter Hooper, 1–17. Cambridge: Cambridge University Press, 1966.

———. "De Descriptione Temporum." In *They Asked for a Paper: Papers and Essays*, 9–25. London: Geoffrey Bles, 1962.

———. *The Discarded Image: An Introduction to Medieval and Renaissance Literature*. Cambridge: Cambridge University Press, 1964.

———. "Donne and Love Poetry in the Seventeenth Century." In *Seventeenth Century English Poetry: Modern Essays in Criticism*, edited by William B. Keast, 92–110. New York: Oxford University Press, 1962.

———. "Edmund Spenser, 1552–99." In *Studies in Medieval and Renaissance Literature*, edited by Walter Hooper, 121–45. Cambridge: Cambridge University Press, 1966.

———. *English Literature in the Sixteenth Century Excluding Drama*. Oxford History of English Literature. Oxford: Clarendon, 1954.

———. *An Experiment in Criticism*. Cambridge: Cambridge University Press, 1961.

———. "Genius and Genius." In *Studies in Medieval and Renaissance Literature*, edited by Walter Hooper, 169–74. Cambridge: Cambridge University Press, 1966.

———. "Hamlet: The Prince or The Poem?" In *They Asked for a Paper: Papers and Essays*, 51–71. London: Geoffrey Bles, 1962.

———. "Historicism." In *Christian Reflections*, edited by Walter Hooper, 100–13. Grand Rapids: Eerdmans, 1967.

———. "Hero and Leander." *Proceedings of the British Academy* 28 (1952) 23–37.

———. "Imagination and Thought in the Middle Ages." In *Studies in Medieval and Renaissance Literature*, edited by Walter Hooper, 41–63. Cambridge: Cambridge University Press, 1966.

———. "Modern Theology and Biblical Criticism" (1959). In *Christian Reflections*, edited by Walter Hooper, 152–66. Grand Rapids: Eerdmans, 1967.

———. "A Note on Comus." In *Studies in Medieval and Renaissance Literature*, edited by Walter Hooper, 175–81. Cambridge: Cambridge University Press, 1966.

———. "On Criticism." In *Of Other Worlds: Essays and Stories*, edited by Walter Hooper, 43–58. New York: Harcourt Brace Jovanovich, 1966.

———. "On Ethics." In *Christian Reflections*, edited by Walter Hooper, 44–56. Grand Rapids: Eerdmans, 1967.

———. "On Reading *The Faerie Queene*." In *Studies in Medieval and Renaissance Literature*, edited by Walter Hooper, 146–48. Cambridge: Cambridge University Press, 1966.

———. "The Parthenon and the Optative." In *On Stories and Other Essays on Literature*, edited by Walter Hooper, 109–12. San Diego: Harcourt Brace Jovanovich, 1982.

Part Three: Literature and Criticism

———. "The Poison of Subjectivism." In *Christian Reflections*, edited by Walter Hooper, 72–81. Grand Rapids: Eerdmans, 1967.
———. *The Preface to Paradise Lost*. London: Oxford University Press, 1942.
———. "Psycho-Analysis and Literary Criticism." In *They Asked for a Paper: Papers and Essays*, 120–38. London: Geoffrey Bles, 1962.
———. "Shelley, Dryden and Mr. Eliot." In *Rehabilitations and Other Essays*, 1–34. Oxford: Oxford University Press, 1939.
———. "Spenser's Cruel Cupid." In *Studies in Medieval and Renaissance Literature*, edited by Walter Hooper, 164–68. Cambridge: Cambridge University Press, 1966.
———. *Spenser's Images of Life*. Edited by Alastair Fowler. Cambridge: Cambridge University Press, 1967.
———. *Studies in Words*. Cambridge: Cambridge University Press, 1960. 2nd ed., 1967.
———. "The Style of Secondary Epic." In *Milton: A Collection of Critical Essays*, edited by Louis L. Martz, 40–55. Englewood Cliffs, NJ: Prentice-Hall, 1966.
———. "Variation in Shakespeare and Others." In *Rehabilitations and Other Essays*, 161–80. Oxford: Oxford University Press, 1939.
———. "What Chaucer Really Did to *Il Filostrato*." *Essays and Studies* 17 (1932) 56–74.
Lovejoy, Arthur O. *The Great Chain of Being: A Study of the History of an Idea*. 1936. Reprint, New York: Harper & Row, 1960.
McGrath, Alister. *C. S. Lewis—A Life: Eccentric Genius, Reluctant Prophet*. Carol Stream, IL: Tyndale House, 2013.
Porter, Stanley E. "C. S. Lewis's Worldview and his Literary Criticism." *McMaster Journal of Theology and Ministry* 16 (2014–2015) 3–50.
———. "Literary Approaches to the New Testament: From Formalism to Deconstruction and Back." In *Approaches to New Testament Study*, edited by Stanley E. Porter and David Tombs, 77–128. Journal for the Study of the New Testament Supplement Series 120. Sheffield: Sheffield Academic, 1995.
Richards, I. A. *Practical Criticism: A Study of Literary Judgment*. New York: Harcourt & Brace, 1929.
———. *Principles of Literary Criticism*. London: Routledge & Kegan Paul, 1924.
Schleiermacher, Friedrich. *Hermeneutics and Criticism and Other Writings*. Edited and translated by Andrew Bowie. Cambridge: Cambridge University Press, 1998.
Stevens, Anne H. *Literary Theory and Criticism: An Introduction*. 2nd ed. Kingston, ON: Broadview, 2021.
Tillyard, E. M. W. *The Elizabethan World Picture*. London: Macmillan, 1942.
Tillyard, E. M. W., and C. S. Lewis. *The Personal Heresy: A Controversy*. Oxford: Oxford University Press, 1939.
Williams, Donald T. "*English Literature in the Sixteenth Century*: C. S. Lewis as a Literary Historian." In *C. S. Lewis: Life, Works, and Legacy, Volume 4*, edited by Bruce L. Edwards, 143–62. Westport, CT: Praeger, 2007.
Yandell, Stephen. "*The Allegory of Love* and *The Discarded Image*: C. S. Lewis as Medievalist." In *C. S. Lewis: Life, Works, and Legacy, Volume 4*, edited by Bruce L. Edwards, 117–42. Westport, CT: Praeger, 2007.

C. S. Lewis and the Art of Criticism

AARON JUNG

INTRODUCTION

WHAT KIND OF LITERARY *critic* was C. S. Lewis? His unique perspective as a literary critic is articulated in his relatively less well-known work *An Experiment in Criticism*, making it an essential volume for anyone interested in Lewis's literary criticism. Published in 1961, this work emerged during a period marked by the proliferation of a multitude of literary approaches, such as existentialism, Russian Formalism, Prague Circle, Frankfurt School, New Criticism, archetypal criticism, feminist criticism, Marxist criticism, Chicago School, deconstruction, and so forth, each of which was shaped, practiced, and waned under the influence of their contemporary philosophical, social, and cultural paradigms.[1] Given this backdrop, it is natural for literary enthusiasts to anticipate a discussion from Lewis's work that delves into technical debates on textual interpretation, reflecting the prevailing scholarly rigour of the time. However, somewhat

---

1. These critical movements operated within diverse socio-political contexts, encompassing distinct academic focuses, theoretical emphases, and spheres of influence. As a result, they cannot always be sharply delineated from one another and, at times, even overlap. Some of these movements embodied expansive intellectual traditions, while others pursued more narrowly defined, specialized approaches or functioned as schools of thought rooted in geographical and cultural contexts. Their historical trajectories also varied—existentialism, for example, evolved from the nineteenth century, whereas deconstruction only began to emerge in the mid-twentieth century. Nevertheless, by the mid-twentieth century, these diverse intellectual currents were not only interacting and competing but also significantly shaping and transforming the landscape of literary studies.

unexpectedly, his work lacks clarity in articulating specific methodologies or formal techniques of literary criticism. Instead, he advocates an interpretive approach that prioritizes an appreciation of the text's intrinsic beauty, thereby aligning, in certain respects, with the Romantic emphasis on aesthetic experience.[2] While he upholds an objective view of literary texts, he deliberately avoids excessively technical and analytical methodologies, urging readers to approach literary works with an open mind and to appreciate them in their own right. To contemporary readers accustomed to highly technical modern literary criticism, Lewis's approach may come as an unexpected yet insightful lesson.

However, the purpose of this study is not to encapsulate or critically evaluate Lewis's argument in *Experiment in Criticism*. Rather, the focus is on Lewis's exhortation for readers to fully immerse themselves in the text, appreciating its beauty in tandem with the author's creative spirit—an approach that resonates with what we perceive as significant in the appreciation of artworks. These significant elements not only enrich the aesthetic experience for both general audiences and professional critics but also influence the assessment of the intrinsic value of both tangible and intangible artworks. With this perception, the present study aims to explore the intersections between Lewis's aesthetic approach and the broader field of human art criticism, offering fresh insights into the scholarly practice of literary studies.

INTO THE EXPERIMENT

Key Concepts

Before one delves into the main discussion about *art* and *literary criticism*, it is essential to clarify the nuanced meanings and interrelations of these key concepts given their multifaceted semantic range and the potential for varying interpretations. The origins of literary criticism can be traced to antiquity, where ancient Greek philosophy framed the critique of both art and literature through the concepts of μίμησις (*mimēsis*) and ποίησις (*poiēsis*). In *Poetica*, Aristotle contends that art, including literature, imitates life not simply to replicate it but to uncover universal truths and convey moral lessons—a mimetic and semi-normative understanding that persisted in

---

2. However, this appreciation is not grounded in the reader's subjectivity, which ultimately distinguishes Lewis's perspective from Romanticism.

religious and moral modes of interpretation until the Enlightenment. The emergence of modern literary criticism, however, is frequently linked to Matthew Arnold, particularly his influential essay "The Function of Criticism at the Present Time." He builds upon Aristotle's perspective, asserting that the critical examination of art is essential for uncovering universal truths and moral insights.[3] Another pivotal figure in the development of modern literary criticism is T. S. Eliot, whose 1919 essay "Tradition and the Individual Talent" articulates the necessity of understanding literary tradition to fully appreciate a work of art.[4] Subsequently, modern literary criticism evolved into a more specialized and academically rigourous discipline through interdisciplinary dialogues with various fields such as philosophy, linguistics, and anthropology. Over time, it diversified into multiple subfields, each emphasizing distinct critical approaches.[5]

Meanwhile, art in general is understood as denoting a skillful activity—an applied craft rooted in human creativity. More specifically, it also refers to human-made creations imbued with aesthetic and cultural significance. Notably, in the realm of literary criticism, the term *art* is frequently equated with *text*, which might imply that a thoughtful consideration of art as an aesthetic creation can yield profound insights into a fresh reconsideration of text as an art form, despite the fundamental distinctions between the broad notion of art and the linguistic construct of text.

The presence of such distinctions does not preclude the possibility of meaningful similarities between art and text. I argue that their most salient commonality lies in their artificiality—both are human-made objects, intentionally created within a particular context, following a specific design, and with a certain purpose. The degree to which the context of the creator influences the form of the created work may vary, and the design of this form itself may be intricate or simple. The intentions behind the act of

---

3. Arnold, "Function of Criticism." It is also known that his discussion on criticism began as early as in 1853 with his "Preface." See also his *Culture and Anarchy*.

4. Of course, beyond Eliot, numerous Anglo-American scholars have played pivotal roles in the development of literary criticism following Matthew Arnold, including Henry James, John Crowe Ransom, I. A. Richards, and William Empson. However, in the present discussion, Eliot will serve as a foundational figure providing a critical framework for understanding Lewis. See Eliot, "Tradition."

5. By the mid-to-late twentieth century, literary criticism was found in biblical studies primarily under the designation of narrative criticism. This terminological distinction appears to be a strategic effort to differentiate it from the existing use of *literary criticism* within the realm of historical-critical biblical scholarship, which did not necessarily share the theoretical premises of modern literary criticism.

creation or the choice of a particular form may be explicit and deliberate or, at times, neutral and incidental. What remains unequivocal is that both artistic artifacts and texts as artifacts do not arise spontaneously in nature. Rather, both necessitate the intervention of a creator and embody a subjective expression.

The second crucial similarity is the function performed by these artifacts. Their primary social function, that is, the social action the creator seeks to accomplish through them, is limitless in scope. Such functions may range from depicting reality or specific phenomena, to conveying prescriptive messages to audiences, to simply providing an aesthetic experience. As a result, they serve countless secondary functions, such as stimulating the imagination, broadening intellectual horizons, and transforming culture, to name but a few.

These functions unfold through a dynamic process that transforms subjectivity into objectivity, only to subsequently reframe it back into subjectivity. Even information grounded in factual reality undergoes a subjective process. It is initially interpreted subjectively by the creator, then transmitted through an objective medium, such as text or artistic representation, and ultimately reinterpreted subjectively by the audience. While one might question the very possibility of a purely objective medium,[6] it is at least evident that the material and linguistic components of an artifact exist independently of the creator before being selected for artistic expression. Likewise, language, including its vocabulary and grammar, is pre-established through social consensus and subsequently chosen and utilized by the creator. This highlights the presence of an objective medium in both artistic and textual creation, making its role a crucial subject for further critical exploration.

With this understanding, art can be defined as an interplay between subjectivity and objectivity, operating through three fundamental stages: the creator's subjective expression, its transmission through an objective medium, and the audience's subjective appreciation. In this relational

---

6. See, e.g., several notable works that provide insightful perspectives on medium: Walter J. Ong maintains that medium, that is, a mode of communication, such as oral, written, print, and electronic, does not merely serve as a passive conduit of a message. Rather, it plays an active role in the communicative process by dynamically interacting with the message itself. He views the medium as a force that shapes human perception and worldview, exerting influence not only on individual cognition but also on the formation of social structures and cultural development (*Rhetoric*, 284–303, esp. 290). Also see McLuhan, *Gutenberg Galaxy*; *Understanding Media*.

dynamic between the creator and the audience, the function of an artifact is inherently social, thus it facilitates communication, conveys ideas, evokes emotions, shares experiences, and fosters relationships. These relational and social dimensions are crucial elements in both artistic criticism and literary criticism, serving as fundamental aspects of interpretation and evaluation.

Criticism as Art in its Context

Beyond an examination of the shared characteristics of artistic works and literary texts, it is equally important to consider how the act of criticism itself functions as an art, requiring skillful engagement. Since this study draws insights from Lewis's work, it is now necessary to trace its intellectual lineage back to eighteenth-century Romanticism and the late nineteenth-century to early twentieth-century movements of Aestheticism and "art for art's sake."[7] Both of these movements also engaged in a reciprocal exchange of influence with Impressionism. Impressionism shares several characteristics with Romanticism, including an emphasis on individual subjectivity, emotion, lived experience, and aesthetic value, while simultaneously rejecting absolute truths and normative values. However, Impressionism departs from Romanticism in its heightened focus on transient experience, deliberately distancing itself from author-centred interpretation, the restoration of humanistic ideals, and moral concerns. Instead, it conceives of literary criticism as a purely artistic expression, one that fosters diverse modes of appreciation and aesthetic experience.[8] As hinted here, aestheticism also bears a direct connection to Impressionism. The nineteenth-century aesthete Charles Baudelaire influenced the Impressionist critic Walter Pater, who, in turn, shaped the representative Impressionist critic, Oscar Wilde.[9]

In addition, Aestheticism shares a strong intellectual affinity with twentieth-century New Criticism. The New Critics prioritized the aesthetic value of the text itself rather than focusing on extra-textual factors such as the author's biographical background. As a result, they were often described

---

7. Baumgarten's *Meditationes* and *Aesthetica* are regarded as works that introduced the term "aesthetics" into philosophical discourse. The aesthetic movement also finds significant philosophical grounding in Kant's *Critique*, wherein Kant, much like Lewis, emphasizes concepts such as beauty, the sublime, and artistic creation.

8. By treating criticism itself as a creative act independent of the author's intended meaning, Impressionism foreshadows certain aspects of the New Criticism and, later, reader-response criticism.

9. See Pater, *Studies*; Wilde, *Intentions*.

as aesthetic critics even though their focus extended beyond the purely aesthetic dimensions of the text.[10] In this context, Lewis, particularly in his engagement with the intellectual climate of his time, likely interacted with and was influenced by the ideas of Romanticism and Aestheticism either directly or indirectly so that this influence ultimately led him to emphasize the importance of appreciating the intrinsic beauty of the text itself, while simultaneously redefining the practice of criticism, either by relegating it to or expanding it into something akin to artistic appreciation.

Given this intellectual trajectory, it is worthwhile examining the connection between Lewis's *Experiment in Criticism* (1961) and Eliot's essay of the same title (1929).[11] It does not appear that Lewis deliberately titled his book in direct reference to Eliot's essay. Nonetheless, both works appear to share a common objective: to critique the limitations of their contemporary literary criticism and to propose alternative approaches to its practice.[12] Remarkably, each author even departs from his own predominant literary critical stance—one adhering to a text-centred approach and the other to an objective framework—to offer a fresh perspective. Perhaps it is this very departure that warrants their use of the term "experiment" in their titles.

Unlike Arnold, Eliot advocated a version of "art for art's sake" in his own right. However, in his essay "Experiment in Criticism," he deviates from his usual emphasis on pure literature and a text-oriented perspective. Unexpectedly, this essay demonstrates a heightened concern with extra-textual elements, particularly the author's context and influence. He may have been apprehensive about the notion that pure literature should be entirely dissociated from utility, acknowledging, albeit cautiously, the inescapable religious, moral, and political dimensions of literary works.[13]

---

10. For instance, another key emphasis of their approach was reading texts with a focus on form, a characteristic they shared with Russian Formalism.

11. As a pivotal figure in the formation of the New Criticism, Eliot played a crucial role in shaping modern literary theory, and his essay reflects his evolving perspective on literary criticism. See Eliot, "Experiment."

12. At the turn of the nineteenth and twentieth centuries, literary critics gradually moved away from prescriptive readings that sought to extract religious or moral principles from texts, instead favouring more descriptive approaches. Naturally, in the early twentieth century, a major point of contention revolved around whether criticism should focus on external elements, such as the author, the reader, and the broader historical and social context, or whether it should remain strictly centred on the text itself. The New Critics championed the latter approach, emphasizing a rigourous and analytical method known as *close reading*.

13. Ashley Marshall attributes this shift to Eliot's involvement in High Church

This apparent departure from his earlier stance was later moderated and even evolved in ways that ultimately reaffirmed a text-centred approach. Over time, Eliot's works played a crucial role in shaping early New Criticism, which emphasized *close reading* and the autonomy of the literary text.

With this historical context in mind, we now turn to Lewis's later work *Experiment in Criticism*, written several decades after Eliot's essay. How does Lewis's perspective on criticism differ from Eliot's, and what unique insights does it offer to the field of literary criticism? These are the questions to which we now direct our inquiry.[14]

Lewis's Experiment in Criticism

In Lewis's succinct discussion of literary criticism, he presents a remarkably novel and distinctive argument, devoting considerable attention to defining the characteristics of unliterary people—those incapable of deeply appreciating a text. Such unliterary readers, according to Lewis, miss the richness of the literary experience by confining their engagement to superficial pleasures such as excitement and curiosity. While good readers may also enjoy these elements, they delve further into the profound emotional, moral, and artistic dimensions of a story. Moreover, unliterary readers focus solely on plot summaries, disregarding the words themselves. This tendency reflects a preoccupation with understanding events at a surface level rather than appreciating the intricate messages and aesthetic beauty accessible only through careful engagement with the text.[15]

Lewis goes a step further by identifying status-seekers as a subset of unliterary readers. These individuals, he explains, read books not "to make [themselves] acceptable, but to improve [themselves], to develop [their] potentialities, [and] to become a more complete [person]."[16] Similarly, he laments the institutionalization of English literature within the educational

---

Anglicanism in 1927 ("T. S. Eliot," 609).

14. To shift the focus more squarely onto Lewis's discussion while bringing the remarks on Eliot to a close, and for the benefit of serious readers who meticulously engage even with footnotes, I will provide a direct answer to the question just posed here before moving on to the next section. One of the key distinctions between Eliot's and Lewis's works lies in the respective nature of their "experiments." Eliot's inquiry primarily centres on the author's role in literary creation whereas Lewis examines the act of reading as an experiment in itself—one that serves as a transformative experience for the reader.

15. This is also where we can observe the underlying intellectual influence of the New Criticism and, more broadly, structuralism on Lewis's work.

16. Lewis, *Experiment in Criticism*, 8 (cited with slight modification).

system, asserting that "[o]ne sad result of making English Literature a 'subject' at schools and universities is that the reading of great authors is, from early years, stamped upon the minds of conscientious and submissive young people as something meritorious."[17] What Lewis argues here is that this entire process distorts the true value of literature. Instead of being a source of intellectual excitement and aesthetic pleasure, it turns into just another academic requirement—something readers feel obligated to engage with rather than something they genuinely enjoy. In the end, rather than cultivating a natural love for literary art, the way literature is taught and engaged with can strip reading of its intrinsic enjoyment, reducing it to a burdensome task.

Lewis's typology of readers further extends to how they interact with texts. He distinguishes between two modes: reception and usage. "A work of (whatever) art can be either 'received' or 'used.' When we 'receive' it, we exert our senses and imagination and various other powers according to a pattern invented by the artist. When we 'use' it, we treat it as assistance for our own activities."[18] While critical reading ideally entails both receiving and evaluating a work, Lewis observes that this balance is often disrupted within the professional practice of literary criticism.[19] He emphatically asserts that readers should prioritize experiencing literature over dissecting it for hidden lessons or moral teachings because the essence of literature lies not in its utility but in the transformative joy it offers during the act of reading. He also rejects the reduction of literature to a vehicle for philosophy, life lessons, or ideological perspectives. Instead, Lewis asserts that its value resides in the immediate impact it has on readers, enriching and transforming them as they engage with it. He encapsulates this idea by stating, "Unless we are fully attending both to sound and sense, unless we hold ourselves obediently ready to conceive, imagine, and feel as the words invite us, we shall not have these experiences."[20]

A Good Critic

It is important to recognize that while Lewis employs the term "reader," his discussion extends beyond the simple act of reading; rather, it encompasses a broader inquiry into textual engagement within an academic framework.

17. Lewis, *Experiment in Criticism*, 10.
18. Lewis, *Experiment in Criticism*, 88.
19. Lewis, *Experiment in Criticism*, 92.
20. Lewis, *Experiment in Criticism*, 32.

Therefore, it is worth considering whether Lewis's characterization of a good reader, regardless of its merits, corresponds with the interpretive techniques of academic critique and, furthermore, what insights we, as practitioners of biblical interpretation, might glean from his conception to refine our approach to the text.

Lewis's core idea on criticism can be discerned through his description of an ideal critic. According to him, critics should provide detailed descriptions of works, assist readers in understanding the texts, and remain open to enjoying even "second-best"[21] works without an insistence on perfection. Therefore, a good critic, in Lewis's view, is "easy to please, but hard to satisfy,"[22] meaning they can appreciate a wide range of works while still expecting high standards of quality. This somewhat paradoxical and seemingly contradictory description of a good critic is characterized by its emphasis on enjoyment.

The joyful appreciation of an artistic object can be considered a broader form of criticism than that which targets texts, and it may align with Lewis's intent to treat texts as an art form. Indeed, Lewis often parallels or conflates literary criticism with the appreciation of art. For Lewis, art serves as a medium for conveying the author's subjectivity including intent, perspective, worldview, and more. Accordingly, one of the primary purposes of art, according to Lewis, is to enable the reader to transcend their own perspective and become immersed in the experiences and viewpoints of others.[23] In light of this, a good critic should be capable of appreciating well-crafted arguments and expressions of the text, even when they disagree with the views presented.[24]

The capacity to engage with a work on its own terms, acknowledging its inherent values without immediate dismissal, is arguably a legacy that certain postmodern critics, such as anti-androcentric, anti-anthropocentric, and anti-hegemonic approaches, have largely abandoned. For these critics, textual appreciation has been supplanted by an exclusive focus on critique—at times, critique for the sake of critique itself. Conducting criticism with a predetermined ideological stance, they inevitably reduce their engagement to an unyielding denunciation of whatever contradicts their own beliefs, often at the expense of acknowledging the aesthetic and

---

21. Lewis, *Experiment in Criticism*, 120.
22. Lewis, *Experiment in Criticism*, 120.
23. Lewis, *Experiment in Criticism*, 85.
24. Lewis, *Experiment in Criticism*, 86.

intellectual merits of the text. However, the first essential step in conducting sound criticism is to suspend one's own ideological predispositions as much as possible and fully engage with the values articulated by the text on its own terms. This applies to both content and form. There is a pressing need to revive discussions on the intricate interplay between form and content—specifically, how a text's formal qualities shape, constrain, and enrich its meaning. Put differently, the endeavour to investigate how the author's subjective construal is transmuted into the text's objective manifestation must be actively reinstated within contemporary critical discourse.

This idea raises a pertinent question concerning the role of the reader's subjectivity in the process of criticism. Lewis addresses the issue of how a reader's subjectivity should function, particularly in cases where an author does not embed a singular perspective or intent in a work, or where the process of interpretation inherently involves the reader's subjective lens. He draws a compelling analogy between modern poetry and a musical score, both of which can be interpreted in various ways by different performers. In such instances, the goal is to discover the most compelling interpretation, rather than the singular correct one. Lewis claims, "The poem, clearly, is like a score and the readings like performances. Different renderings are admissible. The question is not which is the 'right' one but which is the best."[25] In this regard, a mature critic should move beyond a binary framework of right and wrong interpretations and instead adopt a constructive approach—one that evaluates readings in terms of their relative strength, depth, and interpretive richness, striving for what is good and, ultimately, what is better.

Perhaps even more crucial than striving for a better interpretation is maintaining an open-minded attitude—one that remains cognizant of the possibility that what one perceives as a superior reading may, in fact, be a misreading. As Lewis asserts, there is both joy and intellectual value in instances where a reader misinterprets a text. Moreover, by striving for better interpretations, readers can attain a deeper sense of satisfaction that transcends the initial pleasure derived from their misreadings.[26] Another significant consideration arising from this discussion pertains to the

---

25. Lewis, *Experiment in Criticism*, 98.

26. Lewis does not advocate for a Kantian pursuit of a singularly correct interpretation. Rather, he aligns with Schleiermacher's hermeneutical view that inferior interpretations are not inherently beautiful but must be refined and improved to achieve greater interpretive excellence. For a more detailed observation, refer to Lewis's remarks in *Experiment in Criticism*, 100–101.

existence of explicit errors in an author's work. What kind of interpretive approach does such a scenario necessitate from the reader? Should the reader attempt to rectify these flaws, elevate the work's quality, or evaluate it through a corrective lens? Given Lewis's emphasis on fully receiving the author's perspective, what is at stake is not the correction of the error. This discussion, however, warrants further examination at a later stage. For now, we turn to a deeper reflection on the relationship between art and criticism.

ART OF CRITICISM: AN ONGOING EXPERIMENT

Lewis's insights invite a more nuanced exploration of the parallels and distinctions between reading as an artistic experience and reading as a critical endeavour. At its core, a text—an artifact shaped by human agency—can be understood as a human creation imbued with artistic value. From this perspective, equating critical work with artistic experience is not inherently problematic. Hence, it becomes essential to examine, with greater depth, how we can refine and enrich our appreciation of artistic works. In the following discussion, we will focus specifically on music and painting.[27]

Music and Text

Consider the comparison between text and music and imagine attending a live musical performance. Experiencing the music in a concert hall is often regarded as more valuable than listening to a recording in a different setting. This distinction arises in part because a live performance offers a richer, more immersive experience for the audience, engaging multiple senses, such as visual, auditory, and even tactile, while fostering an interactive connection between performers and listeners. These positive aspects are primarily encountered in the immediacy of live artistic expression. Of course, as technology advances, new means of overcoming geographical barriers and facilitating interaction beyond physical presence continue to develop. Digital platforms increasingly enable audiences to engage in

---

27. Among the vast array of artistic expressions, limiting the comparison of text exclusively to classical forms of music and painting may appear unduly restrictive. Contemporary artistic landscapes encompass a multitude of alternative forms, including digital visual art and performance art, which warrant serious consideration. However, due to the constraints of this study's length, an in-depth exploration of these alternative artistic forms will be set aside. Instead, particular attention will be given to the evolving nature of art in the age of AI, a subject that will be addressed in the latter sections of this chapter.

performances in realtime, preserving a sense of participation and presence. Nonetheless, we still live in an era where the value of physical presence often surpasses that of digitally mediated, remote experiences.

Another reason why listening to music in a concert hall is often considered more valuable than hearing a recording lies in the singularity of the live event, which amplifies its sense of uniqueness and rarity. A performance, once played, can never be replicated in the same way. Although subsequent reproductions of the piece may evoke similar emotions, they cannot replicate the exact resonance of the original moment in a specific time and place. For example, on March 9, 2022, as Russian forces advanced on Kyiv, the Kyiv-Classic Orchestra performed in Maidan Square, a historic site of Ukrainian resistance. Their rendition of the Ukrainian national anthem and Beethoven's "Ode to Joy" symbolized national defiance and Ukraine's European aspirations. The temporality and spatial significance of this performance heightened the meaning of the music, creating a profound emotional resonance for its audience. We perceive such musical experiences as valuable due to their singularity and irreproducibility, qualities intrinsic to the ephemeral nature of live performance, especially when intertwined with a moment profoundly shaped by its temporal and situational context.

The qualities of immediacy and ephemerality, which may be seen as reflections of physical limitations, contribute to the perceived value of music, allowing us to appreciate it more profoundly. Of course, we may be able to enumerate some exceptions. The problem arises when the value of live performance is entirely disregarded, as in cases where music is confined solely to recording studios. In such instances, the inherent immediacy and transience of a live performance are lost, leaving behind only the aesthetic form and content of the music. One might also consider cases in which a composer's repeated performances refine and enhance the music, elevating the overall quality of the piece over time. However, even in such instances, the immediacy and ephemerality of the specific performative moment continue to play a crucial role in augmenting the work's experiential value. Countless exceptions could be mentioned, but another crucial factor to consider is how the perceived value of music can be heightened by the listener's personal circumstances, independent of the composer's performance. A listener's perception of a musical work's significance is often shaped by their unique personal context. For example, a wedding march played during a couple's ceremony may hold far greater emotional weight for them, rendering the piece more meaningful than the same composition performed live by its composer in a concert hall. However, even in such cases, the immediacy and ephemerality of the performance remain integral to its artistic value. This relativity of value, wherein the significance of a musical work is profoundly shaped by the listener's specific circumstances, does not diminish the universal artistic worth associated with the composer's context or the broader public reception of the piece. While individual listeners may find a composition more or less appealing based on personal situation or taste, the collective recognition of masterpieces remains largely unshaken. Performances of such works, bound to specific moments in time and space, are often revered and preserved in cultural memory, further reinforcing their enduring artistic significance.

To be sure, there is room for debate on whether the immediacy and ephemerality of a musical performance enhance the intrinsic value of the music itself. Like all other art forms, music derives its significance from its form and content, offering an experience of enjoyment not only to its creator but also to all who engage with it. Throughout history, musical forms have evolved, ranging from Gregorian chant to Baroque, from Classical and Romantic symphonies to contemporary classical compositions, and from jazz and blues to rock and pop, and their content has reflected an even greater diversity across individual works. It is evident that form and content of a musical composition are shaped by the subjectivity of the composer, whose artistic choices give rise to a distinct work. In turn, the piece is received and appreciated through the subjective lens of the listener. This dynamic interplay between the composer's subjectivity, the work itself, and the audience's reception is mediated through the processes of interaction, transmission, and performance.[28] In the case of music, at the very least, the immediacy and ephemerality integral to this process enhance the appreciation of both the content and form of the work, rendering the experience of the art work all the more valuable.

How, then, does this concept apply to texts? Texts, too, exhibit a certain degree of ephemerality, albeit in a different manner from musical performances. Perhaps the enjoyment of a text arises from temporarily immersing oneself in or aligning oneself with the exciting or joyful scenarios it presents. However, unlike musical performances, the presentation and

---

28. While a more extensive discussion on the role of media as an element directly connected to the value of artistic works would be valuable, this essay omits such a discussion due to limitations in length.

reception of a written text allow for greater flexibility in terms of immediacy and temporality, perhaps akin to the artistic experience of engaging with recorded music. What remains are form and content, and repeated readings in different contexts do not diminish the value of them. Rather, repeated engagement often deepens the reader's understanding.

Despite this distinction, texts and music share significant similarities. Foremost among them is the necessity of experiencing both as cohesive wholes rather than in fragmented parts. For instance, Joseph Haydn's *Symphony in G Major, no. 94*, commonly known as the "Surprise Symphony," may initially appear monotonous when only its opening measures are heard. However, when experienced in its entirety, the rationale behind its evocative moniker becomes apparent. Likewise, in literary works, the significance of individual components often becomes fully appreciable only when situated within the whole. Examples of this phenomenon include O. Henry's "The Last Leaf" and Guy de Maupassant's "The Necklace."[29] In "The Last Leaf," the bedridden girl, clinging to the hope symbolized by the tenaciously enduring leaf that refuses to fall, ultimately discovers that the leaf was, in fact, a painting. Similarly, in "The Necklace," the protagonist and her husband toil relentlessly to repay an exorbitant debt for a lost piece of jewelry, only to later learn that the original necklace was a mere imitation. These narrative twists attain their full resonance only when considered within the broader narrative structure. Their poignancy and thematic depth emerge most vividly when read in conjunction with the intricate build-up of their respective narratives. Just as a musical composition cannot be fully appreciated by isolating a single movement or passage, a text is rarely understood through the analysis of individual words or sentences without situating them within the broader context of the discourse. This underscores the need for textual analysis to engage with the text in a more comprehensive and unified manner.

We now turn to a comparison between text and painting.. Unlike music, paintings generally lack ephemerality and immediacy. Rather, much like a written text, they retain a profound sense of uniqueness which arises from elements, such as the artist's physical touch, the texture of the brushstrokes, and the emotions and context embedded in the creation process. As a result, no matter how meticulously a painting is reproduced, its value diminishes when it exists merely as a copy. For example, Vincent van Gogh's *Starry Night* (1889) exemplifies how a painting's singularity is

---

29. See Henry, "Last Leaf"; de Maupassant, "Necklace."

rooted in the artist's physical engagement with the medium, the distinct texture of the brushstrokes, and the emotional and contextual depth woven into the artwork. Created during van Gogh's time in a mental asylum in Saint-Rémy-de-Provence, the masterpiece captures his internal turmoil and extraordinary creativity. The swirling brushstrokes, vivid palette, and dynamic forms are inextricably tied to van Gogh's psychological state and artistic vision. While *Starry Night* has been reproduced countless times, its original texture, energy, and emotional intensity, conveyed through van Gogh's own hand, remain inimitable.

Similarly, two or more literary texts may convey identical content but differ in value based on the author's unique style and how the discourse connects with the author's life. James Joyce's *Ulysses* exemplifies a text whose distinctiveness stems from its author's stylistic innovations and contextual influences.[30] This modernist tour de force reimagines Homer's *Odyssey* within the context of a single day in Dublin, employing multilayered allusions, parody of renowned motifs, an intricate rendering of internal consciousness, an experimental narrative progression, linguistic inventiveness, and meticulous detail. Joyce's imaginative use of language and intimate portrayal of his city reflect his personal experiences and literary craftsmanship. Although *Ulysses* might have inspired numerous adaptations and imitations, its originality remains unparalleled, as its full impact is inseparable from Joyce's style and the cultural and personal contexts that shaped his text as an art.

A work of art may appear ordinary, yet its value is often profoundly elevated by the elements of sacrifice, love, and suffering experienced by its creator in real life. Observing those elements embedded in the author's life may dramatically transform one's perception of the artistic object. Consequently, an awareness of the creative context behind an artwork undoubtedly deepens one's appreciation of its beauty. Likewise, engaging with a text requires more than reading its words at face value. It calls for an attentive consideration of the underlying nuances and an endeavour to read between the lines and contexts, perceiving what is unseen yet integral to its form and content.

---

30. Read Joyce, *Ulysses*.

Part Three: Literature and Criticism

Difficulties

Now, we turn to the discussion of the textual complexity that a good reader must overcome in pursuit of a more refined interpretation. Some texts, even when succinctly summarized, effectively convey their essence and depth. Lewis highlights the story of Orpheus as an example of such a text.[31] Conversely, there are works whose profundity can only be fully appreciated through their complete length and intricate narratives, such as the myth of Odysseus. Additionally, as Lewis asserts, intricate novels like *Middlemarch* or *Vanity Fair* demand prolonged engagement and thoughtful comprehension to grasp the intricate messages carefully woven by their authors.[32] This underscores the distinction between story types that possess inherent value and impact and those that rely on detailed exposition to achieve their full effect.

What warrants particular attention, however, are the limitations faced by contemporary readers in fully engaging with the detailed and complex structures of texts. At least three primary constraints can be identified. First, there is the inherent difficulty of discerning an author's perspective within a text. Readers may struggle to determine whether their interpretation reflects the author's intended meaning or their own subjective projections. This challenge becomes particularly pronounced when interpreting texts such as Scripture, where religious doctrines, theological concepts, and personal faith systems are inextricably intertwined with the act of interpretation. In such cases, the task of discerning the author's intended meaning from the reader's subjective perspective becomes more complex.

Second, contemporary art often exhibits a tendency toward simplicity, eschewing the technical and artistic complexity traditionally found in many classical works. Simplified modern forms frequently allow audiences to derive enjoyment without the need for deep reflection or engagement. Consider, for example, hip-hop music with its repetitive two-chord structures. Its driving basslines and infectious rhythms provide immediate pleasure without necessitating any contemplation of an underlying message. This tendency of modern art leads us to reevaluate the aesthetic value we derive from artistic works and the effort such enjoyment demands from the audience.

Third, the diminished necessity to engage with an author's intent or the subtleties of a text stems not only from the simplification of contemporary

---

31. Lewis, *Experiment in Criticism*, 40–41.
32. See G. Eliot, *Middlemarch*; Thackeray, *Vanity Fair*.

art forms but also from advancements in AI technology. AI now analyzes and distills meaning, sparing readers the effort of grappling with the complex implications in the text. Furthermore, AI can generate a rather fine piece of art devoid of the life, personality, or context of a human creator. At times, entirely fantastical creations detached from realism and situational context captivate contemporary audiences. We now live in an age where not only the metaphorical "death of the author"[33] is assumed, but the author has, in practical terms, disappeared altogether. In this context, criticism rooted in the profound dialogue and reflective interplay between author and reader emerges as a crucial activity that preserves and enhances distinctiveness of human arts in an era increasingly dominated by non-human influences.

BEYOND THE EXPERIMENT

Mistakes, Errors, and Failure

The preceding discussion prompts further reflection on the distinctions between human-created art and AI-generated art. What fundamentally differentiates human artistic expression from its AI-produced counterpart is the presence of error, irregularity, and failure—qualities that add depth and richness to human creations. AI, by design, does not make mistakes, or more precisely, it does not intend to make mistakes. When AI generates flawed results, the model is either discarded or deemed in need of improvement. Human error, in contrast, is something we inherently understand and even appreciate. In fact, an author's mistakes can be a source of delight for critics, as errors often reflect human essence embedded in artistic creation. In Korean, for instance, there exists an idiomatic expression that celebrates such imperfections as "humanistic."

Humanity's history is a chronicle of falsehoods, errors, and failures. Paradoxically, it is through these very mistakes that we have arrived at better answers. At times, we do not even seek better answers but instead savor the beauty of the mistake or the falsehood itself. For instance, Jackson Pollock's artistic journey demonstrates how struggles and mistakes can lead to groundbreaking innovation. Dissatisfied with traditional figurative painting, Pollock sought new methods to express emotion. His accidental discovery of the drip technique while experimenting with paint became the

---

33. See Barthes, "Death of the Author."

foundation of his iconic works such as *No. 5* (1948). This serendipitous innovation revolutionized Abstract Expressionism and made Pollock an admired figure in modern art. Similarly, John Cage struggled with the idea of silence in music and wanted to explore it. He initially believed total silence was achievable in a performance. However, the failure to achieve actual silence led him to realize that environmental sounds, such as shuffling feet or coughing, are integral to music, leading to the creation of *4'33"* (1952). This avant-garde composition, constructed upon the deliberate embrace of mistake or failure, challenged conventional ideas of music and remains a seminal work in experimental composition. Consider another example. Edvard Munch's struggles with anxiety and emotional instability, often viewed as personal deficiencies, became the very essence of his artistic vision. His iconic work *The Scream* channels intense feelings of alienation and existential dread, transforming his personal anguish into a universally recognized symbol of human emotion.

Similarly, irregularities enrich not only art but also the act of criticism itself. Predictability dulls engagement; a person who offers only perfect answers lacks charm. Irregularity, whether in text, art, or critical discourse, adds depth and vibrancy, breaking the monotony of perfection and inviting audiences to discover beauty in the unexpected. These irregularities can often be described using terms like "defamiliarization" or "deviation."[34] The freshness that comes from transforming the familiar into something novel draws attention and fosters a sense of renewal. For instance, in music, the use of major 7 chords often seeks to provide tension for overly familiar harmonies within a measure. Crescendo or ritardando can elevate the atmosphere within a phrase, leaving a profound impact on the audience. Transposition introduces a different mood over a longer section of a musical piece. Such deviating elements bring variation to monotonous musical progressions, enabling a fresh appreciation of the music.

Many transformative works of art also emerge from a deviation from the normative standard. Claude Monet's *Impression, Sunrise* abandoned detailed realism in favour of loose brushstrokes and vibrant colors that emphasized light and atmosphere, sparking the Impressionist movement. Likewise, Pablo Picasso's *Les Demoiselles d'Avignon* shattered traditional perspectives through fragmented, geometric forms, heralding the birth of Cubism. The freshness introduced by either intentional deviations or

---

34. I am using these terms here in a broader sense than that employed by the Russian Formalists. See Shklovsky, "Art as Device." See also Jakobson, "Linguistics and Poetics."

unintentional mistakes, errors, and even failures is equally pertinent to literary criticism. A text is invariably the product of its creator—an unpredictable, flawed, and fallible human being. Paradoxically, it is this very imperfection that endows the text with its unique value and makes the interpretive process enjoyable.

Creativity and Performance

In our final discussion, we need to redirect our focus back to the reader. While AI may now effectively replicate the role of authors, producing beautiful artworks, music, and texts, the role of the audience remains largely within the human domain. Moreover, if we consider that the narrative of the author's life, implicitly woven into a text, significantly enhances its value, the most meaningful form of criticism may well arise from human interaction between author and reader. The reader must engage with the living human author through the text, breathing in tandem with the author—pausing when the author pauses in surprise, quickening when the narrative quickens, and holding their breath when tension stills the author's breathing. This principle extends beyond textual engagement to all forms of human interaction. For instance, if a parent merely logically explains the joys of play to their child and then neglects to actively participate, this constitutes lazy caregiving. Similarly, in romantic relationships, sharing in a partner's joys and resonating with their laughter fosters emotional intimacy and strengthens the bond. Conversely, adopting an overly analytical approach, reducing the relationship to a mere analysis of a partner's actions and preferences, risks ossifying relational dynamics and stifling authentic connection.

While readers attune themselves to the author's rhythm and perspective as essential for fully enjoying the text, the reader's creative engagement remains equally indispensable. Lewis himself emphasizes the need for the reader to maintain an "obedient" attitude while also highlighting "creative" engagement.[35] The reader must fully receive the author's viewpoint yet do so creatively. The process surrounding the production of a text, when understood as an art form, can be characterized by this performative creativity. If text production represents the act of *creation*, text interpretation can aptly be termed *re-creation*. Criticism, therefore, entails not only the creativity of writing but also the re-creativity involved in reading and interpretation.

---

35. Lewis, *Experiment in Criticism*, 19.

In this light, criticism might be justifiably described as *creativism*. For example, while the psalmist exhibited creativity in composing Ps 110, another form of performative creativity would have been at work when the psalm was read aloud to the contemporary congregation. Later, in Acts 2, Peter's citation of the psalm reflects yet another layer of creative engagement. The audience hearing Peter's words, the author of Acts who recorded the situation, the ancient readers of Acts, and ultimately we ourselves, all partake in a spectrum of performative creativity.

In this regard, while *what words mean* is significant, *what words do* is equally vital. A work of art is not merely comprehended intellectually; it moves the body and the spirit. One may engage with music through intellectual analysis, but its true essence often emerges when one physically participates—moving, dancing, or singing along in an act of performative creativity. By "joining in"[36] with an artwork, we experience a transformation, not only in our worldview but also in our very mode of existence.

In this process, the role of emotion is of paramount importance. Although William K. Wimsatt and Monroe C. Beardsley warned against the "affective fallacy,"[37] the emotions elicited by an artwork are a vital component of criticism because both the appreciation and evaluation of a work can often be expressed in emotional terms. However, in many instances, a reader's emotional response must be intertwined with the author's perspective and intention. For instance, admiring the prose of a well-written traffic law while simultaneously violating the law itself could hardly be considered a better act of appreciation. The best forms of emotional engagement remain grounded in the author's purpose and the text's function. We observe that Lewis also criticizes a group of literary critics, known as "vigilants,"[38] who evaluate literature strictly through the lens of their own moral and philosophical beliefs, with little to no regard for the author's intent. Certain strands of contemporary ideological criticism can be regarded as extreme manifestations of this approach. If aesthetic critics, by excluding the author's worldview and focusing solely on the text's beauty, have forfeited the ability to genuinely engage with the beauty of the world, poststructuralists, in their critique of certain ideology, have paradoxically positioned themselves as advocates of their own ideological framework. In doing so, both have ultimately failed to embrace the author's joyful invitation to dance.

---

36. Lewis, *Experiment in Criticism*, 22.
37. Wimsatt and Beardsley, "Affective Fallacy."
38. Lewis, *Experiment in Criticism*, 124–29.

Implications

In light of the above discussion, several key proposals regarding literary criticism can be summarized. First, the necessity of attentive listening to the author is central. Readers must carefully attune themselves to the author's voice, striving to understand the author's intent, ideas, and worldview, even when these diverge from their own perspectives. Effort must be taken to comprehend the broader context in which the text was conceived, as this context greatly enhances the text's value. Achieving such understanding demands rigorous self-reflection to identify and account for one's own preconceptions. Notably, this act of attentive listening to or immersion in the author's perspective should be accompanied by performative creativity, thereby allowing readers to participate in the profound artistic experience surrounding the text. For instance, appreciating the aesthetic qualities of a passage from Proverbs might involve reading it aloud in its original language, while the best way to engage with the doxology in Jude 24–25 could be to recite it as part of a song of praise.

Second, criticism is a holistic engagement. When approaching a text as a work of art, one must resist the temptation of fragmentary analysis and instead examine the text in the context of its overarching discourse and structural coherence. While individual elements may possess inherent beauty, as exemplified by a part of music played during the climactic scene of a film, their emotional resonance becomes more profound when they are situated within the larger narrative. Similarly, Gal 6 should be read in light of the arguments developed in Gal 1 to 5, and Rev 21–22 might best be understood as part of an extended vision that draws from earlier passages, or perhaps even from the long-standing traditions of the Old Testament. However, this holistic approach does not mean that small details should be overlooked. Close attention to subtle linguistic elements is often the starting point for perceiving the broader picture. Criticism must navigate seamlessly between detailed observation and the overarching structure of the text.

Third, discovering value through imperfection, too, is important. Critics should not only recognize an author's excellence or correctness but also appreciate the originality and significance of a text revealed through its mistakes and errors. For example, discovering discrepancies in grammatical agreement between nouns and adjectives or errors in the use of infinitives within Revelation could present the text as a vivid and authentic reflection of its singular author. Similarly, noting inconsistencies among the Synoptic Gospels provides an opportunity to delve into the distinctive features of each account, fostering a deeper appreciation of their individuality. Furthermore, identifying numerical or geographical discrepancies in historical books offers invaluable insights into the authors' identities and the purposes behind their writings. In this sense, every mistake or error becomes a source of enjoyment for critics, enriching their engagement with and appreciation of the Scriptures. Such imperfections do not diminish the value of the texts; rather, they enhance the critical experience.

CONCLUSION

In conclusion, I argue that criticism—more specifically, literary criticism, and in my case, biblical criticism—must reclaim its identity as an artistic practice. A text manifests its artistic value in relation to its creator's context, and when an author's unique experiences and perspectives shape the very form through which meaning is conveyed, it calls for the reader's careful engagement and aesthetic appreciation in its holistic integrity. This approach necessitates not only attentive listening to the text's artificial elements, such as authorial intent, the artist's distinctive touch, and the traces of the author's lived experience embedded in the work, but also a discerning appreciation of the natural substance of the text interwoven into its linguistic form, embracing its logical, truthful, and even imperfect expressions.

Therefore, if we, as critics, have approached a literary work with analytical rigour and an unyielding pursuit of perfection, we have done well. If we have embraced its imperfections, recognizing the insights that emerge from its flaws, we have done even better. But if we have found joy in this entire endeavour and discerned beauty in every critical dialogue, then I believe Lewis—the kind of literary critic who invites us to reconsider the artistic nature of criticism—would affirm that we have done best. The continuing task is to approach criticism not as a merely analytical exercise but as an artistic endeavour. Now then, why not join this joyful experiment in criticism?

BIBLIOGRAPHY

Arnold, Matthew. *Culture and Anarchy: An Essay in Political and Social Criticism*. London: Smith, Elder, 1869.

———. "The Function of Criticism at the Present Time." In *Essays in Criticism*, 1–38. Boston: Ticknor and Fields, 1865.

———. "Preface." In *Poems*, v–xxi. London: Longmans, 1853.

Barthes, Roland. "The Death of the Author." In *Image-Music-Text*. Translated by Stephen Heath. New York: Hill and Wang, 1977.

Baumgarten, Alexander G. *Aesthetica*. Frankfurt: Ioannis Christiani Kleyb, 1750.

———. *Meditationes philosophicae de nonnullis ad poema pertinentibus*. Halle Magdeburg: I. H. Grunerti, 1735.

Eliot, George. *Middlemarch: An Authoritative Text, Backgrounds, Reviews and Criticism*. Edited by Bert G. Hornback. Norton Critical Edition. New York: Norton, 1977.

Eliot, T. S. "Experiment in Criticism." *The Bookman* 70 (1929) 227–33.

———. "Tradition and the Individual Talent." In *The Sacred Wood: Essays on Poetry and Criticism*, 42–53. New York: Alfred A. Knopf, 1921.

Henry, O. "The Last Leaf." In *The Trimmed Lamp and Other Stories of the Four Million*, 198–208. New York: McClure, Phillips, 1907.

Jakobson, Roman. "Linguistics and Poetics." In *Style in Language*, edited by Thomas A. Sebeok, 350–77. Cambridge, MA: MIT Press, 1960.

Joyce, James. *Ulysses*. 1922. Reprint, London: Penguin, 1968.

Kant, Immanuel. *Critique of Judgement*. Translated by J. H. Bernard. New York: Hafner, 1951.

Lewis, C. S. *An Experiment in Criticism*. Cambridge: Cambridge University Press, 1961.

Marshall, Ashley. "T. S. Eliot on the Limits of Criticism: The Anomalous 'Experiment' of 1929." *The Modern Language Review* 100 (2005) 609–20.

Maupassant, Guy de. "The Necklace." In *The Norton Anthology of Short Fiction*, edited by R. V. Cassill, 1131–38. 4th ed. New York: Norton, 1990.

McLuhan, Marshall. *The Gutenberg Galaxy: The Making of Typographic Man*. Toronto: University of Toronto Press, 1962.

———. *Understanding Media: The Extensions of Man*. New York: McGraw-Hill, 1964.

Ong, Walter J. *Rhetoric, Romance, and Technology: Studies in the Interaction of Expression and Culture*. Ithaca, NY: Cornell University Press, 1971.

Pater, Walter. *Studies in the History of the Renaissance*. London: Macmillan, 1873.

Shklovsky, Viktor. "Art as Device." *Poetics Today* 36 (2015) 151–74. Translated and introduced by Alexandra Berlina.

Thackeray, William M. *Vanity Fair: A Novel without a Hero*. 1848. Reprint, New York: Signet, 1962.

Wilde, Oscar. *Intentions*. London: Osgood, McIlvaine, 1891.

Wimsatt, William K., and Monroe C. Beardsley. "The Affective Fallacy." *The Sewanee Review* 57 (1949) 31–55.

Doings, Readings, Thinkings

C. S. Lewis on the Discipline and Reward of Personal Correspondence

Dawn R. Berkelaar

If C. S. Lewis were alive today, I have no doubt that I would write to him. His books and essays were formative for me as a child, teenager, and young adult. After reading them, I felt as though he and I were friends—so, given the opportunity, I would have sent him a letter.

If Lewis were alive today, I feel quite confident that he would write back to me. He was a remarkable correspondent, writing thousands of letters in his lifetime. Most of the ones that still exist have been compiled into three large volumes, together known as *The Collected Letters of C. S. Lewis*, edited by Walter Hooper and published between 2000 and 2007.

Lewis's letters are less well known than his polished published books, which span many genres, including fantasy, theology, philosophy, and literary criticism. As someone who loves to send and receive letters, I wondered what we can glean from Lewis about the art and discipline of letter writing. What did he think was important in a letter? Why did he write letters? What can we learn about him and about his friendships from his own letters?

AN OVERVIEW OF *THE COLLECTED LETTERS OF C. S. LEWIS*

Together, the three volumes of *The Collected Letters* total more than 3,700 pages. Trying to talk in detail about all the letters would be too much. I will briefly introduce the collection but will spend most of my time talking about Lewis's letters to his oldest friend, Arthur Greeves.

The first volume, titled *Family Letters*, contains letters that Lewis wrote from 1905 to 1931—from when he was a young boy of seven, writing to his older brother at boarding school, until he was a man of almost thirty-three. Most of the letters in this volume were sent to Arthur or to Lewis's father, Albert, or to his brother, Warnie. Lewis was an atheist during his late teens and in his twenties, and the final letters in this volume include references to his conversion to Christianity in 1931. The second volume, called *Books, Broadcasts, and the War*, spans the years 1931 through 1949. These letters tend to be shorter, and the recipients are diverse. The third volume, called *Narnia, Cambridge, and Joy*, includes letters written between 1950 and 1963. Many of these letters are even shorter—some were written on postcards—but they were consistently thoughtful. After his books started to be published, Lewis received numerous letters from readers. He felt a responsibility to respond. It took him a long time to do so—up to two hours per day.[1]

Walter Hooper, editor of *The Collected Letters*, was Lewis's secretary for several months during the last year of Lewis's life. In a podcast episode in 2019,[2] Hooper was asked about the sheer volume of Lewis's correspondence. Hooper says, "He [Lewis] believed that . . . if you publish a book, and people buy it, [or, by extension, if you share ideas publicly on the radio], you have a responsibility to those people who write to you . . . In one way, you asked for that, and you are being paid for it as well." Hooper continues, "So you *must* reply to people. [Lewis] took them seriously. He replied by writing in ink, by his hand, and he replied by 'return of post,' which in this country [England] means you write the same day you get the other person's letter."

It was a herculean task to respond to all those letters. No wonder Lewis once wrote, "It is an essential of the happy life that a man would have almost no mail and never dread the postman's knock."[3] In a letter written in 1963, he refers to letter-writing as "loathsome."[4]

---

1. Lewis, *Collected Letters—Volume II*, 789 ("the daily letter writing without W. to help me is appalling—an hour and a half or two hours every morning before I can get to my own work"). Also in the same volume, in a letter written in February 1942, Lewis comments that he had written thirty-five letters that day, to people who had written to him in response to a BBC series of five talks called *What Christians Believe* (509).

2. "Life and Writing of C. S. Lewis" (starting at 15:10).

3. Lewis, *Surprised by Joy*, 116.

4. Lewis, *Collected Letters—Volume III*, 1464.

PART THREE: LITERATURE AND CRITICISM

In the preface to *Letters to an American Lady*, Clyde S. Kilby addresses the question of why Lewis would take the time and effort to respond to the hundreds and thousands of letters sent to him from people around the world whom he did not know. The main reason, writes Kilby, "was that Lewis believed taking time out to advise or encourage another Christian was both a humbling of one's talents before the Lord and also as much the work of the Holy Spirit as producing a book."[5]

Lewis did not consider all letter-writing to be a chore. He considered letters written to personal friends to be his "real correspondence,"[6] and he took remarkable care with them. With one friend, Lewis communicated in mock Tudor English.[7] With another, an Italian priest named Don Giovanni Calabria, Lewis exchanged whole letters in Latin![8] And on at least one occasion, he wrote and sent a carefully composed poem to his friend Dorothy Sayers, in response to an allegorical card that she had sent him.[9] These letters to friends were intelligent, warm, and witty. Sometimes they were also deeply personal. For example, after learning that his friend Cecil Harwood's wife had been diagnosed with cancer, Lewis writes the following to Harwood: "I have nothing to *say*: this letter is only a substitute for a look or a touch. I suppose all that mere friends can do is to prevent (if they can do even that) one very minor by-product of sorrow, the sense of isolation from the whole of one's old world, the feeling that all else goes on the same. Believe me, it doesn't."[10]

ARTHUR GREEVES: AN UNEXPECTED FRIENDSHIP

Lewis's letters to his friend Arthur span almost fifty years.[11] Arthur was Lewis's longest and dearest friend, which is why I want to talk about this

---

5. Lewis, *Letters to an American Lady*, 7.

6. Lewis, *Collected Letters—Volume I*, 692. Lewis writes to Arthur Greeves: "real correspondence (i.e., with my personal friends) is almost impossible in term time now."

7. The first of these is found in Lewis, *Collected Letters—Volume II*, 535.

8. These letters, with English translations, are in Lewis, *Collected Letters—Volume I* and in *Collected Letters—Volume III*. The letters in both volumes were reprinted from Moynihan, *Letters*.

9. Lewis, *Collected Letters—Volume III*, 548.

10. Harwood, *C. S. Lewis*, 117–18.

11. Because of the personal nature of this friendship, I have chosen to refer to Arthur by his first name. For consistency, I ought to refer to C. S. Lewis as "Jack," which is the way his friends referred to him. However, that is not how most people today refer to Lewis, so I have chosen to refer to him by his last name.

correspondence. Lewis's letters to his father were written from duty as well as affection—sometimes mostly from duty, because Lewis's relationship with his father was often difficult. His letters to readers also stemmed largely from duty. His letters to Arthur, by contrast, were personally enriching, and his letters from Arthur were highly anticipated.[12] Lewis's letters to Arthur offer a unique portrait of a rare and precious friendship.

We can learn from this friendship. In 2023, Dr. Vivek Murthy, Surgeon General of the US, declared loneliness and isolation to be epidemic. We live in a hyperconnected world, with social media claiming to connect us to hundreds of "friends." Yet true moments of connection tend to be rare—moments when we feel heard and seen, when we share our thoughts and encounter others' thoughts in return.

In an advisory document about the epidemic, Murthy writes, "Each of us can start now, in our own lives, by strengthening our connections and relationships. Our individual relationships are an untapped resource—a source of healing hiding in plain sight. They can help us live healthier, more productive, and more fulfilled lives . . . The keys to human connection are simple, but extraordinarily powerful."[13] Perhaps Lewis's letters can help us understand some of those "keys to human connection."

As an adult, Lewis had a gift for friendship. We know this from accounts of his meetings with the other Inklings, who were—like him—well-read, creative, intelligent, and fun-loving.

In his younger years, Lewis had few friends aside from his older brother Warnie. Lewis first met Arthur in April 1914, when they were (respectively) fifteen and eighteen years old. Though the two had lived near each other for years, they apparently had not met before this. Their friendship seems to have stemmed from a unique combination of circumstance and shared interests. Arthur was sick and bedridden, and Lewis accepted an invitation to visit. Lewis saw a copy of *Myths of the Norsemen* on the bedside table. Finding out that they both loved Norse mythology was enough to make them fast friends.[14]

In *Surprised by Joy*, Lewis describes Arthur as a "[type] of every man's First Friend." As such, Lewis writes, Arthur was like his "*alter ego*, the man who first reveals to you that you are not alone in the world by turning out

---

12. E.g., in a letter written to Arthur in 1915, "Write soon: you've know [sic] idea how welcome your letters are" (Lewis, *Collected Letters—Volume I*, 119).

13. Murthy, "Our Epidemic," 5.

14. Lewis, *Surprised by Joy*, 106.

(beyond hope) to share all your most secret delights. There is nothing to overcome in making him your friend."[15] He might have been thinking of this very meeting with Arthur when, in his book *The Four Loves*, he writes that a friendship begins when one person says to another, "What? You too? I thought I was the only one."[16]

The anecdote from *Surprised by Joy* can lead a reader to think that Lewis and Arthur were more alike than they actually were. Though they both shared a love of story and myth, they were very different in temperament and abilities. Arthur had little formal education. Arthur's spelling was atrocious. Lewis once wrote of Arthur, "He was not a clever boy, he was even a dull boy; I was a scholar. He had no 'ideas.' I bubbled over with them."[17] Arthur was not like the Inklings, and according to Hooper, Lewis's diary reveals that "Arthur was never quite comfortable with Lewis's companions in Oxford . . . *Alone* they [Lewis and Arthur] usually found much to say, but . . . [Lewis] was often embarrassed *for* Arthur when others were about."[18] The close, life-long friendship between Lewis and Arthur is, in some ways, surprising.

Despite Arthur's lack of education and ideas, Lewis learned much from him. He writes, "I could give concepts, logic, facts, arguments, but he had feelings to offer, feelings which most mysteriously—for he was always very inarticulate—he taught me to share . . . I learned charity from him and failed, for all my efforts, to teach him arrogance in return . . . If I had to write his epitaph, I should say of him what I could say of no one else known to me—'He *despised* nothing.'"[19]

From Arthur, Lewis learned about something the two of them called "homeliness." My associations with the word "homely" are not immediately positive. I think of a person who is plain and unattractive in appearance. What did Lewis and Arthur mean by this concept? Referring to "homeliness," Lewis describes Arthur's "human affection and . . . rich aesthetic relish" for the simple folk around him and for things like "[A] bright hearth seen through an open door as we passed, a train of ducks following a brawny farmer's wife, a drill of cabbages in a suburban garden."[20] "What

15. Lewis, *Surprised by Joy*, 160–61.
16. Lewis, *Four Loves*, 83.
17. Lewis, *Collected Letters—Volume I*, 995.
18. Lewis, *They Stand Together*, 294.
19. Lewis, *Collected Letters—Volume I*, 995.
20. Lewis, *Collected Letters—Volume I*, 994.

[Arthur] called the 'Homely,'" writes Lewis, "was the natural food both of his heart and his imagination."[21] The *Oxford English Dictionary* gives several definitions for the word "homely." The overall connotation is of something simple, familiar, intimate, and commonplace.

In a 1931 letter, Lewis tells Arthur:

> All the "homeliness" [of our old letters] (wh. was your chief lesson to me) was the introduction to the Christian virtue of charity or love. I sometimes manage now to get into a state in wh. I think of all my enemies and can honestly say that I find something lovable (even if it is only an oddity) in them all: and your conception of "homeliness" is largely the route by wh. I have reached this.[22]

One more comment on friendship before we turn to the letters. Lewis's letters indicate that Arthur was gay.[23] Is it possible that Lewis felt the same, and his deep friendship with Arthur was rather a romance? I think not, for many reasons. First, Lewis's early letters to Arthur mention his own (i.e., Lewis's) sexual fantasies, which all involved women. Second, Lewis's long and unconventional relationship with his friend Paddy's mother seems to have included a romantic element for a time.[24] Third, Lewis later fell in love with and married Joy Davidman. There are plenty of indications in the letters that Lewis was not sexually attracted to men. I will not elaborate here for reasons of time and space. I will note, however, that Lewis addresses just this kind of conjecture in his book *The Four Loves*:

> Those who cannot conceive Friendship as a substantive love but only as a disguise or elaboration of Eros betray the fact that they have never had a Friend. The rest of us know that though we can have erotic love and friendship for the same person yet in some ways nothing is less like a Friendship than a love-affair . . . Lovers are normally face to face, absorbed in each other; Friends, side by side, absorbed in some common interest.[25]

---

21. Lewis, *Collected Letters—Volume I*, 994.

22. Lewis, *Collected Letters—Volume I*, 974.

23. See, e.g., <bracketed> references in *Collected Letters—Volume I*, 287, 288, 355, 371, 374, 384.

24. Lewis, *Collected Letters—Volume I*, 339 and 1022; see also Lewis, *They Stand Together*, 346–47.

25. Lewis, *Four Loves*, 77–78.

PART THREE: LITERATURE AND CRITICISM

One person can love another deeply without being "in love" with them. Intimacy in a relationship is not always sexual; other forms of intimacy include the social, intellectual, emotional, and spiritual.[26]

PORTRAIT OF A FRIENDSHIP, IN LETTERS

With all of that as background, here are some characteristics of Lewis as demonstrated in his letters to his best friend Arthur. First, Lewis was interested in more than "small talk." At the end of one of his early letters, Lewis tells Arthur, "Write soon, and tell me all that you are doing, reading and thinking."[27] He repeats this phrase more often[28] and is less interested in the "doings" of ordinary life than in "readings" and "thinkings."[29] His own letters are full of details about what he was reading, which naturally led to an account of what he was thinking.

Lewis realized that sometimes (maybe especially for Arthur), thoughts were not easy to share. In one letter he writes, "I notice . . . that you answer my questions about 'doing' and 'reading' but keep a modest silence about 'thinking.' It is often difficult to tell, is it not?"[30] Lewis, for his part, sometimes found feelings difficult to describe. He tells Arthur, "It is easy to explain a thought, but to explain a feeling is very hard."[31]

Second, Lewis disliked self-pity and complaints in letters. Arthur had a tendency toward self-pity.[32] Lewis warns him in a letter:

> You are drifting into a habit of morbid self-pity lately; all your letters are laments. Beware of the awful fate of growing up like that. I never . . . saw what was meant by such terms as "the releif [sic] of confiding one's troubles" and the "consolations of sympathy": my view is, that to mention trouble at all, *in a complaining way*, is to introduce into the conversation an element equally painful for everyone, including the speaker. Of course, it all depends on the

---

26. See Benner, *Sacred Companions*, 72.

27. Lewis, *Collected Letters—Volume I*, 90.

28. In a letter to Arthur written in January 1915, Lewis refers to his own "theory that a letter should tell of doings, readings, thinkings" (Lewis, *Collected Letters—Volume I*, 103).

29. For example, Lewis writes to Arthur, "You ask me how I spend my time, and though I am more interested in thoughts and feelings, we'll come down to facts" (Lewis, *Collected Letters—Volume I*, 145).

30. Lewis, *Collected Letters—Volume I*, 92.

31. Lewis, *Collected Letters—Volume I*, 245.

32. See the biography at the back of Lewis, *Collected Letters—Volume I*, 993–94.

way it is done: I mean, simply to mention them, is not wrong, but, by words or expression to call for sympathy which your hearer will feel bound to pump up, is a nuiscance [sic].[33]

Third, in his letters to Arthur, Lewis was open about the most personal aspects of his life. For example, for a stretch of time in his late teens, Lewis wrote to Arthur about his sexual fantasies, which leaned toward sadism.[34] It seems that Arthur shared his own fantasies in his letters. After several months of this, Lewis writes:

> I think sometimes we have spoiled everything by starting this subject . . . I happened this morning on an old letter of yours . . . full of enthusiasm about books and music and scenery, which somehow made me feel that we were on a much higher level then, much more removed from the common mob. And yet I do not see that it is sensible to pretend that these things don't exist . . . it would be horrible to keep an artificial silence and feel that there was something there all the time. Let us talk of these things when we want, but always keep them on the side that tends to beauty, and avoid everything that tends to sordid-ness.[35]

A decade or so later, when rereading the letters, Lewis writes, "[confiding] in each other even on this subject . . . has done no harm in the long run–and how could young adolescents really be friends without it?"[36]

Lewis was also open with Arthur about his atheism. At the age of seventeen, he writes, "You know, I think, that I beleive [sic] in no religion. There is absolutely no proof for any of them, and from a philosophical standpoint Christianity is not even the best. All religions, that is, all mythologies to give them their proper name are merely man's own invention—Christ as much as Loki."[37]

Years later, when he had become a theist and then embraced Christianity, Arthur was one of the first people he told. He writes, "I have just passed on from believing in God to definitely believing in Christ—in Christianity."[38]

---

33. Lewis, *Collected Letters—Volume I*, 109.

34. See, e.g., letters starting on January 28, 1917 (Lewis, *Collected Letters—Volume I*, 270); see also 320.

35. Lewis, *Collected Letters—Volume I*, 287-88.

36. Lewis, *Collected Letters—Volume I*, 973.

37. Lewis, *Collected Letters—Volume I*, 230.

38. Lewis, *Collected Letters—Volume I*, 974.

When his father was ill, Lewis shared a heartbreaking confession with his friend, describing "how horrible one feels when the people whom one ought to love, but doesn't very much, are ill and in need of your help & sympathy; when you have to *behave* as love wd. dictate, and yet feel all the time as if you were doing nothing—because you can't give what's really wanted."[39]

In his later years, Lewis's brother Warnie was an alcoholic. Before that was widely known, Lewis told Arthur about it in a letter. Arthur's response was, in Lewis's words, a "most kind and comforting letter—like a touch of a friend's hand in a dark place."[40]

More than once, Lewis admitted to Arthur his struggle with pride, calling it, "my besetting sin . . . There seems to be no end to it. Depth under depth of self-love and self admiration. Closely connected with this is the difficulty I find in making even the faintest approach to giving up my own will: which as everyone has told us is the only thing to do."[41]

While, in his letters to Arthur, Lewis was honest about personal desires and struggles, he also wanted to give and receive honest feedback and criticism about his and Arthur's writing. In the early years of their friendship, Lewis and Arthur included installments of stories they were writing, for each other to read and comment on. In one letter to Arthur, Lewis writes, "There's one thing I want to say: I do hope that in things like this you'll always tell me the absolute truth about my work, just as if it were by someone else whom we did not know: I will promise to do the same for you . . . I have sometimes thought that you are inclined not to. (Not to be candid I mean.)"[42]

Lewis was certainly not afraid to disagree with Arthur. In fact, the former's openness and honesty sometimes meant he was painfully blunt, even while conveying deep warmth and appreciation. I think Lewis got away with it because he was as honest about his own strengths and shortcomings as he was about those of others. He once told Arthur:

> *Weakness* is your danger, as *Pride* is mine. (You have no idea how much of my time I spend just *hating* people whom I disagree with—tho' I know them only from their books—and inventing conversations in which I score off them.) In other words, we all

---

39. Lewis, *Collected Letters—Volume I*, 805.
40. Lewis, *Collected Letters—Volume II*, 952.
41. Lewis, *Collected Letters—Volume I*, 878–79.
42. Lewis, *Collected Letters—Volume I*, 186.

have our own burdens, and must do the best we can. I do not know which is the worse, nor do we need to: if each of us could imitate the other.[43]

One topic Lewis and Arthur argued about related to the role and limitations of sentiment/feelings.[44] Books were also sometimes a source of disagreement; Lewis writes, "When one has read a book, I think there is nothing so nice as discussing it with some one else—even though it sometimes produces rather fierce arguments."[45]

Of course, arguments can lead to hurt feelings. Lewis's letters reveal that he was willing to apologize when that was warranted. In one case, Arthur had given Lewis an "awful dressing down" over negative comments the latter had made about a book Arthur liked. While Lewis wanted to respond with a "very rude" letter, instead he writes, "real friendships are very, very rare and one doesn't want to endanger them by quarreling over trifles. We seem to be always [sparring] now a days: I dare say its [sic] largely my fault ... but anyway do let us stop it."[46] On another occasion, he writes, "I am ... sorry that I wrote you rather a snarky letter when we last communicated, and tried to turn an apology into an accusation, which was a very unhandsome thing to do."[47]

One of the most striking things I noted about Lewis's and Arthur's friendship was Lewis's longstanding commitment to regular correspondence with his friend. As I mentioned previously, Lewis and Arthur corresponded for almost fifty years. For stretches of that time, Lewis wrote to Arthur weekly. Arthur also wrote regularly, though shorter letters and less often. As a teenager, Lewis's days were full from morning until evening with lessons and activities. He wrote his letters to Arthur late at night. Once, he comments, "Do you know ... that it is at great cost I write hard like this up to the very moment of going to bed? I never sleep well on the nights of writing—all the ideas buzzing in my head keep me awake."[48] Finding time

---

43. Lewis, *Collected Letters—Volume II*, 125–26. Note also a bracketed comment at the end of Lewis's response to the first letter Charles Williams sent him: "(I embrace the opportunity of establishing the precedent of brutal frankness, without which our acquaintance begun like this would easily be a mere butter bath!)" (186–87.).

44. See, e.g., Lewis, *Collected Letters—Volume I*, 118.

45. Lewis, *Collected Letters—Volume I*, 173.

46. Lewis, *Collected Letters—Volume I*, 253.

47. Lewis, *Collected Letters—Volume I*, 794.

48. Lewis, *Collected Letters—Volume I*, 286.

to write only became more difficult when Lewis was deployed in World War I, when he was a student at Oxford, and when he became a professor.

While reading Lewis's letters to Arthur, I was curious how their frequency changed over time. I checked the dates of the letters in *They Stand Together: The Letters of C.S. Lewis to Arthur Greeves*. So far as I know, this volume contains all the existing letters from C. S. Lewis to Arthur Greeves. (The same letters are also found in *The Collected Letters*. Some of Lewis's letters to Arthur were likely lost or destroyed[49] over the years.)

Appendix A shows what the dates of the existing letters look like when mapped for frequency. Months are in columns and years are in rows. The number in each cell shows the number of letters sent in that particular month. Lewis's letters were most consistent early in his and Arthur's friendship. From October 1917[50] until the end of 1918,[51] Lewis was in the army—training, fighting, or recuperating from illness or injury. Letters during that time were a little less frequent. Though Arthur lived most of his life in Ireland, in the early 1920s he lived for a few years in London, where he attended the Slade School of Fine Art. During this time, it is likely that he and Lewis saw each other in person occasionally; perhaps they felt less need to keep in touch through letters as a result.[52]

Lewis and Arthur had another intense period of letter writing from the end of 1929 through 1931. This portion of their correspondence began shortly after Lewis's father died. It also included the time when Lewis embraced Christianity. During this time, Lewis experimented with writing letters to Arthur in diary format, adding a little each day,[53] trying to establish the habit as part of his daily routine.[54] He also seems to have asked Arthur if they could commit to weekly letters again, but Arthur declined. In a letter in 1935, after a long hiatus, Lewis writes, "I believe I could still make a fair

---

49. Arthur's cousin destroyed at least a few of the letters. See Lewis, *They Stand Together*, 41.

50. Lewis, *They Stand Together*, 199.

51. Lewis, *They Stand Together*, 240.

52. See Hooper's note in Lewis, *They Stand Together*, 294.

53. Lewis, *Collected Letters—Volume I*, 830-38, 849-64.

54. Lewis, *Collected Letters—Volume I*, 838 ("In spite of the failure so far I intend to keep up the effort of continuing a journal letter to you. In the [vacation] it shd.[sic] be easier than in the term, and perhaps habit will at last teach me to fit a portion however small into my day's routine").

attempt at a *regular* correspondence, but you yourself vetoed that, and odd letters, like odd bills, I do find it hard to meet when I'm busy."[55]

In his later years, Lewis's letters to Arthur tended to be shorter and less frequent. Many of these were sent in order to make and confirm vacation plans, or to cancel them due to illness. Throughout his life, Lewis made it a priority to see Arthur in person regularly. These visits helped keep the friendship strong. Initially the two saw each other during Lewis's breaks from boarding school, since their families lived across the street from each other. After Lewis's father died in 1929[56] and the Lewis home in Ireland was sold, Lewis often vacationed with Arthur.

These regular in-person visits were important to Lewis. In 1931, when Arthur indicated that he might cancel his first planned visit to Lewis's home at the Kilns, Lewis writes:

> I certainly don't wish to press a visit on you as a duty. All the same ... I would remind you that there is a good case for coming to see me even at the cost of some discomfort; because it is important to the continuance of a friendship that each should have some experience of the other's life ... now that I am in quite new surroundings I shall never feel at ease till you have shared them with me. How can I write to you about places you have never seen?[57]

Appendix B shows the previous data (the dates of Lewis's letters, mapped over time) with added indications of when we have evidence that the friends saw each other, and when it seems likely that visits between the two happened.[58] The friends might well have seen each other more often than this. These visits, combined with the letters, illustrate Lewis's long-term commitment to his friendship with Arthur.

In the last year of Lewis's life, he and Arthur had been planning a vacation that had to be cancelled due to Lewis's ill health. About a month before he died, Lewis writes to Arthur, "It looks as if you and I shall never meet again in this life. This often saddens me v. much ... oh Arthur, never to see you again!"[59]

Lewis's appreciation of his oldest friend is clear throughout his letters, but sometimes Lewis expressed in words how much his friendship

---

55. Lewis, *Collected Letters—Volume II*, 169.
56. Lewis, *They Stand Together*, 16.
57. Lewis, *Collected Letters—Volume I*, 962.
58. Compiled from information from Lewis, *They Stand Together*.
59. Lewis, *Collected Letters—Volume III*, 1455–56.

with Arthur mattered to him. In 1930, he writes, "In the act of writing to you those things naturally come uppermost which I can only imperfectly share with anyone else."[60] And in March 1931, "Do try and write me a long letter soon. You are constantly in my mind even when I don't write, and to lose touch with you would be like losing a limb."[61] In September 1933, he writes, "I remember you at least once a day whatever happens and often in between, and wish we could see more of one another."[62]

Finally, we come to a characteristic of Lewis, revealed in his letters, that I respect greatly, but that makes me somewhat uncomfortable given the topic of this chapter! Lewis carefully protected his friends' privacy and reputations. For example, shortly after Albert Lewis's death, Warnie undertook to document family history, compiling diary entries, letters, and more into eleven unpublished volumes now referred to as *The Lewis Papers*.[63] At Warnie's request, Lewis borrowed his own letters back from Arthur and chose a few to include. Lewis was careful to keep back all the letters that referred to sexual fantasies and also any letters which implied that Arthur had "said foolish things."[64]

Lewis protected the privacy of other friends, too. In 1961, when asked for copies of the Latin letters he had received from Don Giovanni Calabria, Lewis replied that he no longer had the letters. He writes, "It is my practice to consign to the flames all letters after two days—not, believe me, because I esteem them of no value, rather because I do not wish to relinquish things often worthy of sacred silence to subsequent reading by posterity."[65]

Lewis's protectiveness of his friends' privacy is sadly ironic, given that the same courtesy was not extended to him. Granted, as a young man, Lewis had read books of published letters without expressing any ethical scruples about the publication of those letters. And in a letter to Arthur in 1916, when Lewis was seventeen, he writes, "I think you and I ought to publish our letters (they'd be a jolly interesting book by the way)."[66] Perhaps these are clues that Lewis would not have minded having his letters published.

60. Lewis, *Collected Letters—Volume I*, 892.
61. Lewis, *Collected Letters—Volume II*, 103.
62. Lewis, *Collected Letters—Volume II*, 120.
63. See Lewis, *Collected Letters—Volume I*, 1013.
64. Lewis, *Collected Letters—Volume I*, 973.
65. Lewis, *Collected Letters—Volume III*, 1221. Translation from the original Latin was done by Martin Moynihan.
66. Lewis, *Collected Letters—Volume I*, 173.

However, Lewis's letters contain much more evidence to suggest the opposite. I have already mentioned some of that evidence, namely Lewis's comment about burning letters and his careful selection of letters to include in *The Lewis Papers*. In addition, consider the following: before he lent Lewis's own letters back to him, Arthur went through and scratched out sections in the letters that he did not want others to read. He had kept the letters over the years and seems to have reread them often.[67] However, he took clear and concrete steps to keep certain sentences and phrases from being read by outside eyes.

Decades later, after Arthur died in 1966,[68] his cousin Lisbeth sent Warnie the letters Arthur had received from Lewis over the years, along with instructions that they should be given to the University of Oxford Library.[69] Arthur may have realized before he died that the letters would one day be published, but I imagine he was comforted by the thought that the letters were self-edited. However, in the course of preparing Lewis's letters for inclusion in *The Collected Letters*, efforts were made to restore the words that Arthur had scratched out long before. As Hooper describes it, "Using the techniques of infra-red and ultra-violet fluorescence photography the deleted passages, for what they are, have been almost completely restored."[70] In the text, they are marked with angled brackets (< and >). Far from protecting the privacy of these two men, the most salacious bits of their correspondence now stand out in the text as if marked with a highlighter.

I suspect Lewis would be a bit disgusted at the knowledge that his letters were collected and published. In January 1948, he replied to an American minister who had asked him for "back-ground material"—presumably meaning details about his personal life. In response, Lewis writes, "The only thing of any importance ... about me is what I have to say." He added the following:

> I can't abide the idea that a man's books [should] be "set in their biographical context" and if I had some rare information about the private life of Shakespeare or Dante I'd throw it in the fire, tell no one, and re-read their works. All this biographical interest is only

---

67. Lewis, *Collected Letters—Volume I*, 972.
68. Lewis, *They Stand Together*, 38.
69. Lewis, *They Stand Together*, 39–40.
70. Lewis, *They Stand Together*, 44.

a device for indulging in gossip as an excuse for not reading what the chaps *say*, [which] is their only real claim on our attention.[71]

CONCLUSION

I used to feel a bit sad that my life did not overlap in history with C. S. Lewis's. After reading his letters, I feel much less wistful than I did before (though I look forward to talking with him, and perhaps even exchanging letters, someday "beyond the stable door"[72]).

Rather, I am thankful for the delight he took in friendship, and for the lengths he went to in order to maintain friendship. I find myself wanting to do the same. Though letter-writing for us today tends to look quite different (and I do not think Lewis would approve of email[73]), I am inspired by his example to nurture the friendships that God has granted to me, based on circumstance and shared interests.

I think Lewis would approve. In *The Four Loves*, he suggests that the idea that we choose our friends is largely an illusion. He writes, "Friendship is not a reward for our discrimination and good taste in finding one another out . . . At this feast it is He who has spread the board and it is He who has chosen the guests. It is He, we may dare to hope, who sometimes does, and always should, preside. Let us not reckon without our host."[74]

APPENDIX A

C. S. Lewis's Letters to Arthur Greeves mapped over time (1914 to 1963)[75]

	Jan	Feb	Mar	Apr	May	Jun	Jul	Aug	Sep	Oct	Nov	Dec
1914						1			1	4	3	
1915	1	2	1		3	3	1			2	1	
1916		3	3		3	4	4		2	3	7	

71. Lewis, *Collected Letters—Volume II*, 830–31.

72. See Lewis, *Last Battle*, 119 and elsewhere.

73. I think this for at least two reasons. One is that Lewis never learned how to type. Another is the speed with which an email can be transmitted. Can you imagine how overwhelming it would be to reply by "return of post" (i.e., on the same day you received a message), when the recipient might turn around, still on the same day, and do the very same thing?

74. Lewis, *Four Loves*, 114–15.

75. Lewis, *They Stand Together*.

	Jan	Feb	Mar	Apr	May	Jun	Jul	Aug	Sep	Oct	Nov	Dec
1917	2	7	2	1	4	2	2	1		1	1	2
1918		3			2	2	1	2	1	3	1	1
1919	1	2	1		1	1	1	1	1	1		
1920		2		2	1	4						
1921						1						
1922							1					
1923				1								
1924												
1925												
1926												1
1927						1		1				
1928												
1929			1	1	1		3			1	4	2
1930	4	3	2	3		5	2	5	1	2		1
1931	2	2	1	1	2	1	2	2	2	2	1	1
1932	1	1	1			1	2					2
1933		1	1			1		1	2		1	
1934										1		1
1935				1		1						2
1936		1			1							
1937			1			1						
1938						1						
1939									1			
1940					1							1
1941					1							1
1942												1
1943	1					1						1
1944	1	1										1
1945		1										1
1946					1							
1947	1						1	1				
1948												
1949	1					2	4			1		

PART THREE: LITERATURE AND CRITICISM

	Jan	Feb	Mar	Apr	May	Jun	Jul	Aug	Sep	Oct	Nov	Dec
1950				2	1							
1951	1		1	2		1						
1952			1			2			1	2	1	
1953		1	3				1			2		
1954			1	2	1			2				
1955						1		1	1	1		1
1956		1			3	1	1			1		
1957				1				1	1		1	
1958			1	1	1				1		1	
1959			1	2	1							
1960			1				1					
1961	1				7	2					2	
1962						1					1	1
1963			4				1		1			

APPENDIX B

C. S. Lewis and Arthur Greeves—Letters and visits mapped over time (1914 to 1963)[76]

	Jan	Feb	Mar	Apr	May	Jun	Jul	Aug	Sep	Oct	Nov	Dec
1914						1			1	4	3	V
1915	1	2	1	V	3	3	1	V	V	2	1	V
1916	V	3	3	V	3	4	4	V	2	3	7	V
1917	2	7	2	1	4	2	2	1	V	1	1	2
1918		3			2	2	1	2	1	3	1	1
1919	1	2	1	V	1	1	1, pV	1	1	1		V
1920		2		2	1	4						
1921	pV	pV	pV	pV	pV	1, pV	pV	pV	pV	pV	pV	pV
1922	pV	pV	pV	pV	pV	pV	1, pV	pV	pV	pV	pV	pV
1923	pV	pV	pV	1, pV	pV	pV	V	pV	pV	pV	pV	pV
1924	pV	pV	pV	pV	pV	pV	pV	pV	pV	pV	pV	pV
1925	pV	pV	pV	pV	pV	pV	pV	pV	pV	pV	pV	pV

76. Compiled from information in Lewis, *They Stand Together*. Note: V ("visit"); pV ("possible visit").

	Jan	Feb	Mar	Apr	May	Jun	Jul	Aug	Sep	Oct	Nov	Dec
1926	pV	pV	pV	pV	pV	pV	pV	pV	pV	pV	pV	1, V
1927						1		1	V	V		V
1928	V							V	V			V
1929	V		1	1	1		3			1	4	2, V
1930	4	3	2	3, V		5	2	5	1	2		1, V
1931	2	2	1	1	2	1, V	2	2, V	2	2	1	1
1932	1	1	1				1	2, V				2
1933		1	1			1		1	2		1	
1934				V						1		1
1935				1		1	pV					2
1936		1			1		pV					
1937			1			1						
1938						1	pV					
1939									1			
1940				1								1
1941				1								1
1942												1
1943	1					1						1
1944	1	1										1
1945		1										1
1946				1								
1947	1					V	1	1				
1948												
1949	1					2	4			1		
1950					2	1						
1951	1		1	2, V		1						
1952			1			2		V	1, V	2	1	
1953		1	3				1	V	V	2		
1954			1	2	1			2	V			
1955						1		1	1, V	1		1
1956		1			3	1	1		V		1	
1957			1					1	1	1		
1958			1	1	1		V		1		1	

Part Three: Literature and Criticism

	Jan	Feb	Mar	Apr	May	Jun	Jul	Aug	Sep	Oct	Nov	Dec
1959			1	2	1	V	V					
1960			1				1					
1961	1				7	2, V					2	
1962						1					1	1
1963			4				1		1			

BIBLIOGRAPHY

Benner, David G. *Sacred Companions*. Downers Grove, IL: InterVarsity, 2002.

Harwood, Laurence. *C. S. Lewis, My Godfather*. Downers Grove, IL: InterVarsity, 2007.

Lewis, C. S. *The Collected Letters of C. S. Lewis: Books, Broadcasts, and the War, 1931–1949—Volume II*. Edited by Walter Hooper. HarperSanFrancisco, 2004.

———. *The Collected Letters of C. S. Lewis: Family Letters, 1905-1931—Volume I*. Edited by Walter Hooper. San Francisco: HarperSanFrancisco, 2004.

———. *The Collected Letters of C. S. Lewis: Narnia, Cambridge, and Joy, 1950-1963—Volume III*. Edited by Walter Hooper. HarperSanFrancisco, 2007.

———. *The Four Loves*. 1960. Reprint, New York: HarperCollins, 2017.

———. *The Last Battle*. 1956. Reprint, London: Fontana Lions, 1986.

———. *Letters to an American Lady*. Edited by Clyde S. Kilby. Grand Rapids: Eerdmans, 1967.

———. *Surprised by Joy*. 1955. Reprint, London: Fontana, 1973.

———. *They Stand Together: The Letters of C. S. Lewis to Arthur Greeves (1914–1963)*. Edited by Walter Hooper. New York: Macmillan, 1979.

"The Life and Writing of C.S. Lewis—Part One," the first episode of Eric Metaxas's interview with Walter Hooper, produced by *Socrates in the City Podcast*, 2019. Online: https://socratesinthecity.com/listen/the-life-and-writing-of-c-s-lewis-part-1.

Moynihan, Martin, ed. *Letters: C. S. Lewis and Don Giovanni Calabria—A Study in Friendship*. Translated by Martin Moynihan. London: Collins, 1989.

Murthy, Vivek H. "Our Epidemic of Loneliness and Isolation: The U.S. Surgeon General's Advisory on the Healing Effects of Social Connection and Community." Office of the U. S. Surgeon General (2023). Online: https://www.hhs.gov/sites/default/files/surgeon-general-social-connection-advisory.pdf.

Index of Authors

Adey, Lionel, 150, 153–54, 158, 163–65, 169–70
Adlerstein, Yitzchok, 61–62
Arnold, Matthew, 177, 180
Auerbach, Erich, 169
Auffenberg, Walter, 34
Austen, Jane, 160

Bai, Feng, 85
Bandura, Albert, 79
Barbour, Brian, 158
Barfield, Owen, 7
Barkman, Adam, 12, 28–29, 45
Barr, James, 162
Barthes, Roland, 191
Bartlett, Robert, 48
Baumgarten, Alexander G., 179
Beardsley, Monroe C., 194
Béguin, Albert, 169
Benner, David G., 204
Berkeley, George, 28
Berry, Zachariah, 79
Bibby, Reginald W., 54
Blanken, Irene, 79
Boccacio, Giovanni, 153
Bohr, Niels, 28
Booth, Wayne C., 156
Brink, Gijsbert van den, 21–22
Browning, Don, 114–15
Bultmann, Rudolf, 53
Bunyan, John, 6

Cage, John, 192
Calabria, Don Giovanni, 200, 210
Calhoun, Scott, 163

Calin, William, 10, 155–56, 158, 160, 164, 169–70
Chapman, George, 156
Chaucer, Geoffrey, 8, 150, 152–53, 169
Collins, Susan, 48
Curtius, Ernst Robert, 169

Darwin, Charles, 24
Davidman, Joy, 2, 203
Davies, Brian, 36
Davies, Jamie, 34
Davis, Lanta, 111, 113
Dawkins, Richard, 78–79
Dean, Robert J., 115
Dembski, William, 30
Dennis, Sherry K, 60
Descartes, René, 25, 27, 37, 41
Devries, Ben, 24
Draper, Paul, 44
Dryden, John, 157
Duriez, Colin, 1, 149

Edwards, Bruce L., Jr., 164
Edwards, Michael I., 164
Einstein, Albert, 28
Eliot, George, 190
Eliot, T. S., 3, 157–58, 177, 180–81
Empson, William, 158, 163, 177
Emudianughe, T. S., 34

Faner, Jhon Marc V., 43
Fox, James, 34
Frye, Northrop, 169

Gadamer, Hans-Georg, 14, 110–12, 114, 117, 122

Index of Authors

Goldingay, John, 124
Goering, Marlon, 85
Gordon, R. K., 153
Gower, John, 150

Haidt, Jonathan, 74–76, 79
Harrison, Peter, 31
Harwood, Laurence, 200
Hawking, Stephen, 62
Henryson, Robert, 153
Hooper, Walter, 158, 160, 198–99, 202, 208, 211
Howard, Evan B., 112
Hume, David, 75
Hunter, James Davison, 54

Illingworth, J. R., 22
Iser, Wolfgang, 164
Ivanhoe, Philip J., 67

Jakobson, Roman, 192
James, Henry, 177
Jamieson, Dale, 42
Jauss, Hans Robert, 164
Johnson-Delaney, Cathy, 34
Joyce, James, 189
Judd, Andrew, 110–11

Kant, Immanuel, 40–41, 45, 73–74, 80, 179, 184
Keats, John, 105
Keltz, Kyle, 36
Kierkegaard, Søren, 21
Kilby, Clyde S., 200
Kohlberg, Lawrence, 74
Kosma, Maria, 110
Kreeft, Peter, 59

Larkin, Philip, 3
Latimer, Hugh, 161
Leavis, F. R., 157–58
Lederman, Janine, 34
Lehner, Christopher, 28
Lewis, C. I., 113
Locke, John, 67
Lorenz, Konrad, 26
Lovejoy, Arthur O., 152, 166
Luther, Martin, 53

Lyotard, Jean-François, 53

Machiavelli, Niccolò di Bernardo dei, 153
MacInnis, John, 94
Marlowe, Christopher, 156
Marshall, Ashley, 180
Matthiessen, F. O., 169
Mayor, Andrienne, 46
Mazar, Nina, 79
McGrath, Alister, 1, 149, 154
McLuhan, Marshall, 178
Merritt, Anna, 85–86
Mill, John Stuart, 74
Milton, John, 8, 154–58, 167, 170
Monin, Benoît, 85–86
More, Thomas, 161
Mowat, Harriet, 115
Moynihan, Martin, 200, 210
Murray, Michael, 24, 26

Newton, Phil A., 122
Nietzsche, Friedrich, 68

O. Henry (William Sydney Porter), 188
Ong, Walter J., 178
Osmer, Richard, 114
Otto, Rudolf, 45

Pater, Walter, 179
Pascal, Blaise, 62
Petrarch, Francis, 153
Pike, Mark A., 113
Plantinga, Alvin, 27–28, 30
Porter, Stanley E., 15, 128, 149, 154
Prior, Karen Swallow, 112

Rachels, James, 73
Rachels, Stuart, 73
Ransom, Elwin, 60
Ransom, John Crowe, 177
Reid, Thomas, 28
Reilly, R. J., 33
Richards, I. A., 158, 164, 177
Root, Andrew, 122

Sagan, Carl, 62
Schakel, Peter, 95

Index of Authors

Schleiermacher, Friedrich, 154, 184
Schneider, John, 27
Scott, Walter, 160
Shakespeare, William, 8, 153–54, 160, 162, 167, 211
Shelley, Percy Bysshe, 157
Shippey, Tom, 32
Shklovsky, Viktor, 192
Sidney, Philip, 161
Singer, Peter, 41
Sousset, Jean, 169
Southgate, Christopher, 24, 38
Spenser, Edmund, 8, 150, 156, 161, 168–70
Spitzer, Leo, 169
Sterba, James, 21, 28
Stevens, Anne H., 151, 171
Studdock, Mark, 60
Swinburne, Richard, 21, 27, 40, 44
Swinton, John, 115

Thackeray, William M., 190
Tillyard, E. M. W., 154–55, 158, 166, 171
Tolkien, J. R. R., 7, 32, 109, 111, 152
Tyndale, William, 161

Usk, Thomas, 150

Van Norden, Bryan W., 67
Visscher, Lukas, 43

Ward, Michael, 95, 99
Ware, Kallistos, 91–93
Webbe, William, 162
Westbeau, Georges, 35
Wilde, Oscar, 179
Williams, Charles, 7, 207
Williams, Donald T., 161
Williams, Raymond, 164
Wilson, F. P., 160
Wimsatt, William K., 194
Wolterstorff, Nicholas, 30

Yandell, Stephen, 150

Zuboff, Shoshana, 83–84
Zuckerman, Miron, 79

www.ingramcontent.com/pod-product-compliance
Lightning Source LLC
Chambersburg PA
CBHW051642230426
43669CB00013B/2402